FRIENDS OF LIBRARIES

SOURCEBOOK

THIRD EDITION

Sandy Dolnick

Editor

American Library Association
Chicago and London
1996

While extensive effort has gone into ensuring the reliability of information appearing in this book, the publisher makes no warranty, express or implied, on the accuracy or reliability of the information, and does not assume and hereby disclaims any liability to any person for any loss or damage caused by errors or omissions in this publication.

Project editor: Joan A. Grygel

Cover designer: Tessing Design

Text design and composition: **the dotted i** in ITC Galliard and ITC Avant Garde on Xyvision

Printed on 50-pound Victor Offset paper, a pH-neutral stock, and bound in 10-point C1S cover stock by Victor Graphics, Inc.

The paper used in this publication meets the minimum requirements of American National Standard for Information Sciences—Permanence of Paper for Printed Library Materials, ANSI Z39.48-1992. ∞

Library of Congress Cataloging-in-Publication Data

Friends of libraries sourcebook / edited by Sandy Dolnick. — 3rd ed.
    p.   cm.
   Includes index.
   ISBN 0-8389-0685-0 (alk. paper)
   1. Friends of the library—United States—Handbooks, manuals, etc.
I. Dolnick, Sandy.
Z681.7.U5F75   1996
021.7—dc20   96-3384

Printed in the United States of America.

00 99 98 97 96   5 4 3 2 1

Contents

Contents

Contents

Figures

Foreword

Friends help libraries in a number of ways. Each of us comes from a different community with its own expectations, and our goals vary accordingly. What we share is a passion for libraries and a desire to help them meet the challenges of the day, as well as remain vital far into the future. Here, to set the stage for this book, is one vision of what that future holds, written by the vice provost and director of libraries for the University of Pennsylvania. This *Sourcebook* will give you the tools to help you achieve *your* vision for your library.

Future Fate: The Library in the Twenty-First Century

Dr. Paul Mosher

A dozen years ago, technologists thought they would bury libraries, ushering in a paperless, mainframe computer-based society in which books and libraries would wither and then disappear, replaced by a vast, seamless electronic information network on the Internet, negotiated by "knowbots": search engines guided by artificial intelligence. It hasn't happened that way, of course, and those of us who follow the recent progress of libraries have begun to get a pretty good picture of the libraries of the early twenty-first century.

If we visited a library in the year 2010, what would we see?

The library will still be there, and it will still be filled with books. Publishing statistics reveal that publishing is still profitable; the Book Industry Study Group predicts that by 1999, libraries will spend about $2 billion on books—and total domestic expenditures for books will exceed $30.5 billion—big numbers, reflecting ongoing health. The number of titles published continues to increase rapidly, and this trend will continue into the next century. Publishers are investing in electronic publishing ventures—some heavily—but no one has made any big money yet from electronic publishing. Unless there is a breakthrough, change will be slower than the technopundits would have us believe—culture changes more slowly than technology.

The book is still more efficient than the computer screen for long text, for the novel, literature, and the transmission of complex ideas. Long text on the computer screen behaves—paradoxically—very much like the scrolls that preceded the appearance of the codex book—then a revolutionary technology—in the third century A.D. Try reading Proust, Joyce, or St. Augustine on a computer, and your eyes will ache, as will your muscles. Three hundred pages on the computer screen is sheer, backbreaking boredom. But you can always reformat it and print it out: another half hour gone, and 300 loose pages stacked around your printer—what a deal!

So what changes will there be?

In place of the old paper catalog you will find a growing number of desktop computers that will contain the library catalog, access to catalogs of other libraries and utilities (like OCLC), and a good many reference works (encyclopedias, dictionaries, subject indexes, abstracts, and other finding aids). The desktop computer will also provide access to a growing array of online forms and services—and you will be able to access much of this information and carry out many functions from your home or workplace via networked PC without going to the physical library. In other words, access to the electronic dimension of the library will be distributed rather than centralized.

You will be able to ask reference questions, request books or journals, place holds or renewals, file complaints or compliments, and find out whether paper books or journals are on the shelf—all by desktop computer. The twenty-first century library will be a hybrid—a fusion of paper and electronic resources, with many formerly paper-based transactions carried out electronically. And your local library system will be distributed—connected to you and to other libraries such as the Library of Congress through the Internet—promising access to a vast world of Internet-linked information resources throughout the country and, gradually, other parts of the world.

Librarians will increasingly become more technologically skilled, linking electronic technology with the skills they have possessed: understanding the creation, production, communication, and consumption of information with basic applications of information technology. They will combine this knowledge with new information technology skills and will assist patrons with basic issues of the applications and uses of information technology as well as the information itself. These trends are currently visible in public, special, and academic libraries, but they will accelerate and intensify: The new graduates of our library and information technology programs possess a deeper mix of these skills, and the rest of the profession will increasingly need to upgrade their skills and acquire education in information technology and its applications.

Many libraries will offer a free basic set of information resources and distant services—such as reference, renewal, and access to some online information bases. There is likely to be an additional set of resources—value-added resources, such as the law and news service Lexis-Nexus, which will be subscription or fee based: There are considerable market efforts to change the financial base of the information market to provide increasing revenues for property rights owners at the expense of free and open exchange of information that has been the base of copyright law in the paper publishing world and the foundation of the public library paradigm.

The role of the library in the electronic age will thus resemble in many ways the library of the paper age: It will acquire information, knowledge, and entertainment resources most appropriate for the patron community within the limits of the library budget. However, instead of the two layers of the present—paper and media—the library will have three or more: An electronic layer will be added to the traditional ones.

The library of the twenty-first century will have successfully bridged the gap between information (the ends) and technology (the means) to create a new and productive fusion. Librarians will also bridge the division between paper-based and electronic information. This successful process of integration and fusion will create a new kind of library; one that will remain familiar, even though its tools and modalities will change profoundly over the next two decades.

Preface

The word *collaboration* easily comes to mind when thinking about the third edition of *Friends of Libraries Sourcebook*. The book draws on the ideas and energy of people in libraries, businesses, and especially Friends groups from all types of libraries. While as editor I take responsibility for the choices of material in this book, experts from the field contributed most of the writing. As executive director of Friends of Libraries U.S.A. (FOLUSA), I am privy to many sides of the same story and have occasionally supplemented the contributors' perspective with my own interjections.

Since the last edition of this book, Friends are still the "caring core" of the library community and increasingly have taken an active posture in performance of their mission. Their substantive efforts resulted in the expanded attention given to branch libraries, gift shops, volunteers, school and junior Friends, advocacy, fundraising, and foundations in this edition.

The changes in our everyday lives are mirrored in the volunteer world of the Friends. People are busier than ever before. Changes in federal, state, and local government have eroded fiscal support significantly. Technology has entered most lives so that almost no one thinks of a small, furry rodent when hearing about mouse problems.

It is exciting to read of the challenges met and conquered by the resourcefulness of groups with small budgets and great plans. The vitality of the successful Friends of the Library groups with their accrued wisdom and leadership we vicariously experience in these pages provides direction for future successes by Friends of Libraries. Selected examples of successful Friends endeavors are highlighted throughout this book in brief Action Points and more-detailed Focus sections.

A strong framework for the growing significance of these groups is Friends of Libraries U.S.A. As the national voice for library volunteers, FOLUSA is the depository for ideas and resources used by Friends; its files have provided material for this edition. Highlighted throughout this book are interesting design layouts and logos from FOLUSA files that reflect the best from its 3,000 plus members.

The *Friends of Libraries Sourcebook* third edition is designed as a practical manual to help both beginning and experienced Friends. Many of the chapters have only one author designated, but authors of previous editions have indeed left their marks on the manuscript. The *Sourcebook* is truly a group effort, and the work of many individuals from many groups is gratefully acknowledged, including Judi Baker, Scott Bennett, Herbert Bloom, Lillian Bradshaw, Ernestine Clark, Roger Downward, Graham Finney, Joan Grygel, Shirley Helfrich, Patrick Hogan, James Houck, Susan Linder, Ruby Ling-Louie, Caroline Loose, Hazel Maxwell, Laura Murru, Evy Nordley, Sara Parker, Dianne Rooney, Ruth Rejnis, Frederick Ruffner, Paul Scupholm, Richard Torbert, Perry White, Jane Winslow, Christine Wise, Steven Wooldridge, and Cecil Young. I would like to thank my many teachers from past and present boards of Friends of Libraries U.S.A. The various contributors and I hope that readers will learn what has worked and adapt it to their particular needs. Learn, grow, prosper, and help our libraries move into the next century.

Sandy Dolnick

Contributors

Peggy Barber, associate executive director, development and communications, American Library Association

Dale Buboltz, American Association of School Librarians; former librarian, South Gate Junior High School, Los Angeles

Christy Connelly, director, Cincinnati Zoo and Botanical Garden Gift Shop

Sandy Dolnick, executive director, Friends of Libraries U.S.A.

Roseann Gill, vice president, Friends of the Free Library of Philadelphia; liaison, Alliance of Friends

Kay Harvey, director, Broward County Library Foundation

Sarah C. Hite, past president, Friends of the Denver Public Library

Joan Hood, director of development, University of Illinois-Urbana Library

Marcia Kuszmaul, assistant vice president, Marcy Monyek and Associates

Carolyn McReynolds, executive director, Friends of the Library, Metropolitan Library of Oklahoma

Sara Oates, head, community relations, Carnegie Library of Pittsburgh

Charlotte O'Dea, past president, Empire State Friends; director, United Way of Chenango County, New York

Peter Pearson, executive director, St. Paul Friends of the Library; board of directors, Friends of Libraries U.S.A.

Jane Rutledge, president, Friends of Indiana Libraries; board of directors, Friends of Libraries U.S.A.

Ira Shucker, CPA; chair, board of trustees, Atlanta-Fulton Public Library

Jane Turner, president, Turner and Associates

1

What Friends Are For

Sandy Dolnick

Friends are a necessary part of life for institutions as well as for people. Support and recognition are important elements of any friendship. The basic assumption of this book is that organized Friends of the Library groups can and should supply these elements to all libraries and represent the library to its community.

While people tend to think of Friends of the Library as nonprofit institutions benefiting public libraries, Friends groups are also relevant to academic, school, and special libraries. Library communities, broadly defined, may be made up of citizens, students, parents, alumni, patrons, and business and professional groups. Whatever the constituency, the potential effectiveness of a group with no vested (monetary) interest cannot be overestimated. The library, which is often taken for granted, can multiply the support from its community if it is willing to establish and perpetuate a Friends organization.

Changes in public attitudes toward government spending have brought intense pressures to bear upon library budgets. At the same time the value of many endowments has diminished to unforeseen lows. In many cases Friends of the Library groups, by mounting advocacy campaigns, raising funds from private sources, or providing volunteer labor, have made it possible for the library to continue services that would otherwise have been eliminated.

Although the initial reasons for having a support group may differ among various types of libraries and communities, they generally fall within the following parameters.

Money—Friends groups have traditionally raised funds for projects or acquisitions in excess of the general library budget.

Services—There is no limit to the services that a dedicated volunteer group can provide, short of substituting members for specialized staff. These services can be hands-on help or in-kind support made available through connections to the business community. (See chapter 12.)

Public relations—Each Friend is a walking public relations vehicle for the library to its community. Each event, media mention, public activity, advocacy effort, or community involvement adds to the library's stature.

Advocacy—An informed, active citizen lobby provides the public library with its strongest weapon. Budgets are not the only area where advocacy is necessary. Increasing assaults on library collections by interest groups seeking to impose their particular views on communities can be nullified by an informed Friends of the Library group and a current materials-selection policy. Other libraries also have strong support from their patrons.

Community involvement—An organized Friends group is essentially validation of the library's importance to its community. The group members' increased awareness of the collections and inner workings of the library further strengthens their ties to the institution.

Each of these areas is covered in depth elsewhere in this book. The rationale for individual Friends groups may change over time. A group that begins as a purely social organization, for example, may shift its orientation as the library's needs grow.

Friends of Libraries, therefore, are many different things to many different communities. They all may be loosely defined as groups of citizens that are associated on behalf of libraries.

The interest and need for Friends groups has grown steadily over the past ten years. Each year the American Library Association and Friends of Libraries U.S.A. receive increasing numbers of queries about such groups. Friends of Libraries U.S.A., the national volunteer network for library support, was formed to further the growth of new groups and to exchange information among existing ones.

The following capsule histories may best describe typical activities of Friends groups.

FOCUS

East Brunswick Friends of the Library
East Brunswick, New Jersey

The success of the East Brunswick Public Library during its twenty-eight-year history has been achieved with the help of the Friends of the Library, established, not coincidentally, the same year the library opened. This group has contributed enormously to the improvement of library services, worked to promote the use of the library by the community, and been instrumental in providing funding for many important programs and services beyond those the library budget could provide.

The East Brunswick Friends of the Library is one of the largest Friends groups in New Jersey, with more than 1,600 members—individuals, families, organizations, and businesses. The Friends group contributes to the improvement of library service by providing gifts of equipment and materials, supporting staff development activities, providing initial funding for innovative new collections and services, and underwriting major library programming.

The Friends group promotes library development nationally through its membership in Friends of Libraries U.S.A. and by participating in American Library Association programs. On the regional and state levels, Friends leaders provide guidance and assistance to Friends groups in other communities and work for state legislation to improve library service. The Friends group is a generous supporter of the Literacy Volunteers of Middlesex and of Books to Keep, a holiday book-distribution project of Middlesex County public libraries. The group also sponsors a Book Endowment Fund to help supplement the annual materials budget and, in 1991, established a scholarship for high school seniors who have exhibited an interest in library services.

Recent contributions by the Friends include the group's sponsorship of the library's twenty-fifth birthday celebration, a storytelling festival, and the donation of a special classical music collection in memory of a longtime board member and library supporter. Through its annual book sale and other fund-raising efforts, the Friends group has provided computers for both public and staff use; circulating video game, computer software, and CD-ROM collections; funding for handicap-accessible computer furniture throughout the building for a computerized public access catalog; an electronic directory; after-hours videotape return and drive-up book return; and funding for a Fall Foreign Film Festival. The Friends group has funded the library's Summer Foreign Film Festival for the past thirteen years.

It is difficult to imagine what the East Brunswick Public Library would be like without the Friends. The group's many and varied contributions benefit each library user.

Friends of the Georgia O'Keeffe Elementary School Library
Albuquerque, New Mexico

In 1993 the Georgia O'Keeffe Elementary School was the first public school to organize a Friends group in New Mexico. Its purpose is the enrichment of the total resources and facilities of the library. The group's energies are directed to literacy promotion, library advocacy, and fund-raising.

What Friends Are For

The group calls itself the School of Readers, and the school's 980 students celebrated the seventy-fifth anniversary of Children's Book Week with the Friends by participating in a month-long program called Read across America. Students read two hundred books with distinct regional themes, answered quiz questions for each book, and held special events during Book Week. They formed a human fence around the boundaries of the school, each with book in hand, then they sat down and read. The week ended with celebration parties for each grade level that were organized by the Friends. Readers were honored for their achievements, and everyone wore red, white, and blue or stars and stripes. The Friends provided a cake to feed one thousand.

The Friends organized a Night of a Thousand Stars that included seventeen authors and illustrators visiting, selling, autographing, and reading out loud to a crowd of one thousand. They also organized a Brown Bag Book Exchange.

The group's advocacy included letter-writing campaigns and speeches before the school board to successfully protest budget cuts. It influenced the hiring of a professional librarian, and blew the whistle on the district's diversion of $1.7 million earmarked for updating library collections. In addition, the Friends were successful fund-raisers, and they provided volunteers to the library.

Academic Friends of the Library

Many types of academic libraries have successful Friends of the Library groups, sometimes called *Associates*. They are part of both large and small institutions: universities, colleges, community colleges, and two-year campuses for urban populations. Their activities vary, depending on the tone they want to convey and the population mixture of town and gown they serve.

FOCUS

Wright State University
Dayton, Ohio

More than seven hundred individuals attended the book fair at which more than forty authors and illustrators were on hand to autograph a wide variety of new books. Authors included Arnold Adoff, Steven Birmingham, Tom Crouch, Virginia Hamilton, and Sherrie Szeman. These authors were joined by some thirty antiquarian dealers from seven states who offered a cornucopia of rare, old, out-of-print, and collectible titles. Plans are under way for the Second Annual Wright Book Fair.

OF THE OCALA PUBLIC LIBRARY
OCALA, FLA.

The Friends of the Libraries are selling brass bookmarks featuring the Wright flyer—at $5.85 they make great gifts. Also available are T-shirts, canvas totes, and visors.

Friends members receive discounts on purchases at several area bookstores, including the Wright State University Bookstore.

Friends in Relation to Others in the Library

The Library Director

The relationship between the library director and the Friends group should be characterized by mutual respect, basic understanding of goals and objectives, appreciation of each other's individual potential for achievement, and the shared enjoyment of ultimate success.

All parties must clearly understand their respective roles in order to work together toward common goals. The primary responsibility for bringing about this favorable state of affairs rests, in large measure, with the positive attitude of the library director.

The library director must be prepared to respond to some fundamental questions and concerns relative to Friends. Among these are

1. The director's desire for a Friends group and belief in the benefits of having such a group. Unless the library's leadership really wants a Friends group, it is less than fair to encourage its formation.
2. Availability of time to work with Friends. Continuous communication, information, and encouragement are needed to sustain interest on the part of volunteers; the director or a designated liaison must be available for such leadership.
3. Willingness to assist Friends in understanding the legal and organizational structures of the library. If the Friends group is not told how it fits into the organization, disillusionment, frustration, and chaos can result.
4. Necessary staff leadership in helping the Friends formulate long-term goals and short-term objectives. The Friends program is most valuable when it moves the total library program forward. The Friends group should be challenged to think and plan on a broad scale. (See chapter 4.)
5. Representation at all Friends meetings, whether they be executive committee, board, or membership gatherings. The Friends group must be made to feel that the library director is an important and indispensable part

of its endeavors. This relationship should cultivate leadership by the Friends and not dependence on the director.

6. Praise and publicity for the achievements of the Friends group. All appropriate governing bodies should learn of its achievements.

7. Awareness of how the community views the Friends. A group that becomes elitist, overspecialized, or simply social may antagonize voters in important library elections and bond campaigns. The director should encourage broad-based and varied Friends activities.

8. Most importantly, the realization that the director's performance can and should inspire faith in the library program and, therefore, increase and inspire the Friends' willingness to work for the program.

Cooperation is vital. Without it, a library director can destroy a Friends group. On occasion, a Friends group has broken a library director. By understanding each other and working together, the library director and an effective Friends group can produce the most desirable of improved library services for the taxpayer and the user.

The Trustees

The powers and duties of library trustees are established by law and, consequently, are not subject to delegation to another body. The basic duties and responsibilities include the employment of a competent and qualified librarian/director, the formulation of library policy, and the development of both long-range and strategic planning with an annual adjustment of goals and objectives. The trustees must develop library leadership skills to be advocates for libraries and must generate adequate funding for the library's facilities, programs, and services. They must monitor the operating budget and protect the assets of the library.

To fulfill these duties, the board of trustees must serve as a liaison between the public and the library. In so doing, it must create a broad base of support. This support can be effectively strengthened and broadened through the establishment of organized groups, especially the Friends, that can serve as ambassadors of the board.

The fund-raising role of a Friends group should be determined in consultation with the board and the library director. Often fund-raising can either be a joint venture between the trustees and the Friends or be a project that involves the Friends solely. Whatever the form, the purpose and the means by which fund-raising is carried out should be a common decision by all parties.

Of course, the important role Friends play in public relations and building good will for the library should be appreciated by the trustees and library director alike.

What Friends Are For

The Staff

Although the library director and the staff may be involved with the Friends group on several levels, the director and staff may work most closely with those individual Friends who volunteer for work within the library. The staff will expect that no special favors be given to a Friend who is performing the same job that a paid employee performs. Early on, the staff should be assured that the presence of Friends as co-workers will not endanger the staff's future employment. For a successful work experience to be achieved for both the paid employee and the Friend, attention should be directed to ensuring that each is treated equally in the workplace. (See chapter 19.)

Cementing the Relationships

Cooperation and understanding can be accomplished through definite lines of communication. Depending on the size of the library, meetings may include the president of the Friends, the library director or liaison, the president of the board of trustees, the outreach librarian or the library's public relations officer, and a representative of the development office or the library foundation. Such meetings provide an opportunity for all concerned to keep abreast of library activities and any current needs that might be possible projects for the Friends, to hear of proposed projects the Friends would like to undertake, and to deal with any problems that might arise that would affect library operations.

Above all, library boards of trustees need to express their appreciation to Friends for their valuable support and service. This can be expressed in many ways—by letters, certificates, receptions, special honor programs, and media recognition. Words of thanks, however expressed, are always welcome.

In addition to "general" thanks, particular importance should be placed upon recognition, both inside and outside the library, of volunteers who serve the library as unpaid staff. They render an individually significant contribution to the library and to the community. An evaluation of their work and an expression of appreciation by the departmental supervisor are equally important in giving the volunteer Friend proper recognition.

One final important aspect of the trustee-friend relationship is that the partners may well find their positions reversed in the future, for the Friends of the Library organization is an excellent training ground for future library trustees. Moreover, after trustees complete their terms on the library board, they may continue distinguished service as Friends, thereby solidifying a relationship that will continue to provide for the local library the kind of support so necessary to its continuing and successful operation.

RICHMOND, VA.

The Downside Hazards

There are times when the best intentions in the world have been frustrated; everyone is sorry that a Friends group was started. Following are some typical problems described in quotations from Friends and from librarians.

From the Friends:

Our funds are considered to be the property of the trustees (or library director) who wish to spend them as they please.

On one hand we get the feeling we are not doing enough—and on the other that whenever we develop our own ideas, we are overstepping.

Our director is very defensive and unsure and refuses to let us communicate with the library trustees. We are given a role only in a budget crisis.

The library staff is very supportive of us, but we have a weak director and a public relations person who is jealous of our popularity in the town.

The need for mutual respect between the Friends and the professional staff, director, or librarian is partly the librarian's responsibility, too. The librarian's graduate work does not usually include training in the need to work well with laymen who are Friends and trustees.

Our City Council wants to review our budget to determine their funding responsibility. Do they have that right?

From the libraries:

Our Friends are more concerned with book selection than with the needs of the library. They aren't friends of mine.

If the Friends aren't going to give us the money they raise, what is the point of having them?

This is an insider group: members are, to a person, hand-picked by the group leadership and are already accustomed to the forceful personalities that predominate. They will not recruit those they do not know or those who do not appreciate the way they function. They turn off potentially strong members who could be of great help to us.

The Friends need to recognize that the work in a library is never finished and yet records must be kept and reports made to funding agencies at certain intervals, no matter what else is pressing. Friends should remember that personal time given for a Sunday afternoon program is a piece paid out of the librarian's life that cannot be recovered.

Anyone who has ever used a library on a regular basis seems to think he knows how to be a librarian.

The majority of librarians are overworked and underpaid. Dealing with groups of people is time-consuming and can be nervously exhausting. Many librarians would prefer to be allowed to do the job without interruption.

How often does your Friends group recognize the extra time the library staff has given you? If gratitude is due, it should be given publicly.

Many of these problems could have been avoided—or easily solved. Simple courtesy, planning, and communication are the keys to success.

When professionals and laypeople work in an atmosphere in which authority is loosely defined, there can be some resentment. Whether it is caused by an imagined slight or is simply the neurotic reaction of a particular individual, the resentment and resulting hostility are real to the people involved. If a librarian begins to feel that a Friend threatens his or her job, interferes with library work, or opposes policy, it is time to find another place for the volunteer.

Few volunteers intend to provoke ill will. If there is a personality conflict, however, it is the volunteer who must adjust. Sometimes the problem can be overcome by changing assignments. It is also possible that some area of the library will never be good for volunteers. If so, they should be removed completely. Difficulties that persist should be brought to the library director's attention. If no help is forthcoming from that source, it is time to reassess the situation.

Friends can be a valuable work force. They donate their time, perhaps instead of money, to perform tasks that professionals cannot, because of time, money, or space limitation.

What Friends Do

The primary purpose of the Friends organization is to be of service to the library and to the community. Types of libraries and communities are different, with different needs and different talents available. These needs can range widely, from fund-raising to lobbying for a local referendum or providing snacks for the children in story hour. Each community is unique and so, therefore, is each Friends organization.

The library director must work closely with the Friends organization, especially with a newly formed group. The director must ensure that both have the same service goals in mind, that adequate guidelines exist so that Friends can work productively, and that Friends are adequately supervised.

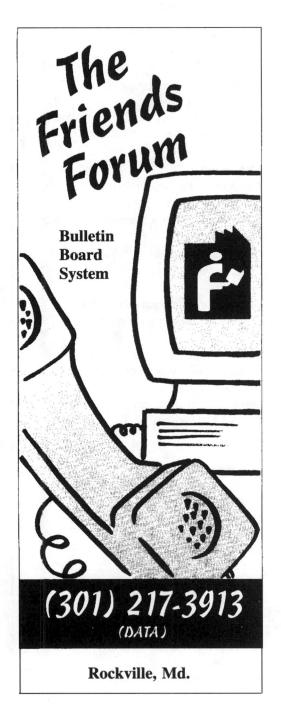

The services that Friends organizations provide fall into three broad groups: fund-raising, service to the community, and service to the library. Within these broad categories there are jobs for those who wish to work with people; for those with special talents; for those who like to work with books; and for those who like to work with local, state, and federal governments. Some of the services performed by existing Friends organizations are listed in figure 1.

One of the reasons why Friends organizations succeed is that many people are willing to work for a cause and accept recognition instead of a salary. A Friends organization can provide an opportunity for individuals to make an identifiable contribution to their community and to their own self-esteem. It provides an outlet for those who wish to be of service, those who wish to polish job skills for reentry into the working world, retired citizens, and the public's relations to the library. The library is thereby using the community to help itself.

National Resource for Friends

As the growing number of libraries with Friends groups demanded some central source of information, a national resource was formed: Friends of Libraries U.S.A.

Figure 1. *Services Performed by Existing Friends Organizations*

Service to the Community

Christmas open house
Produce and host television series or
    radio show
Exhibit booth at county fair
Volunteer for the blind
High school essay contest
Parade float
Outreach program at retirement
    center
Film program for elderly in public
    housing
Oral history
Teachers' tea
Newcomers' day
Survey on library use
Shut-ins brought to the library for
    National Library Week lunch to meet
    staff and the mayor
Send librarian to ALA Convention
Help for "mother's morning out"
Story-phone
Rare-book appraisals

Dress-pattern exchange
Art and craft fairs
Senior citizen teas
Author days
Hobby shows
Coffee hours
Programs for special groups: children,
    senior citizens, young adults,
    business people, homemakers, etc.
Film festivals
Lectures
Study groups
Seminars
Workshops for church librarians
Special anniversary programs
Concerts
Sunday afternoon musical programs
National Library or Book Week
    programs
Series of conservation programs
Vocational seminars

Service to the Library

Advocacy
Clerical help
Coffee and refreshments at programs
Decorate for holidays
Docent program
Tours of the library
Clipping and setting up magazine file
Arrange displays
Manage grounds and shrubs
Painting
Shelving
Assist with mailings
Tune piano
Maintain memorial gift procedure

Clip articles for vertical file
Free paperback book exchange
Typing
Mend books
Run library switchboard
Index newspapers
Index microfilm
Telephoning
Maintain community bulletin board
Care for plants
Make telephone calls to publicize
    important library events
Take special surveys
Present special story times

ROME, GA.

Purchases for the Library

Film programs
Computer hardware
Software
CD-ROMs
CD-ROM players
VCR tapes
Special audiovisual equipment
Matching funds for Reading is
    Fundamental grant
Books
Funds to increase endowment
Special furnishings
Rare books
Printing
Hospital book carts
Rare book repairs
Elevator

Fiscal agent for Humanities Grant
Building repair
Security system
Rental book collection
Copy machine
Large-print books
Landscaping
Shades
Rugs
Magazine subscriptions
Holiday decorations
Art works
Plants and planters
Puppets, toys, and games for children
Story hour treats
Special library brochures

Fund-Raising

Advocacy
Membership drives
Book sales
Bazaars

Special events
Memorial funds
Grant writing
Auctions

Adapted from Iowa Library Friends Conference, 1994.

FOCUS

Friends of Libraries U.S.A.

As the rate of growth of Friends of the Library groups accelerated in the late 1970s, it became clear that some way to increase communication among groups and help them become more visible was necessary.

The first attempt at forming a link among existing groups was the publication in 1978 of the *Friends of Libraries National Notebook,* a quarterly newsletter. Its seventy subscribers included individuals, libraries, and organized Friends groups in large and small libraries, both public and academic. In

1979 Friends of Libraries U.S.A. was organized from that core group as a membership organization. It was formed with the support of the American Library Association (ALA) and remains an affiliate of ALA.

For many years ALA served as FOLUSA's mailing address and provided office services. In 1994 all office and financial functions were transferred to FOLUSA's new Philadelphia headquarters, but the two organizations continue to cooperate and support one another's missions and goals.

Today, as a network of more than 2,800 Friends groups involving more than one million individuals, FOLUSA has become the national volunteer network of support for libraries. It seeks to develop and support local and state groups, and it encourages grass-roots advocacy. It serves as the national voice of local Friends, and provides ideas and information through a comprehensive array of useful and practical publications, videos, and online communications. The newsletter, now named *Friends of Libraries U.S.A. News Update,* provides national news of concern to library Friends, how-to-do-it articles, and an exchange of ideas from across the nation. Its publications guide Friends in their efforts, and its many *Fact Sheets* (see appendix C) provide basic information on a multitude of topics. Popular videotapes produced by FOLUSA cover basic questions such as how to start a group and how to plan successful activities. Annual workshops, programs, and author events are held by FOLUSA in conjunction with ALA's annual convention. In cooperation with Baker & Taylor, FOLUSA administers a program of annual awards for Friends groups.

Speakers, materials, and programs are available from FOLUSA for regional gatherings. Its popular author programs, held at ALA conferences, are also offered to state library association meetings. FOLUSA's services are also requested on a regular basis by libraries in foreign countries eager to form Friends for their libraries. Recently, the Friends of Libraries Australia was formed.

Special programs are held periodically in conjunction with Library Legislative Day in Washington. FOLUSA also recognizes national library supporters for outstanding service to libraries with its annual Public Service Awards.

Today, deciding to go forward with a Friends of the Library group is much easier than it used to be. FOLUSA is a resource for the nation with its collection of materials about successful Friends for all types of libraries. When questions arise, a history exists that will help guide newcomers along the path to successful Friends.

2

Friends on the State and National Level

Jane Rutledge

Local-library Friends groups can expand their horizons and take advantage of good ideas for programs, membership drives, fund-raising, and advocacy from other groups all over the country by joining their state Friends group and Friends of Libraries U.S.A. This chapter presents the steps for organizing a state group, the advantages of state groups, and information on services of Friends of Libraries U.S.A. and by the American Library Association.

Specifics of State Friends of Library Groups

A statewide Friends of Libraries organization is a structured association formed to assist local Friends and to undertake projects on a statewide level. State Friends members are local Friends groups and individual citizens who are dedicated to supporting and strengthening library services and programs throughout the state. A state Friends group provides for communication and collaboration between its members; assists in the formation of new local Friends groups; enables local Friends to be more effective in their support of libraries; and advocates local, state, and national legislation that will benefit libraries.

A state Friends group is usually organized as a not-for-profit, educational, 501(c)(3) corporation. Because the state laws and procedures governing incorporation and sales tax vary, state Friends groups are especially useful in helping local Friends groups through the process of incorporation and getting sales-tax-exempt status.

State legislation often affects local libraries, financially and otherwise; therefore, a state Friends group serves as a legislative information and action network. Advocacy activities include participation in state legislative days, direct lobbying of congress members, providing testimony on library legislation, organizing letter-writing campaigns, and providing library supporters with continuing education for effective advocacy. The following list describes some additional activities of state Friends groups.

Serving as a clearinghouse for speakers, advice, and information. State Friends board members make themselves available to assist local groups who are starting a Friends organization, reviving one, or experiencing problems. State Friends newsletters let local groups and other library supporters know what's going on throughout the state, highlight available resources, and educate members on library issues. Most state Friends groups keep their members in touch with a regularly published newsletter.

State Friends groups in California, Arizona, Minnesota, and Mississippi have published handbooks for the use of local groups.

Friends of Connecticut Libraries made videos on topics of interest to local Friends.

Friends of Maine Libraries have starter packs of Friends information available.

Friends of Indiana Libraries maintain resource materials in five loose-leaf notebooks that are available by interlibrary loan from the state library.

Friends of Michigan Libraries are online with a computer linkup.

Helping new Friends groups get started.

State Friends groups in Kansas, California, Minnesota, and elsewhere go beyond providing information. They offer small "seed money" grants to help emerging Friends groups get on their feet.

Sponsoring programs and workshops.

The "Friends Helping Friends Workshop" (Pennsylvania Citizens for Better Libraries) included a presentation on fund-raising; sessions on strategic planning for membership recruitment and publicity; and sessions on the basics of writing bylaws, filing for incorporation, and registering as a state charitable organization.

Holding gatherings for Friends to share information.

Friends of Michigan Libraries hold periodic meetings, called "Linkings," at various locations around the state. The group presents a program on a topic of interest, such as book sales or newsletters, followed by group discussion and show-and-tell.

Hosting legislative gatherings.

Friends of Tennessee Libraries use a "Pie Day" theme to remind their legislators that libraries deserve a larger slice of the pie.

Citizens for Maryland Libraries cosponsor Legislative Day with the state library association.

The potluck dinner held by Friends of Connecticut Libraries for its legislators has become a tradition.

Sponsoring statewide projects such as public awareness campaigns.

Friends of Connecticut Libraries arranged for the governor to proclaim April as "Library Friends in Connecticut Month."

**To serve the People of Tennessee
here's what the PUBLIC LIBRARY provides
with its piece of the pie:**

* Access to technology
* Genealogical records
* Children's story hours
* Cost-free "how-tos"
* Summer reading programs
* Career information
* Information about legislative issues
* Travel guides
* Information about colleges
* Cookbooks
* Literacy tutoring
* Computers and software
* Investment information
* Special materials for the blind
* Legal information
* Reference books
* All kinds of maps
* Current newspapers/magazines
* Back newspapers/magazines
* Small business information
* Tapes and CDs
* Videotapes
* A quiet place to read

*and MORE

BUT →

Here's how Tennessee
stacks up with the
rest of the country:

47th

in per capita funding
for
PUBLIC LIBRARIES

Tenn. average: $7.44 per capita

Nat'l average: $17.83 per capita

From the state budget
libraries get less than
1/10 of 1%

We deserve a **BIGGER**
piece of the pie

**FRIENDS OF
TENNESSEE
LIBRARIES**

Friends of Libraries in Oklahoma arranged for an influential library supporter to address the legislature.

Friends of Indiana Libraries cosponsored a public-awareness campaign asking citizens to invest in Indiana's information future.

Giving recognition awards for special service to libraries.

Pennsylvania Citizens for Better Libraries recognizes outstanding leadership in the library community with annual awards to a citizen, a Friends group, a local public official, and a legislator.

Friends of California Libraries offer Brag Time Awards, presented at its annual conference to local groups who have been especially successful in supporting their libraries.

Friends of North Carolina Libraries give Outstanding Friends Awards.

Ohio Friends of the Library give Recognition Awards to Friends groups in various size categories.

Developing special programs. In some states the Friends group applies for and receives funds from the Library Services and Construction Act (LSCA) or state humanities councils to conduct or administer statewide activities.

The Minnesota Association of Library Friends sponsors a program on Minnesota writers that is available to local libraries.

Friends of Kansas Libraries created an exchange of children's art with the former USSR, and the children's art from the USSR was exhibited in libraries across the state.

Each year Friends of Mississippi Libraries selects a site to dedicate as a literary landmark in honor of National Library Week; the first ceremony was held at Rowan Oak, the William Faulkner home in Oxford, Mississippi. (The Literary Landmark program is a service of FOLUSA.)

Participating in White House Conference planning. Friends at the state level provided leadership and momentum for planning the White House Conferences on Libraries and Information Services (WHCLIS). Their energy was vital and their long-standing commitment necessary in securing passage of legislation for the White House Conferences. Some state Friends groups were formed as a result of the two White House Conferences, and they have maintained communication and continuity with the citizens who participated in WHCLIS events and in the Governors' Conference activities preceding them. State groups will again play key roles as the states conduct planning activities and mobilize resources for the next conference.

Friends on the State and National Level

Starting a State Friends Group

The establishment of a state Friends group usually begins with a gathering of a few active Friends from many areas in the state. An important partner in the genesis of a state Friends group is the state library; another may be the state library association.

When a broadly based group of library supporters has discussed the formation of a state Friends group and determined to go ahead with it, the group appoints interim committees to work on organizational matters such as bylaws and incorporation, membership and officer recruitment, and programs and projects. Incorporation, gaining not-for-profit status, developing working relationships with other library organizations, and building statewide support are important first tasks. After approval of bylaws and election of its first board of directors, a state Friends group is ready to take on the challenges of developing and nurturing local groups and rallying citizen support for library issues.

Most state Friends groups are supported only by membership dues, which are usually kept low so that all Friends groups in the state, however small and hard-pressed, can afford to join. Some are beginning to augment their modest budgets by going after grants to support special projects, by soliciting support from large individual and corporate donors, and by asking for in-kind assistance (for instance, office space and mailing help) from the state library and the larger Friends groups in the state.

> **From Friends of Indiana Libraries:**
>
> ## *Indiana Book Sales 1995*
>
> **Listing more than 80 book sales, plus ongoing sales and library shops across Indiana**
>
> **8½ × 11, calendar format**
>
> ### $5.00 postpaid
>
> **Orders to: FOIL, 40 Brynteg, West Lafayette, IN 47906. Make checks payable to: Friends of Indiana Libraries.**

An alternative pattern for state Friends is affiliation with the state library association, often in tandem with library trustees as a Friends and trustees roundtable. Friends groups who are affiliated cite the advantages of being part of an established organization with a permanent address, support staff, publications, and a broad membership base. The costs of such affiliation need to be carefully considered, especially the registration fees for statewide meetings.

State Friends groups that have chosen to function as independent groups often mention finances as a determining factor; affiliation may mean larger dues and less control over the Friends' budget. Also, many groups feel that their voice in legislative matters is stronger coming from an independent, citizen-based organization.

Those state Friends groups that opt not to affiliate with the state library association usually do, however, develop strong bonds of cooperation with the association. Often the two groups will hold their annual meetings together, or the Friends will be invited to present programs at the association's meetings. Many state library associations, recognizing the importance of Friends to the libraries of their states, offer Friends reduced rates at their conferences and workshops. Some state groups reduce meeting costs significantly by holding meetings at a library rather than a conference site.

Besides the state library and the library association, other important liaisons may include the trustees organization, the State Center for the Book, other library organizations, and the White House Conference Task Force.

Friends of Libraries U.S.A. offers support and advice to state Friends groups and helps keep them in touch with one another by way of the State Friends Network, which serves as a clearinghouse for state Friends information.

State Friends and the State Library

An important field of activity for state Friends, in cooperation with their state libraries and state Centers for the Book, is literacy and the promotion of reading. State Friends are able to sponsor and promote literacy and reading programs, participate in coalitions, work on public relations campaigns, and encourage citizen involvement.

State Friends groups may sponsor literacy and reading events, including book and author dinners, "read-ins" with notable people reading aloud as part of a public program, receptions honoring their state's authors, and book festivals. Some state Friends have participated in the creation of the state Center for the Book and cooperated in its activities.

FOCUS

Friends of Maine Libraries

Friends of Maine Libraries has established a grants program for its organizational members. The initial grants were offered for the purchase of "Books for Babies" kits, a Friends of Libraries U.S.A. program that was adapted for local use.

A second grants program has been added that provides funds for books on tape. Winning libraries may purchase audiocassettes for children or adults with their grant funds. A list of recommended titles is provided, but libraries are free to select any titles they wish.

Local libraries and Friends groups are encouraged to apply for the awards by submitting a brief application. The grants are awarded at the Friends of Maine Libraries annual meeting to libraries in each of the three regional library districts.

The grants program, which is planned to continue for the foreseeable future, provides another reason for local libraries and Friends to join the newly organized state Friends group. Because grant applicants must be current dues-paying members, the program has been a membership builder. The grants are funded in part from the Friends of Maine Libraries operating budget and in part from contributions.

The state Friends usually support the state library association's legislative agenda, and the two groups work together closely on advocacy activities.

Action Point

Friends of Connecticut Libraries

Friends of Connecticut Libraries has maintained a close relationship with its state library's Division of Public and Cooperative Library Services. In 1992 the two groups put into writing an agreement between the Friends and the state library. (See appendix E.) The state library agreed to plan, coordinate, and fund one workshop annually for Friends, to meet regularly with the Friends program committee, to include Friends in appropriate statewide planning activities, and to house the Friends archives and resource materials. The Friends agreed to conduct annual needs assessment for the state library, to serve as liaison for the state library with Friends throughout the state, and to support the state library's continuing education activities.

Challenges Facing State Friends Groups

Because they are usually volunteer, dues-supported organizations, state Friends groups are vulnerable to certain problems.

Leadership

Recruiting and retaining officers and board members may be difficult in a statewide organization. Many devoted and enthusiastic Friends feel that their first loyalty is to their local group, with little time and energy left over for another organization.

Because board meetings will involve travel, the outlay of time and expense may discourage potential board members. Also, the personal relationships that help in recruiting at the local level may be lacking when the organization tries to find the right volunteers from a wide geographic area. It is a challenge, too, to develop good working relationships among board members who may see one another only a few times a year.

As is the case with any volunteer organization, leadership recruitment and development must be a full-time concern, with all current board members actively involved in searching for the next generation of officers. Officers of local groups are often able to represent their areas with significant leadership skills.

Geography

Solutions must be found for the problems inherent in an association whose officers may be scattered from one end of the state to another. It is important for a state Friends group to establish a permanent mailing address so that important communications do not get lost with every change of officers. Often the state library will agree to serve as a mailing address and forward mail to the current officers.

It is also important that a statewide organization draw its leadership from a wide geographic area, and that it be committed to serve libraries and Friends groups of all sizes. In large states, regional gatherings may be a solution to the problems of travel for representatives of remote groups.

Communication

Keeping in touch is becoming easier for officers, with greater use of the telephone, conference calls, and increasing E-mail opportunities. However, members also need to hear from the organization with some degree of regularity, either through a newsletter or special mailings. Informing and involving the members of a state group is a continuing challenge.

A Perspective for the Millennium

Statewide Friends groups take with them into the year 2000 the problems of the 1990s. As libraries face the concurrent demands of new technology and fiscal restraints, citizen support becomes even more vital for their continued health and growth. At the same time, citizen groups face the challenges posed by the drying up of the traditional volunteer pool and public discouragement about the possibility of making a difference. State Friends groups will play a strong role in creating adequate legislative and local support for libraries.

Local Friends groups must find ways to be more effective with increasingly limited resources. Sharing ideas and, just as important, sharing energy and enthu-

siasm, with other Friends helps keep local groups energized. State Friends groups will continue to foster these exchanges and provide services to maintain the health and vigor of local Friends.

State Friends groups will increasingly find themselves filling new roles and expanding old ones, as technological and societal changes bring new challenges to the library community. Among these may be

> emphasizing the important role of Friends of the Library groups as advocates for legislative action and continuing financial support for libraries
>
> expanding the awareness of the role of Friends groups in the overall mission of the library and assisting local groups in finding new ways to help the library reach its goals in areas such as literacy, outreach programs, and the importance of technology and information access in a free society
>
> publicizing activities and partnerships available to Friends groups that will provide support for library development and enhance citizen advocacy

As we approach the year 2000, technology will further change the ways in which citizens receive and use information. Some issues of public policy must be resolved:

> What information is provided without cost to the user and what is fee-based?
>
> What government information is given to the private sector for later sale to users?
>
> What information remains public and what is sealed by the government as confidential?

Libraries will also be coping with decisions about the delivery of information to people in their residences, workplaces, and classrooms. Adequate funding—to preserve collections, to enable libraries to play their traditional and current roles well, and to provide the ability to begin new ones—will be crucial.

Given these challenges, statewide Friends groups have a vital and necessary role. They ensure that libraries are responsive to the society in which they are situated, that there is broad public support for libraries and their services, and that libraries survive as keepers of the human memory and benchmarks of our values.

The American Library Association

Linda Wallace, director, Public Information Office, ALA

The American Library Association (ALA), founded in 1876, is the oldest and largest library organization in the world. Its 57,000 members are primarily librarians, but membership also includes trustees, publishers, Friends, and library supporters. Its mission is to ensure the highest quality library and information service for the American people and to advocate for the public's right to a free and open information society.

The ALA Office for Information Technology Policy provides counsel and support materials to policymakers, librarians, and the public in dealing with issues such as public access to government information, copyright, and fair use.

The association's Washington office educates and works with legislators to obtain the federal support necessary for libraries to flourish. Library supporters from all fifty states gather each year for Library Legislative Day to discuss key issues of concern with members of Congress.

ALA maintains a vigorous program to defend the public's right to read, listen to, and view library materials representing all points of view. A "Library Bill of Rights," first adopted in 1939, serves as an interpretation of the First Amendment to the Constitution.

ALA also sponsors National Library Week every April to celebrate the contributions of America's libraries and librarians. The association publishes a variety of materials to support schools and libraries in promoting the importance of libraries and literacy year around. A free ALA graphics catalog offers posters, banners, bookmarks, booklists, T-shirts, jewelry, and other gift items with proceeds going to support the work of the association.

The ALA Public Programs Office works to develop exhibits and programs such as Writers Live at the Library to support libraries as centers for culture, literacy, and learning, often with the help of major foundations and corporations.

The ALA's foundation, the Fund for America's Libraries, founded in 1995, seeks major gifts to support ALA and the nation's libraries in fulfilling their mission.

The ALA headquarters is in Chicago. Two major membership meetings are held each year, an annual conference in June and a midwinter meeting in January, offering exhibits and programs on wide-ranging topics related to libraries and information issues.

For more information call or write:
    The American Library Association
    50 E. Huron St.
    Chicago, IL 60611
    Tel: (312) 944-6780
    Toll-free: (800) 545-2433

Friends of
Michigan
Libraries

Friends of Libraries U.S.A. Programs

Many programs have been designed by Friends of Libraries U.S.A. to help local and state groups enjoy the benefits of a larger group, so that their efforts can be concentrated on local affairs. Following are some of these national programs.

> Books for Babies is a program initiated by FOLUSA to make literacy materials available to local groups for distribution. Kits for parents of newborns include baby's first library card and a book.

> Literary Landmarks programs provide plaques and advice on planning events to honor significant literary figures and locations in every state. Handsome brass markers are placed on the designated sites.

> Literary Tours of Britain provide high-quality, custom-tailored tours of interest to readers. Friends groups may sponsor tours or join already established ones. "Myth and Mystery of Great Britain" is one popular itinerary, including visits to homes of mystery writers and places of interest to readers of that genre. Other tours are available. A special feature of the FOLUSA tours is the ability to get travelers behind the scenes and to provide events that are unavailable to other tourists. Each traveler makes a donation to the library.

From time to time FOLUSA is able to arrange special programs that are made available to local Friends through national corporations seeking partnerships.

Outlook for the Future

The voice of the citizen is often the most effective medium for reaching politicians and decision makers. However, the voices of library Friends may be overlooked by professionals at the local and state level unless mechanisms are in place to give this interest group a chance to express its interest and opinions.

In many states, Friends are becoming involved in citizen-trustee councils and occupy liaison positions in library organizations. State library associations and state divisions for library service need to learn to include Friends in their meetings so that an educated group will exist well before the last budget meeting is held and the cry for citizen input is heard.

FOLUSA is committed to helping Friends help their libraries and equally committed to helping communities and decision makers know and understand the special role and contributions of Friends groups. FOLUSA's efforts and activities continue to bring the name of Friends of the Library to the attention of the public.

FOLUSA's state Friends network keeps in touch with state Friends organizations and provides information, resource-sharing, and advice. Figure 2 lists the network's participants as of 1995.

Figure 2. *1995 State Friends Network Participants*

Friends of Alabama Libraries

Arizona Library Friends

Friends of Arkansas Libraries

Friends of California Libraries

Colorado Library Association Trustees and Friends Division

Friends of Connecticut Libraries

Friends of Delaware Libraries (in progress)

Federation of Friends of the District of Columbia Public Library System

Florida Library Association Friends and Trustees Caucus

Georgia Library Friends

Friends of the Library of Hawaii

Friends of Illinois Libraries

Friends of Indiana Libraries

Iowa Library Friends

Friends of Kansas Libraries

Friends of Kentucky Libraries

Friends of Libraries of Louisiana

Friends of Maine Libraries

Citizens for Maryland Libraries

Massachusetts Friends of the Library

Friends of Michigan Libraries

Minnesota Association of Library Friends

Friends of Mississippi Libraries

Trustees and Friends Council of the Missouri Library Association

Nevada State Friends

Association of New Hampshire Library Friends

New Jersey Friends of Libraries

New Mexico Library Association Friends and Trustees Interest Group

Empire Friends (New York State)

Friends of North Carolina Public Libraries

Ohio Friends of the Library

Friends of Libraries in Oklahoma

Oregon Friends of the Library

Pennsylvania Citizens for Better Libraries

Rhode Island Coalition of Library Advocates

Friends of South Carolina Libraries

Friends of Tennessee Libraries

Friends and Trustees Roundtable of the Texas Library Association

Vermont Friends and Trustees Committee

Friends of Virginia Libraries

Washington Library Friends and Trustees Association

West Virginia Friends of the Library

Friends of Wisconsin Libraries

3

Getting Organized

Sandy Dolnick

There is no magic formula for organizing a Friends of the Library group, but there is an old one. It is given by Alexis de Tocqueville in *Democracy in America* (1835, 1840) in his description of the American character:

> These Americans are the most peculiar people in the world. You'll not believe it when I tell you how they behave. In a local community in their country, a citizen may conceive of some need which is not being met. What does he do? He goes across the street and discusses it with his neighbor. Then what happens? A committee begins to function on behalf of the need. You won't believe this, but it's true: all of this is done without reference to any bureaucrat. All of this is done by private citizens on their own initiative.

Amazingly, the customs mentioned have not changed significantly since then. Some public positions change, but the American experience still includes an important role for volunteerism to right wrongs, better the community, and make the best place possible for one's home and family. Americans feel they are empowered to make things better if they do not like the society in which they live. They still talk to their neighbors and find ways to make a positive change as a Neighborhood Watch, Mothers Against Drunk Driving, or Friends of the Library group. We are very fortunate to live in a society in which conditions can be changed by the positive actions of a small group of people.

This ability to call the community to action is not something easily carried outside our borders. The attitudes of expectation in a socialist environment are directed toward the government, not to the individual within the society. Advocacy pressures at the local levels do not have the same accountability in other countries. Many new citizens to the United States have to be educated about charitable giving and community responsibility.

The First Leaders

The force that is the natural starting point for formation of a Friends organization in any given community varies from situation to situation. Initial leadership can come from the library director who calls interested citizens together, from a member of the community who may have had prior experience with a Friends group or who just sees a need, or from an established community organization. Groups that have a history of assisting include library trustees, local charities or foundations, civic leagues, Rotary Clubs, Jaycees, the American Association of University Women, the League of Women Voters, school parent-teacher associations, the Junior League, literary clubs, and the Federation of Women's Clubs. Someone must recognize the need for action and must provide enthusiastic leadership.

Friends of Libraries are a diverse group of people. The members span all age groups and other demographic characteristics. Their reason for joining may be because they are aware of how important it is to support the library. It may be for more-selfish reasons: to combat loneliness and to meet people, to learn job skills, or to make business or social contacts. Usually, Friends love books and enjoy being around them and around people who are also interested in them. It is important to provide a means for all of these needs to be satisfied.

Principles for Success

If adhered to and reviewed annually, certain principles, as listed in figure 3, will develop a nurturing atmosphere and pleasant environment for Friends and library staff. The ten commandments were learned through the combined experiences of hundreds of groups.

Groups being organized should be able to check off each item listed in figure 3; established groups will find this list a good yearly evaluation. By renewing its principles each year, a group can retain the vitality of a new organization and reap the benefits of experience.

Steering Committee

Once the decision has been made to form a Friends group, a steering committee or planning group should be established as soon as possible to maintain the initial enthusiasm. This committee should represent the library's constituency. The steering committee will work in close consultation with the library leadership and with the board of trustees, as appropriate.

Figure 3. *The Ten Commandments of a Successful Friends Group*

1. The library director must be in favor of a Friends group. If this is not the case, do not proceed any farther. There is no use in continuing.

2. The library staff must be willing to work with Friends—at least that part of the staff that comes into contact with the Friends.

3. All parties involved must realize that a time commitment is involved and that a successful group is no accident. The activity level of the group will determine the amount of time involved; if there is only one book sale a year to worry about, for example, there will be minimal time involved *once the group is organized.*

4. The library must agree on which of its resources (e.g., space, staff time, paper, and telephone) will be used by the Friends.

5. A committed core group must exist. This core group may be only two or three people.

6. The authority to which the library director reports must recognize the Friends group.

7. Communication must be open to the full library community; the Friends should not have an exclusionist policy.

8. All those involved in the Friends must realize that the Friends group does not make library policy, which is the function of the trustees. Trustees and Friends have separate functions, and liaisons should be developed between the two groups.

9. The library must decide, in discussion with the Friends, the roles it wishes the group to play: advocate, social, fund-raising, volunteer, or a combination. These roles change as needs change, so they should be reviewed annually.

10. Money raised by the Friends should be disbursed by them as they see fit according to information on the library's needs, provided by the library director and the trustee's liaison.

Formal Organization

All planning will flow from the mission statement adopted by the Friends. It is usually restated in the purpose section of the constitution of the organization; many examples are found throughout this book. The statement is what defines the Friends and makes them unique from other similar organizations working with libraries. Although you may have a general idea of what is expected of the Friends, you want a statement that will allow for some flexibility as the organization matures. Therefore, statements such as "to support better library services" are used rather than "to supplement the book budget." Other decisions will be needed.

SAN BERNARDINO COUNTY LIBRARY
FRIENDS OF THE LIBRARY

MISSION

To build a partnership between the library and the community to advocate for quality library service for all of the people of San Bernardino County.

PURPOSE

To maintain an association of persons interested in the library, to focus public attention in a positive manner on library services, facilities and needs, to help promote the use and enjoyment of the library, to develop supplemental funding for the library and to actively support the policies and procedures of the San Bernardino County Library in the community and at the local branch library.

MEMBERSHIP

Residents or business members of a community who value the service of public libraries join an organized Friends of the Library group to volunteer their time and talent, to promote the use of the library, to assist the library staff and to augment and enhance library service.

PROGRAM

- Recruit members from the community on a continual basis seeking representation that reflects the community's population.

- Sponsor library programs provided for children, youth and adults.

- Plan and implement fund-raising activities including book sales.

- Provide funds to purchase materials and equipment as recommended by library branch manager.

- Represent the library point of view to legislators and the media.

- Acknowledge and support the library's plans, progress, decisions and future needs.

- Develop and provide social and educational activities as requested by members for the Friends.

- Encourage the unrestricted donation of gifts, endowments and bequests to the library.

Decide upon a fiscal year. The steering committee will probably decide to set up the Friends as a not-for-profit corporation. Consult a lawyer about the procedures involved in doing so. Not-for-profit status will enable the Friends to make mass mailings at third-class rates, a considerable savings. More importantly, not-for-profit status also qualifies the group to file for tax exemptions. If granted an exemption, the group will pay no tax on its income. Contributors to the Friends will also be able to deduct their donations from their income tax. Virtually all religious, charitable, or educational institutions are not-for-profit corporations with tax-exempt status. It is extremely difficult to raise funds for an organization that is not tax-exempt.

Another extremely important reason for having the group incorporate is to defuse any potential problems about where the money that is raised belongs. While in the initial flush of enthusiasm it may seem incomprehensible that there may be conflict about the use of funds, that is the most common problem expressed by librarians, trustees, and Friends in calls to the FOLUSA office. While it may only reflect personality conflicts that are inevitable in human relations, or misuse of power in the worst possible instance, there are ways to make it a nonissue. One way is to incorporate as a nonprofit. Then the monies will not become part of the general operating budget of the municipality or of the library. Funds must, of course, be spent in accordance with the mission statement on behalf of the library.

Before a Friends group can incorporate, it must write a constitution and bylaws that include the name of the organization and its purpose, membership, dues classes (not amounts), and officers. Committees, size of the board, and specific dues amounts do not need to be expressed except in general terms. The constitution and bylaws should also provide for meetings and activities, include procedures for amendment, and include a clause stipulating that upon dissolution of the Friends the remaining monies fall to the library. See appendix B for examples of Friends constitutions.

Once the organization is incorporated, it will be necessary to notify the federal and state government to change the constitution. Therefore, it is best to make the constitution as basic as possible. It is easier to change the bylaws than the constitution, but even they should be general enough that the board does not have to go through a delay to change general operating procedures. The constitution and bylaws should be short, concise, and flexible enough to be functional as the organization grows and expands. They should also reflect long-range goals. A group that is formed for the specific purpose of raising funds for a new library, for example, will find its task complete when the building is a reality. But since that is the time when volunteers are needed most to extend library services and to provide extra support for new projects, the constitution and bylaws should make long-term library support the goal of the organization rather than raising funds for a library building. The documents should be carefully phrased so that the Friends can obtain tax-exempt status without delay. Again, consult a lawyer about these matters.

Another important point to consider in the group's bylaws is provision for regular board turnover. If such provisions are not made, the board may become

FRIENDS OF THE MACOMB PUBLIC LIBRARY DISTRICT

Winter 1994/95

Historic Occasion: First Annual Meeting

When: Monday, January 30, 1995

Where: Bailey House, 100 S. Campbell

What: Social hour: 6 p.m. - Wine and hors d'oeuvres
             Dinner: 6:30 p.m. - Catered by the Bottenberg Inn
                     Cost: $10 per person, including gratuity
          Business meeting (brief)
          Program

We may seem to be full of ourselves as we draw to the close of our first year -- and we should be! We have made some great starts. Now it is time to move forward into our second year. You, the members, need to give the organization direction. That is done through the annual meeting. The basic business that must be done includes adopting by-laws changes, adopting a budget, and electing officers and directors. All of these items are detailed elsewhere in this newsletter. We hope you will come prepared to make your decisions and take advantage of the opportunity to tell the Board of Directors what you would like the Friends to accomplish this next year.

To cap off the evening and still get you home in good time, Dennis has arranged for Brent Crossland, Specialist for Rural Library Affairs from the Illinois State Library, to give us his view of current happenings and how we, as Friends, fit into the picture.

THANKS GO TO THE MACOMB
ROTARY CLUB, SPONSOR OF
THIS NEWSLETTER.

self-perpetuating. The bylaws should stipulate that board members have staggered terms and should limit the length of service allowed.

Getting organized obviously takes a great deal of planning by the founders beyond their initial desire to start a Friends group. A knowledge of the community served by the group is fundamental.

All interested parties should review and comment on the constitution and bylaws. The steering committee may write a draft, make it available at the library for study, and present it to the inaugural meeting of the Friends. Alternatively, the documents may be formulated at the inaugural meeting. However, this can prove time-consuming, and most members are not that interested. Drafts should be sent to the library leadership and the board of trustees, as appropriate, before they are formally adopted by the Friends membership.

Fiscal Policy

Prudent governance requires wise fiscal conservancy. Record keeping is essential to trace the flow of money donated and to keep track of the organization's expenses. Decisions regarding expenditures over an agreed-upon amount should be a joint responsibility of a finance committee or of the treasurer, president, and concerned committee chair. Large organizations may have an executive director who would share the responsibility with the president.

Collect receipts listing the amount, reason for expense, and signature of the responsible party, even for petty cash. There have been occasions of flagrant abuse where the Friends have chosen to ignore their fiscal responsibility. Very simple accounting methods, now often computerized, should preclude any such oversight.

To effectively accomplish a mission, any organization must have good financial procedures, a reporting process, and audit controls. Nonprofit organizations, due to limited resources of staff and budgetary needs, may fall short of giving this infrastructure the attention it must have. Viability of the organization is dependent upon reasonable and adequate financial and audit controls.

The responsibility lies with the board of directors to ensure that comprehensible, accurate, and timely financial reports are presented to the board with full disclosure of all matters. Additionally, reasonable audit controls should be in place. A key to ensuring adequate controls is to engage a professional accounting/auditing firm. This is a critical first step in ensuring full accountability to the board of directors of the day-to-day operations of the organization.

Financial Statement

Every board meeting should include a report of the financial state of the Friends. The statement should list income and expenses grouped by category. Any simple accounting program, such as Quicken, will easily produce this report if each financial transaction is recorded as it occurs. Income could include items such as dues, donations, grants, income from sales, and interest income. Expenses may be supplies, telephone, postage, printing, wages, insurance. Cash on hand or unallocated funds should be indicated, and the ending balance should be included.

All petty cash slips, receipts, and checks should be saved and filed. Donation checks should be photocopied as well as entered into the bookkeeping program.

The First Board of Directors

After the steering committee has presented the constitution, bylaws, and a slate of officers to the inaugural meeting of the Friends, a new board of directors must be elected. The steering committee may wish to be a part of it, or they may feel that their contributions are complete. The board should take into account the suggestions found in Fact Sheet 14 in appendix C, one of a series of Fact Sheets published by Friends of Libraries U.S.A.

Most Friends groups have a president, vice-president, secretary, and treasurer who perform the traditional duties associated with these positions. Some also have executive or advisory boards of ten to twenty-five members that include the officers and chairs of such committees as membership, program, publicity, finance, and publications. Organizational guidelines help in board transitions from one year to the next. In a well-organized board all members have a responsibility. People will drop off a board if they feel they are not being appreciated or are wasting their time. The policies of two Friends groups appear in figure 4.

The board should represent the overall community's background and education. Well-known people should be encouraged to join the Friends. Even though they may have little time to give to the organization, their community contacts will be valuable. Also actively recruit a lawyer to help with legal matters and a person with publicity experience and media contacts.

Make a special effort to expand the board by recruiting minorities and members of other groups that form natural allies with the Friends. Ask specific groups to appoint liaisons to the Friends board. It is also a good way to identify future board members. Groups to consider asking include members of the clergy and members of the Woman's Club, Rotary, PTA, Chamber of Commerce, and Junior Chamber of Congress. Recruit a student representative from area high schools, school administration, etc. It is easier to fill a liaison position than you might think, since the liaison carries no responsibility except to report on the Friends organization and to report back to the Friends.

A typical agenda for a board of directors meeting is presented in figure 5 on page 37. The chairperson should be familiar with parliamentary procedure for clari-

SAINT PAUL, MINN.

Figure 4. *Sample Policies*

Friends of the San Francisco Public Library
Board Responsibilities

Board members have four responsibilities, that of

     governors
     sponsors
     ambassadors
     consultants

As governors, board members carry out their legal and fiduciary responsibilities. They must attend monthly board meetings (usually held on the second Wednesday of each month at noon in the Main Library). It is understood that occasionally meetings will be missed. However, when three consecutive meetings are not attended, the president or his/her representative may ask the member to resign from the board to allow someone else to be appointed to fulfill the responsibilities.

As sponsors, the primary activity is fund-raising. The board is chosen to reflect the city's economic, racial, social, and gender diversity. All board members must be FOL members in good standing. While all may not be able to make additional financial donations, this should not keep them from participating in revenue-gathering efforts. Some possibilities include membership recruitment booths, calling lapsed members, sharing personal and professional contacts, etc.

As ambassadors, board members are expected to articulate FOL's role and mission, especially as it relates to the Library, the Commission, and the Library Foundation. With prior authorization of the president or executive director, they may also be asked to speak at public gatherings; however, they exercise authority as board members only when designated by the board to do so.

As consultants, board members truly show their uniqueness, contributing in ways and areas best suited to them. The board does most of its important work in committees. Board members are expected to actively participate in one or more of them.

I understand and will fulfill my FOL Board Member responsibilities to the best of my ability.

          Name   Date

(continued)

Figure 4. *Sample Policies (cont.)*

Friends of the Berkeley Public Library
Guidelines

1. Board members shall become informed of library practices and services and shall interpret these to the community as opportunities may arise.

2. Board members shall participate in monthly board meetings.

3. Board members shall attend one or more trustees' meetings during the year.

4. Most board positions shall have assigned duties; however, as circumstances dictate, up to one-fifth of the board members may be designated members-at-large. Members-at-large will be given committee assignments by the president.

5. At the end of each term in office, board members shall hand on to the next person holding that position a written description of the job, detailing the procedures followed and the activities undertaken that year.

fication of correct procedures for handling various motions and discussions. Even in a small, informal group, adherence to the general etiquette of parliamentary procedure will enhance the conduct of business and will satisfy requirements for propriety.

Committees

Some committee descriptions develop as time allows the group to evolve. For example, the following committees may be formed to handle specific aspects of the organization.

Advocacy committee to formulate and oversee advocacy efforts in conjunction with library staff

Awards committee to nominate and designate worthy library supporters

Book Sale committee to plan sale and collect, process, and sell books

Budget and Finance committee to track the budget and fund-raising financial balances and to oversee expenses

Development committee to seek new sources of income

Executive committee usually made up of officers, to function when the whole board is not available but action is necessary

Figure 5. *Sample Agenda*

Agenda

Call to order

Minutes of the previous meeting*

Correspondence (may be read, summarized, or circulated)

President's report (report on activities undertaken on behalf of group)

Treasurer's report*

Standing committee reports (e.g., volunteers, program, membership, publicity, or any committee that is part of the group's regular structure)

Special committee reports (include such special efforts as fundraising, book sales, receptions, National Library Week, etc.)

Old business

New business

Adjournment*

*Motion called for

Hospitality committee to welcome attendees at programs, involve new members, and see to refreshments for meetings

Membership committee to increase membership by finding new opportunities to reach nonmembers

Nominating committee to work with the board to find representatives of the library population and geographic area to join the board

Publications committee to produce and evaluate written materials and newsletters

Special Projects committee to see to such projects as community fairs, memorial donations, and one-of-a-kind projects

Volunteers committee to coordinate schedules and sign up members

Publicity

With organizational questions out of the way, it is time to tell the community about the Friends and to seek support and membership. The news media are usually willing to use their public-service time and space on behalf of library activities and Friends groups. The Friends' publicity developers should do their homework first, however, if they expect media cooperation. (See chapter 7 for more information on publicity.) Editors are best approached by a person who has publicity experience, media contacts, and a press release in hand. If the Friends group wants free print space or air time for membership recruitment advertising, it should prepare the advertisement first and submit it to the appropriate person. Comments or suggestions from media professionals should be welcomed. If the Friends organization wants to be represented on a community radio or television program, it should have available a list of knowledgeable speakers.

Many business firms and community organizations can provide valuable publicity support to Friends. Banks, public utilities, fast food restaurants, chambers of commerce, churches, and service clubs may have bulletin boards, newsletters, or regular meetings through which membership in Friends can be promoted.

Clarifying Roles

Friends groups exist to help implement the policies of the trustees and library director. The group is free to function in many ways as public relations agent and volunteer workers to extend library services and information that could not be handled by the regular staff. From the very start, therefore, it is imperative that the library staff understand the purpose of the Friends organization and accept it as an ally. Likewise, members of the board of trustees or governing board should know about the organization and should keep open channels of communication between the Friends and themselves. At no time should actions of the Friends appear to infringe upon the policy-making privileges of the trustees.

To facilitate cooperation, the Friends group should send a regular observer or liaison to trustee meetings. In turn, a trustee may be an ex officio member of the Friends board. As for the library staff, the director is responsible for interpreting the activities of the Friends to the staff and for enlisting the staff's support and cooperation for these activities.

Growth and Changes

Building an active, growing Friends organization is often a slow process. A noon film program, for example, may start with a small group. If the first participants become involved in film selection and learn of other Friends activities, participation may grow each year. Most fund-raising beginnings are also modest. The used book sale may not raise as much money in the first year as the one in the next town. The

important thing to remember at the beginning is that each activity should make new Friends. As membership grows and the Friends group becomes better known, its activities will gain more support. The ways that Friends can help to promote library services are limited only by the imagination of the membership.

Bylaws

After the Friends group has been in operation for a year or so, experience may indicate that the bylaws need to be amended. For instance, the board may need to increase or decrease in size, meeting times may need to be changed, or election procedures altered. Some groups have found that their constitution and bylaws needed revision because they were cumbersome and did not allow the group to adapt to changing needs. (See the example in figure 6.) The bylaws are the means by which the group operates to reach its goals. The group's guidelines evolve through experience; each organization is different. It may well be several years before the Friends group has bylaws that are completely satisfactory.

Administrative Assistance

As groups mature and grow, they often find it necessary to hire a paid employee. This is no longer a luxury enjoyed by only a few university and public library Friends groups. This person may work part-time or full-time serving as executive secretary or executive director. Keeping the financial and membership records and carrying on the correspondence for the group are some of the duties he or she may perform. The employee can provide continuity and help in planning special events. Two of the employee's most important services are answering the telephone and answering the questions of a member. The library often provides the office space, equipment, and supplies.

Hazards

If a Friends group is founded without the support of some existing community organization, it is important that the first people chosen to speak for the Friends are representative of the types of people who can be expected to join. The entire tone of a Friends group is determined by its nucleus of organizers. A group where founders are truly representative of the community will be more successful. But the wrong person speaking for the group, even with the best of intentions, can harm or destroy a new organization. One librarian found out too late that the person she

Figure 6. *Sample Proposed Bylaws Change*

In a process that began early in the fall, the Friends board debated and discussed a series of amendments to the Friends bylaws. Friends familiar with the laborious and lengthy procedure through which those bylaws were adopted might well regard board members as gluttons for punishment, but the year of experience operating under the bylaws for the first time suggested the wisdom of change.

At the Friends annual meeting in January the board will offer the following proposed changes in the bylaws, following the procedure prescribed in the bylaws in Article VII, section 1, and Article VIII, section 2. This method requires a four-week, written notice of the proposed amendments and a two-thirds majority of those present and voting at the annual meeting.

Amendment #1. Section 2 of Article VII (which covers membership meetings) currently reads: "Regular meetings of the membership shall be held once each month, on the third Thursday, prior to the meeting of the District Library Board. In addition to the conduct of regular business, membership meetings shall include informational programs consistent with the stated purpose of the Friends organization." Your board proposes to replace section 2 with the following new paragraph: "Membership meetings, other than the annual meeting, are held at the discretion of the board, with the time, place, and agenda announced at least thirty days in advance of the meeting. Ten percent of the membership may, by petition, require the board to call a membership meeting within forty-five days of submitting the petition and require one or more agenda items for that meeting. In addition to the conduct of the regular business of the organization, membership meetings may include informational and social programs consistent with the stated purpose of the Friends organization."

Rationale: *At first glance this change may look like a naked power grab on the part of the board. Not so! Friends members in 1994 clearly demonstrated their lack of interest in monthly meetings held to conduct routine business only, meetings held solely because the bylaws required them. To avoid this robotic and mechanical routine attended by a small fraction of the membership the board proposes this amendment that will eliminate the necessity of regular monthly meetings. As a safety valve the proposed amendment includes a means by which a relatively small number of members can require a meeting in the absence of board action. It is the intent of this amendment to have fewer general membership meetings and make them more meaningful and interesting.*

had entrusted with the job of building a Friends group was antagonizing both the community and her staff.

Respondents to a survey of Friends groups indicated that careful choice of leadership, judicious planning for the long term, and continuing review of the Friends' goals and accomplishments are vitally necessary. "We had a 'false start' several years before actual organization," one respondent wrote. "We started with a 'committee' and the chairman didn't carry through. . . . The librarian and board representative selected the beginning group. The first chairman or president must be dependable." Another respondent stated that "Our library director has placed his wife in charge of a very important project for our group. She has no organizational ability and refuses help when it is offered. It reflects on us, but we have no way out."

One respondent complained: "It has been my experience with the present group and with others that after they have been established for many years, the active members tend to form a tight little unit that seems unwilling to make a concerted effort to get new blood into the organization. This situation can be very difficult to overcome!" Another declared that "I'm fairly new to the group, and I find a small group of long-time library supporters somewhat ingrown. (This is especially true of book-sale workers.) New ideas and workers are welcomed with reservations. A desire to retain the old tasks, friendships, relationships, etc., at the expense of attracting board members from a broader base in the community stifles vitality. Resistance to formal procedures and decision making is another problem."

It is heartening to note the growing numbers of groups that have succeeded at this task. A large number of aids designed to provide help in the formative period and beyond are contained in subsequent chapters of this book.

Again, there is no one correct way to proceed in organizing a Friends group—if one method does not work, another will. The winning combination is made up of those personalities and elements unique to each community.

4

Management by Objectives

Sarah C. Hite

Management by objectives (MBO) is a management system that is used extensively and successfully by corporations, government agencies, and libraries. It also is a very effective tool for Friends groups. Although many Friends boards and their committees are already doing systematized planning, the boards may not define as clearly the steps for efficient organization that MBO represents. Although MBO will not revolutionize Friends activities, it is a tool that when used properly helps the group define its goals, evaluate its accomplishments, and make its plans. If Friends groups take the trouble to learn and apply MBO, they can save hours later on. Like anything else, the more MBO is practiced, the easier it becomes.

Definitions

Following are definitions of several terms used in the MBO process.

Alternate plan: A contingency plan should the original fail.

Control: A check; an assessment that warns of problems in advance.

Evaluation: Both the first and the final step. As the first step, one reviews current resources and possible directions. As the final step, one reviews the results, the use of resources, and the effectiveness of management.

Goal: Statement of intentions; general direction.

Leadership: The art of getting people to do things. Leaders understand and make use of the motivations, needs, and emotions of others; they find ways to get people to work with enthusiasm.

Management: The use of an organization's five basic resources: money, workforce power, materials, time, and authority.

Management process: An analytical system of organizing resources to get results.

MBO: Management by objectives, a five-step cyclical management process. (See figure 7.)

FRIENDS
ATLANTA, GA.

Figure 7. *The Process of Management*

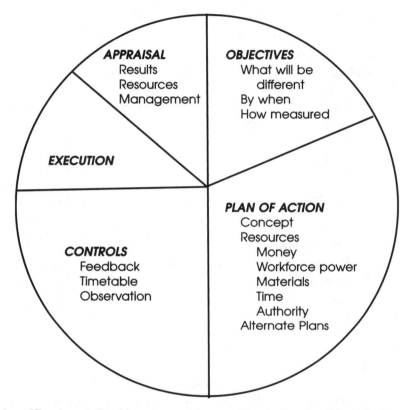

Adapted from "The Association Management Process: How to Practice What We Preach."

Method: Plan; how to reach objectives.

Objective: Specific statement of what is to be accomplished (or what will be different or changed), by when (the specific future time), and how results will be measured.

Purpose: The reason for being; why the group exists.

An Outline of Management

The steps involved in the process of management are shown in outline form.

Purpose: The mission that the organization is intended to fulfill

Goal: A general aim implied by the mission (What you want to do)

Objective: A measurable outcome for reaching the goal

Management process (management by objectives)

A systematic way of organizing resources to get something done

A five-step cyclical process

    I. Define and communicate objectives

   II. Organize for action

       A. Develop and define concept (how are we going to do this)

       B. Allocate resources

           1. money

           2. workers

           3. materials

           4. time

           5. authority

       C. Alternate plans

  III. Create controls (sensing devices to warn of impending failure)

       A. Feedback

       B. Timetable

       C. Observation

   IV. Execute plans

    V. Evaluate

       A. Did we or did we not meet our objectives?

       B. How were resources used?

       C. How well did we manage?

       D. As a result of this appraisal, what recommendations about future goals and objectives might we make?

The Steps

First Evaluation

The evaluation is both the beginning and ending step of MBO, a process the Friends board and each committee should carry out at the beginning of each new officer's term. The board should ask itself:

What are our present achievements?

Where does the Friends group want to go?

What do we think is important?

What volunteers, money, materials, and time do we have available?

What do our members want?

What needs to be done?

What can we do?

These and other questions need to be answered before a group can set objectives. A group has to know its philosophy and its capabilities before beginning its work.

Goals and Objectives

A Friends group should first have firmly in mind its purpose, the reason for its existence. The group's main task is to assist the library, to help provide good library service to the community. In the next MBO step, the goals and general operating direction are formulated. (See figure 8 for one Friends group's goals and objectives.) These are probably stated in the bylaws (which should be examined occasionally to see if they are still timely). Possible goals might be to

promote the library in the community

sponsor community events and activities

provide special items for the library

encourage gifts, endowments, and memorials

promote volunteer activities

raise funds

act as an advocate

inform the community about programs, activities, resources, and needs

These goals are very general statements of intent, things a Friends group would like to see come about. Accomplishment of some or all of these goals demonstrates that the group is meeting its purpose.

The most difficult job in management comes next: translating these goals into defined and specific objectives before initiating, planning, or tackling a specific task. Objectives not only state *what is to be accomplished,* they also define *by when* and *how they are measured.* By establishing specific objectives at the beginning of new officers' terms, the Friends board knows what it is trying to do. The objectives become the blueprint for decisions, policies, and priorities. Loosely organized Friends boards and committees often try to follow general goals. Conversely, boards and committees that set and follow specific objectives are generally well organized and operate with a minimum of wasted effort and resources. A high esprit de corps develops because they know their goals and can later measure their achievements.

Figure 8. *Sample Goals and Objectives*

Friends of the Monroe County Public Library

Goal I.   Expand membership in numbers, diversity, and
involvement

Strategic Objectives

1. Create a program for membership development
2. Develop an overall marketing strategy for a membership drive
3. Increase member involvement with the organization

Goal II.   Raise funds for the special needs of the Library

Strategic Objectives

1. Establish more opportunities for annual giving
2. Create more opportunities for contributing to the endowment
3. Develop special events for the purpose of raising funds
4. Initiate a program for planned giving for the endowment and
   restricted projects
5. Create a program that promotes and recognizes gifts-in-kind

Goal III.   Educate and advocate for the library with the
community

Strategic Objectives

1. Sponsor as a minimum, quarterly programs that address a
   variety of issues
2. Create a biweekly column in the *Herald Times* on library
   activities and issues
3. Develop a newsletter
4. Create a speaker's bureau

CHAPEL HILL, N.C.

Following are some examples of objectives a Friends board/committee might establish for the organization after its self-appraisal and general goal setting.

Goal: To raise money for the library

Objective: To conduct a used book sale by June of next year that will net $5,000

Goal: To provide programs in the library

Objective: To sponsor four programs on "How the West Was Won," to be held on the first Thursday in September, November, January, and March, with an average attendance of 100 people

Goal: To increase the Friends membership

Objective: To increase membership by 200 before May 31

Goal: To have an annual meeting

Objective: To host a dinner meeting with a well-known author in March for 150 people

Goal: To act as an advocate for the library

Objective: To increase next year's city funding for the library by 6 percent, including funds to promote literacy

Each of these objectives describes what changes will occur, states when the objective is to be reached, and includes a standard of measurement. Once the objectives have been determined by the board and assigned to a committee, the group is ready for the next step.

Organizing for Action

How will objectives be accomplished? What is the plan? How will it happen? Five resources are available: people, money, material, time, and authority. Management is essentially the allocation of these resources.

Some questions need to be asked about each resource.

How many people are needed? Who will select them? Who will do what? What training is necessary?

How much money can be allocated? How much is really needed to do the job? Where could additional funds be obtained, if necessary? What, if any, budget cuts could be made? What safeguards should be employed to protect the organization?

What materials are needed? How will they be selected, allocated, and produced?

How much time is there? How much is needed? Is there any flexibility in the deadline? Is there a critical time sequence on which the plan hinges, or a series of deadlines?

How shall authority be delegated? How many restraints should be put on the committee? What is its relationship with the board? What decisions need board approval?

For any objective there obviously can be several approaches to achieve it. Each approach dictates a different mix in the allocation of the five resources. Planning requires that the Friends organization assess all its resources and capabilities and then draw up a plan that takes maximum advantage of these. One thing to remember in allocating resources, however, is to keep some in reserve. The group should never allocate all its resources; there may be an emergency, or some portion of a plan may need to be strengthened.

Considering Alternate Plans

Inaccurate assumptions, unknown factors, or simply a change in circumstances might call for a change in plans. To the extent that contingencies can be thought out ahead, a Friends group should have alternate plans to alleviate much worrying. What if the guest speaker cannot make it at the last moment? What if the outdoor event is rained out?

Planning, then, might be defined as simply thinking ahead to the desired outcome. Try to anticipate certain likelihoods. Those who are most effective discipline themselves to think through future situations step by step. Effective planners also consider the possibilities for failure and plan accordingly.

Controls

Successful managers not only consider what might go wrong but establish warning systems that tell them in time to take action. A manager who becomes aware that things are not going well during the course of a project can make corrections early. Conventional controls are budget, time, costs, and written or oral reports. If a budget has been made and costs are excessive, the manager must take action. Serious deviations from the schedule are another warning. Progress reports give the group a sense of direction and measurement. Other controls include:

Standards of performance: Everyone should know and accept what is expected of everyone else before the committee or group starts to work. These standards can be used to determine if each person is doing his or her job.

Personal observation of the manager: The more the manager can observe a situation personally, the more easily adjustments can be made in the plan.

Feedback: In addition to the manager's observation, informal evaluation by others is important. The manager may ask participants: How do you feel things are going? How do you think plans are shaping up?

Control systems can be very expensive in time, effort, and in the negative atmosphere they sometimes engender. Hence, the simpler the controls, the better—as long as they work!

Execution

In executing the plan, the manager or the board steps back and watches events take their course. The hardest part of this step is to let people who have been assigned jobs do them without interference. Motivated people provide the key to effective execution, which is where leadership really counts. Courage, commitment, dedication, and enjoyment make the difference.

Final Evaluation

Evaluation is the final step in MBO. Management by objectives is cyclical and returns to the point where it started. It is very important to determine both positive and negative results. The final evaluation has three parts.

First, were the objectives achieved? Were resources used effectively? Did the group overcommit its money? Were volunteers undercommitted? What was the cost in time versus the return? Were the results worth the effort and use of resources? Was the management process followed? Were members' needs met? Did they have fun meeting the objectives?

Second, where do the Friends go from here? This internal appraisal looks again at the Friends' resources and policies and how to use them.

Third, how were the library and the community affected? Was the project important to them? Are the Friends fulfilling a real need in the library and the community?

The final portion of this last evaluation is to coordinate the assets and capabilities of the Friends with the needs of the library and the community. The Friends group should determine what it can do best that will help the library the most. New goals and objectives can then be set for the next year. Each board should write a set of objectives and plans for its successors for the forthcoming year. Though the new board may accept, modify, or create its own objectives, it should be able to get under way quickly and continue on a successful course.

Conclusion

Some people are concerned that if management is approached as a science and as a defined process, individuality, personal flair, and fun will be stifled. This concern is unwarranted. Within a defined framework, Friends groups can be creative, innovative, and challenged. Everyone will know and understand where the organization and its committees are going, how it plans to get there, and what is required. MBO does not replace or displace imagination or good judgment. It is simply an organized way of doing things that will ensure the continuity of the Friends operations, ensure directed activities, and provide a framework for progress.

5

Friends and the IRS

Ira Shucker

The Internal Revenue Code is a complex document that cannot be easily understood even in its many paraphrasings. The purpose of this chapter is to give you not only the answers to some of your questions about taxes but also to help you become familiar with the concepts that govern tax-exempt status for Friends groups, as expressed in everyday terms.

Advantages and Disadvantages of Tax-Exempt Status

Section 501(c)(3) of the Internal Revenue Code grants a general exemption from the payment of federal income tax for corporations such as the Friends that are organized and operated exclusively for educational purposes. Receiving federal tax-exempt status generally results in the same status under state and local law. There are two main reasons your organization would desire tax-exempt status:

1. Your organization can accomplish more with the money it gets if it is exempt from having to pay income taxes by being able to hang on to surplus funds.
2. Your group can raise money more easily if it also qualifies as a tax-deductible organization because contributors may deduct their charitable contributions. Also, additional funds often can be obtained in the form of grants from government agencies or private foundations.

Tax-exempt status means that funds may be raised through solicitation efforts without any tax consequences to the Friends group so long as no part of the gross receipts goes to the benefit of any member or employee of the organization (except as reasonable compensation for services performed in connection with tax-exempt activities).

Besides these advantages, there are other, lesser-known advantages to tax-exempt status. An exemption from federal unemployment taxes is available to tax-exempt Friends groups, as are reduced-rate bulk mailing privileges. Most states also offer exemption from income, property, and sales taxes, and federal exemption can help show that you qualify for these exemptions on a state level. However, be careful: even if you're exempt from state sales tax on what you buy, that does not always automatically make you exempt from collecting sales tax on what you sell.

One disadvantage of exemption is its definite limitations upon the political and lobbying activities of an organization. Such limitations may pose real problems if your goals require these activities; thus, a separately funded companion group may have to be organized. Organizations that qualify for tax-exempt status also are still required to pay tax on unrelated trade or business income. Therefore, the exemption is not absolute. Furthermore, to maintain its tax-exempt status, an organization must comply with extensive annual reporting requirements.

Qualifying for Tax-Exempt Status

For a Friends group to meet the requirements for tax-exempt status, it must be organized and operated exclusively for one or more of the exempt purposes listed in Section 501(c)(3) of the Internal Revenue Code. Education, which is defined by regulations under the Code as "instruction of the public on subjects useful to the individual and beneficial to the community," is a likely choice of exempt purpose for Friends groups.[1]

Generally essential for application as a tax-exempt organization is that the group be formally organized as a corporation or an association. Incorporation requires a creating document (articles of incorporation or a constitution) that establishes and governs the organization and sets out its purposes and powers. Along with the creating document, bylaws provide for the organization's internal rules of operation and procedure. The preferred form for Friends groups is a corporation, or a foundation in corporate form, to allow for greater legal and operational flexibility.

In determining whether an organization qualifies for tax-exempt status, the Internal Revenue Service employs two basic tests. One is the organizational test: Is the group organized exclusively for exempt purposes? The group's articles of incorporation or constitution—not the bylaws—are relevant. This governing document must limit the entity's activities to those purposes for which it is applying for

1. Treas. Reg., Sec. 1.501(c)(3)-1d3.

exempt status and may not expressly allow for activities not in furtherance of the organization's exempt purposes. Insubstantial activities are not prohibited. The articles of incorporation or constitution may state purposes narrower than those prescribed in the Code. However, the governing document may *not* provide a broader description of purposes than is provided for in the Code, regardless of how the organization actually restricts its operations. The articles of incorporation or constitution must also provide for the distribution of the Friends' organizational assets for tax-exempt purposes if the organization dissolves. The failure to make such a provision will prevent the granting of tax-exempt status.

The second basic test is a determination of whether the organization operates exclusively for tax-exempt purposes. The organization demonstrates its operation under one or more tax-exempt purposes by engaging primarily in activities that accomplish these purposes. If a substantial part of the group's activities do not further the organization's exempt purpose, this requirement will not be met. And if part of the organization's net earnings benefit private individuals, the organization will not be operating exclusively for a tax-exempt purpose. However, the charitable nature of the organization will not be destroyed if private individuals or organizations incidentally derive a benefit from charitable activities.

Additionally, an organization is not operated exclusively for tax-exempt purposes if it is an action organization that attempts to influence legislation by propaganda or by contacting, or urging the public to contact, members of legislative bodies for purposes of proposing, supporting, or opposing legislation. Furthermore the organization may not, as a substantial part of its activities, attempt to influence a political campaign on behalf of or in opposition to a candidate for public office. (See Political and Legislative Activity later in this chapter.)

Charitable and educational organizations related to the parent tax-exempt organization are also tax-exempt. However, organizations whose activities are oriented toward assisting two or more unrelated tax-exempt organizations are not looked upon favorably. Typically, providing business-like services by one tax-exempt organization to one or more other unrelated tax-exempt organizations is considered an unrelated trade or business.

When the Internal Revenue Service alleges that an organization is not operated exclusively for a tax-exempt purpose, it frequently asserts that the organization's operations are similar to a commercial business enterprise conducted for profit. The key to the substantiality test for nonexempt activities is the fact that the term *exclusively* has been interpreted by the court system to mean "primarily," so that a nonexempt purpose or activity will disqualify a group from exemption only if it becomes a "substantial" part of the group's purpose or activities. Thus, the mere presence of profit-making activities is not a bar to tax-exempt status. The best defense against the accusation that a substantial activity is "really" a business is to show convincingly that it is actually carried on to further or accomplish a tax-exempt purpose.

Applying for Tax-Exempt Status

Friends organizations wishing to apply to the Internal Revenue Service for recognition of their tax-exempt status must do so on Form 1023, preferably within fifteen months of the effective date of their governing document. Form 1023 is filed with the district director for the Internal Revenue Service district in which the organization is principally located or operated. Extensions may be granted, but they should not be relied upon. If the organization applies within fifteen months, its exemption and the deductibility of contributions to the organization will be granted retroactive to the governing document's effective date. Otherwise, the exemption, if granted, would start at the date of the postmark of the application, unless the organization has a good excuse for filing late. Failure to apply will result in taxable status for the organization. If your group is a chapter or unit of a larger organization that has been previously issued a "group exemption letter," the group may file its own independent Form 1023, or it may simply rely on the existing group-exemption letter. Only organizations that do not ordinarily receive more than $5,000 in gross receipts and are not private foundations are exempt from filing. However, even if exempt, your Friends group may choose to file to reassure contributors and assure the group's officers that the organization has no liability for income tax.

Form 1023 is designed to elicit from your group the information needed to show that you qualify for the tax status you are claiming. It asks about your group's structure, purpose, officers, activities, plans, and finances. Don't just answer the exact questions and then stop. Bring up things that might help your position in the course of answering the questions.

Accompanying Form 1023 must be an updated copy of the organization's governing instrument, bylaws, a statement of receipts and expenditures, balance sheets for the years the organization has been in existence, a statement of proposed activities, and an application for employer identification number (Form SS-4). If bylaws or similar internal rules do not exist, include a statement attesting to their absence. If the organization has not yet begun operations, a proposed budget for two full accounting periods and a current statement of assets and liabilities are required.

A subordinate organization affiliated with and subject to the general supervision and control of a central organization may be relieved of filing its own Form

1023 application if the central organization applies for a group exemption. While the caveat of applying for the subordinate group's own exemption still applies, a group exemption letter is a second way of achieving tax-exempt status. The central organization must first obtain recognition of its own tax-exempt status and must establish the following for each subordinate organization to be included in the group exemption.

1. All are affiliated with the central organization.
2. All are subject to the central organization's general supervision and control.
3. All are exempt under the same paragraph of the code that exempted the central organization.
4. None are private foundations or organized and operated in a foreign country.
5. All have the same accounting calendar as the central organization.
6. All will be formed within the fifteen-month period subsequent to the date the group exemption application is submitted.
7. All have organizing documents.
8. All authorize in writing that the central organization can include them in its application for group exemption.

It is important to note that the central organization is responsible for evaluating the tax status of its subordinates and for annually furnishing the Internal Revenue Service with a list of qualifying subordinate organizations. To extend tax exemption to subordinate groups, the central organization must submit with its application a letter signed by its principal officer outlining the principal purposes and activities of subordinate groups as well as a sample governing document and attestation that the subordinates are operated in accordance with their stated exempt purpose, have authorized their inclusion in the group exemption letter, and are not private foundations.

Once a group exemption letter is issued, the central organization must resubmit annually, at least ninety days before the close of its fiscal year, a continuing statement of the subordinate organizations' principal purposes and activities as well as information regarding any changes in their purpose, character, method of operation, name, or location. If there are no changes, the central organization must include a statement to that effect.

For subordinate organizations to consolidate their tax returns with the central organization, all the subordinates must be exempt under the same federal tax law provisions and have no unrelated income items. Note that since organizations with gross receipts not normally in excess of $25,000 are not required to file an annual information return (Form 990) the central organization may exclude from its group return those subordinates with gross receipts less than $25,000.

A user fee associated with the application for exemption depends on the level of your group's annual gross receipts. The result is a determination letter, or ruling, concerning the group's tax-exempt status. Successful applications, including all attachments, are public documents and are available for public inspection unless public inspection would adversely affect the organization. The organization must make a specific request to prevent public inspection.

Advance Rulings

Until it receives a determination letter, the organization is required to file income tax returns and pay the applicable tax. If a newly created organization has a first tax year of at least eight months, it can get a definitive ruling from the Internal Revenue Service. However, advance rulings may be obtained prior to an organization's becoming operational. Advance rulings are issued for educational organizations like the Friends if they can reasonably be expected to meet the requirements for "public support" set forth in either Section 170(b)(1)(A)(vi) or 509(a)(2) of the Internal Revenue Code. Even if your first tax year is eight months or longer, it may be a good idea to request an advance ruling rather than an immediate determination, unless it is clear you can meet the Code's public-support test based on your first year's numbers.

Advance ruling periods are not always permitted by the Internal Revenue Service. Your answers to the questions about your activities and operational information on Form 1023 are looked at not only to determine if you qualify for exemption but also to determine if there is a reasonable likelihood of your group's raising sufficient public support to meet the support tests by the time those tests are made. Therefore, it is a good idea to tell the Internal Revenue Service about the ways your group will gain the necessary public support for qualification.

To meet the requirements for public support contained in Code Section 170(b)(1)(A)(vi), an organization must normally receive a substantial part of its support from governmental units or the general public and meet the requirements of one of two tests. The first test, called the one-third of support test, requires the organization to demonstrate that normally at least one-third of its total support will be received from governmental units, direct or indirect public contributions, or a combination of both over a continuous four-year period. An extended advance ruling period can also be requested to extend to the group's first six tax years. However, an extended ruling period must be requested at the outset—you can't switch back and forth. If the organization cannot meet the one-third test, it may

nonetheless be able to qualify under the second test, called the *facts and circumstances test.*

The facts and circumstances test requires the organization to demonstrate that it can reasonably expect to receive at least 10 percent of its total support from governmental units, or direct or indirect public contributions (like United Way), and that it will operate in a manner to attract new public or governmental support on a continuous basis. In the case of Friends groups, the inclusion of directors elected by the membership helps, and membership solicitations and dues should be designed to encourage membership by a broad cross section of people interested in the Friends' activities. Any contributions to the Friends from an individual, corporation, or trust that exceed 2 percent of the organization's total support will be included only to the extent of 2 percent of total support. Total support consists of amounts received as gifts, grants, contributions, membership fees, net income from unrelated business activities, and gross investment income.

Under Internal Revenue Code Section 509(a)(2), an organization must receive more than one-third of its support from gifts, grants, contributions, membership fees, and gross receipts from any tax-exempt activity that is not an unrelated trade or business. Gross receipts from an individual or governmental agency may be included in the one-third support total only to the extent of the lesser of $5,000 or 1 percent of the organization's total support. Contributions from what is termed a "disqualified person"—an individual, corporation, or trust that contributes 2 percent or more of total support—are included in total support but excluded as a source of support used to meet the one-third test. Additionally, the organization must not receive more than one-third of its support from gross investment income and unrelated business net income.

If either of the two Internal Revenue Code section tests is met, the new Friends organization will receive an advance ruling and be treated as a publicly supported organization, not a private foundation, for the advance-ruling period. At the end of the advance-ruling period, the Internal Revenue Service will determine if the statutory tests for public support have been met.

The failure to meet the public support test will result in the normal foundation excise tax on any net investment income for the period covered by the advance ruling. In addition, it is possible that failure to meet the support tests can result in loss of a group's tax exemption because such groups are considered to be "private foundations." To qualify as a tax-exempt organization, foundations must have more required clauses in their governing documents than do nonfoundations. Therefore, inclusion of the language required of foundations for tax exemption in your governing documents ensures that your group maintains its exemption and deductibility under the Internal Revenue Code.

Friends and the IRS

Since the requirements under Section 170(b)(1)(A)(vi) are less stringent and more advantageous, an organization should apply under this section rather than Section 509(a)(2) if the organization can reasonably expect to meet the former section's requirements. Note, however, that the Internal Revenue Service has issued a determination letter designating the Friends of Libraries, International, as an organization meeting the more stringent requirements of Section 509(a)(2).

If the Internal Revenue Service, represented by the district director, rules against your organization, you have the right of appeal. Timely appeal can be made within the Internal Revenue Service, and that failing, you can take the Internal Revenue Service to court under certain circumstances.

The Tax on Unrelated Business Income

Frequently, when the Internal Revenue Service challenges a nonprofit organization's exemption, it asserts that the organization's operations are all or in part similar to a commercial business enterprise conducted for profit. Hence, the income is unrelated business income—unrelated to the organization's tax-exempt purpose. The idea is to prevent tax-exempt organizations from competing unfairly with tax-paying businesses. Realistically, it is difficult to formulate unrelated business income guidelines to determine when a group's activities are educational or in the nature of a business, since what may be educational in one context may be a trade or business in another.

The classic example concerns a newsletter that your group publishes to further its goals by promoting and coordinating its activities. The newsletter is sold by subscription to members and is further subsidized by paid advertisements. The subscription income would be "exempt-function income" because selling the newspaper contributes importantly to your exempt purposes. The Internal Revenue Service may challenge the advertising income, however, and call it a separate unrelated business. It would then tax the organization on any excess of advertising revenue over advertising costs even if your organization were losing money overall.

There are exceptions to this scenario. If, for example, the advertising depended upon the newsletter's existence, if subscriptions didn't cover costs, then that loss could be used to offset any profit made on advertising. However, a group cannot create a loss to offset unrelated business income from other activities that do not directly depend upon the newsletter's existence.

Another group of exceptions is key to Friends groups. Such exceptions relate to activities excluded from being classified as unrelated trades or businesses because substantially all the work is performed by volunteers or because substantially all of the merchandise is donated to the organization for it to sell. There are also specific exclusions related to the specific purpose of other nonprofit organizations such as employees' associations, business leagues, and health organizations.

It is worth remembering that if a business activity is substantial and of a commercial nature and becomes a highly effective business venture, the tax-exempt status of the organization may be revoked. The existence of profits, while not conclusive, is some evidence that a business purpose is primary and that the services associated with the organization are those commonly associated with a commercial enterprise. The fact that profits obtained from the activity are then used for exempt purposes is irrelevant. If the activity is insubstantial, tax-exempt status may be maintained, but an unrelated business tax would apply, at standard corporate rates, on net income (after exclusion of the first $1,000) from such activities.

Political and Legislative Activity

Tax-exempt organizations have to limit carefully their political and legislative activity even if it directly contributes to the accomplishment of a group's tax-exempt purposes. If your group's efforts serve to support or oppose legislation or a referendum, you are lobbying—even if you never contact a legislator and merely urge your members through your newsletter to get involved or to involve their friends. Giving a telephone interview to a reporter concerning a legislative controversy could constitute lobbying.

The law limits political and legislative activities that tax-exempt organizations can engage in because of the economic leverage tax-deductible charitable organizations have. It is not surprising then that tax-deductible charitable organizations are entirely prohibited from attempting to influence elections for public office and that even an analysis of a candidate's voting record may be scrutinized by the Internal Revenue Service for bias in the framing of questions or the selection of topics.

Congress has tried to channel organizations conducting political activities (the influencing of elections) into a different section of the Internal Revenue Code. The purpose is to keep the political intervention apart from and thus less able to be subsidized by the funds that support other tax-exempt activities.

A Friends group exempt from taxation as a 501(c)(3) organization can undertake legislative activity, but in a limited way. The group's legislative activities must be balanced with its objectives to determine whether a substantial part of its activities attempt to influence legislation lest it lose its exempt status. An organization that loses its tax exemption due to excess lobbying expenditures will be subject to an additional 5 percent tax on the lobbying expenditures for the year in addition to its liability for any tax resulting from its change in status. Further, the group's manager will also be subject to the tax if he or she knew that such an expenditure would result in the organization's loss of exempt status.

This liability does not apply to organizations that have made a special election, referred to as a Section 501(h) election, or "lobbying" election. This election can be made or revoked using Internal Revenue Service Form 5768. Your group can make the election at any time during the tax year to which it applies, and the election will continue in effect until you revoke it.

The election provisions replace the uncertainty produced by a substantiality test with a sliding-scale percentage of exempt-purpose expenditures test. It also provides a distinction between grass-roots lobbying, attempting to influence the opinions of the general public, and direct lobbying, where the efforts involve direct communication with individuals involved in the legislative process. In addition, election provisions include lobbying expenditure ceilings that limit spending even if an organization is willing to pay the tax.

The obvious advantage of election is a reduction of the risk associated with an Internal Revenue Service challenge if your group engages in "influencing legislation." However, election requires a reasonable administrative commitment to analyze the time spent by each paid staff member who devotes part of his or her time to lobbying. Furthermore, the administration must distinguish between lobbying and nonlobbying and between direct and grass-roots lobbying.

Tax-exempt organizations have been allowed to donate to libraries' campaign speeches, interviews, and other materials of an individual who was a candidate for a "historically important elective office," and to conduct public forums at which debates and lectures on political questions were conducted. However, in performing these activities, an organization must present a full and fair exposition of relevant facts sufficient for the public to form its own independent conclusion.

There are also specific exceptions from the definition of "influencing legislation" for making available the results of nonpartisan analysis, study, or research in a balanced manner; providing technical advice or assistance to a governmental body at its written request; making appearances before a legislative body with respect to a possible decision that might affect the organization (the right of petition); and communicating to an organization's members the actual or proposed legislation. However, the organization cannot encourage its members to lobby or urge nonmembers to lobby.

If your group attempts to communicate with someone in government outside the legislative branch, it will be considered lobbying only if the main reason you are communicating is to influence legislation. But if your group communicates with

someone in the legislative branch, it is lobbying unless you avoid influencing legislation.

Even if it doesn't make the lobbying election, your group would be well advised to maintain factual backup to show that it has not engaged in a "substantial" amount of lobbying—and activities would have to be monitored and controlled as well as expenditures.

Annual Information Requirements

A tax-exempt organization must file an annual return with the Internal Revenue Service, albeit usually an information return, generally on Form 990 or its short-form counterpart, Form 990-EZ. The due date for filing either form is the fifteenth day of the fifth month after the end of the organization's accounting year, which is either the calendar year or an elected fiscal year. The failure to file or the filing of an incomplete return can result in penalties to the organization. If the filing date falls due while the organization's tax-exemption application is still pending, the organization should still file Form 990 and simply indicate that the application is pending.

To request an extension of time to file Form 990, use Form 2758, which must be completed and filed on or before the due date of the return. The extension is generally for a sixty-day period, with six months the maximum extension.

If the organization normally has gross receipts of $25,000 or less, Form 990 need not be filed. Many states, however, accept a copy of Form 990 in satisfaction of all or part of the state's own reporting requirements, although the state's minimum filing requirements may differ. Additionally, many states require that a tax-exempt organization with contributions above a certain level must have an annual independent audit of its financial statements.

All organizations eligible for tax exemption under the Internal Revenue Code must file a Form 990 Schedule A. Additionally, any organization that has unrelated trade or business income of $1,000 or more must file Form 990-T.

If an organization has employees, it may be required to file a number of forms, including Forms W-2 and W-3 (Wage and Tax Statements), Form 941 (Employer's Quarterly Federal Tax Return), and Form 5500 or 5500C (relating to employee benefit plans). The Form 1099 series are information returns for reporting payments such as dividends, interest, and miscellaneous income. Form 1096 is an annual summary of Form 1099 information return filings. Form 8282 (Donee Information Return) is required of donees who sell, exchange, or otherwise dispose of charitable deduction property, for example, donated books, within two years after the date of receipt.

The organization must make available for public inspection a copy of its annual return for three years after the due date of the return. A contributor list need not be disclosed. A copy of the organization's exemption letter must also be available for public inspection.

Furthermore, fund-raising events that are designed to solicit contributions that are in part a donation and in part the purchase price of an article (for example, providing contributors with copies of collector books or an admission ticket to an event) require specific disclosure. The organization must disclose that a contribution is being solicited and the amount that represents payment for the value of the item received (e.g., the fair-market value of the book or event admission). The remaining balance reflects the actual deductible portion of the amount contributed.

Compliance—Avoiding Audits

The best way to avoid audits is to fulfill your reporting requirements on a timely and accurate basis. For nonprofit organizations such as the Friends, there are three possible dire consequences of an adverse investigation by government authorities: (1) denial of tax exemption, (2) an end to your right to raise funds publicly, and (3) cancellation of your corporate charter, if incorporated.

The reasons for an audit center around three areas. One is the suspicion of ineligibility for tax-exempt status. This could result from a misrepresentation of your activities and purposes in your original application for tax-exempt status or from engaging in prohibited transactions after or even while waiting for exemption. The second cause for an audit is failure to comply with the requirements for unrelated business income, political activity, legislative lobbying, or self-dealing. Finally, failing to file timely and accurate payroll or information returns when required will often engender an inquiry.

In an audit the supporting documentary evidence of operational activity and financial transactions that took place during the period under review will be examined. Interviews with persons knowledgeable about the organization's practices may also occur, especially concerning questionable items and activities. The organization's legal documents will almost certainly be examined. In addition, it is not uncommon that an organization's press releases and clippings, program publications, and correspondence are surveyed for clues to the organization's activities that are not apparent through the financial and legal records.

The level of investigation will depend on the evidentiary information originally supplied to the auditor in support of the audit and on the findings in the early stages of the audit. It is obvious that this is an occasion for the organization's professional counsel—legal, tax, and accounting—to be intimately involved.

Conclusion

Obtaining tax-exempt status is neither impossible nor difficult despite the requirements for qualification. An advance ruling may be obtained for a new organization shortly after it has been formed if the organization's purposes are clearly defined and relate to an exempt activity. Additionally, the entity must reasonably expect to meet the support tests through its fund-raising programs. Maintenance of tax-exempt status is a never-ending vigil to ensure that the organization's purposes and activities are in full compliance and that no significant benefit or part of the organization's assets go to a private individual or corporation. The advantages of tax-exempt status are too great to be overlooked or treated cavalierly.

While this chapter is intended to be a general outline of the relevant issues and concerns of Friends groups applying for tax-exempt status as an educational organization, it is no substitute for professional representation. The application of the law may vary with the facts and circumstances of a particular organization as well as with time. Consequently, while this chapter can be used as a primer to the issues surrounding tax-exemption, independent legal and tax counsel should be retained.

6

A Friend in Deed: Advocacy

Roseann Gill

ADVOCACY, the act of pleading for, supporting, or recommending a cause or course of action; active espousal.

Random House Webster's College Dictionary

This chapter will provide ideas for advocacy by Friends groups, followed by actions used during successful campaigns to reduce proposed major service cuts in both a small and large city library system. This is a starting point, not an all-inclusive listing of actions that a Friends group could take to support a library. Each community is unique, and each needs an approach that is personalized to its specific characteristics.

Advocacy Interpreted

Advocacy means standing up for the library system and for the users of the library system. It means promoting the efforts of the Friends. It means support, promotion, and awareness for all libraries: public, school, college, special interest, city, county, town, and the Library of Congress.

Advocacy is not outside the mission of the Friends. It is not something unusual. Advocacy is something each Friend does, often not realizing the effect. One of the most powerful advocacy opportunities we have is used completely without effort: at social gatherings or during the course of ordinary activities when we spread the word about libraries. When standing in line or speaking to someone at a social event, talking about the library and our personal involvement with it makes the public aware of the library as a public necessity. The more Friends there are who care, the more the community takes notice.

For advocacy to be effective there has to be some groundwork laid. The community will respond better to urging from responsible friends and neighbors they know in a broader context. Steps that should be taken to put Friends of the Library groups in an advantageous situation should a need arise are outlined in Fact Sheet 15 in appendix C.

At times advocacy becomes an intense effort because of a special situation. The extra efforts to support a new program or to fight off cuts in service, for example, build on the ongoing regular advocacy program of your group.

As with other Friends activities, advocacy is planned and carried out in coordination with the library administration, ensuring that the public and elected officials get the same message from both sources. The message may be more effective if it comes from supporters, not employees, of the library system. Also, the Friends may be able to do some things that the library staff is prevented from doing by law, regulation, or potential conflict of interest.

A note of caution: The amount of money that your Friends group can spend on advocacy efforts is limited by your status as a not-for-profit organization under the IRS codes and any state or local regulations. Therefore, it is strongly recommended that you confer with your lawyers or tax advisers on the limitations.

Everyday Advocacy

Everday advocacy is easy—it can take place as children are dropped in day care or when playing golf or tennis. The next level of involvement includes a measure of commitment, advertised for by the following group.

Action Point

Bronxville, New York

The Friends' newsletter includes a help wanted notice inviting applications for the position of library advocate:

> Responsibilities include communicating at least three times yearly with legislators at all levels of government by letter and by telephone. An advocate must be a strong supporter of libraries. Information about funding, background information, and whom to contact will be provided.

Everyday advocacy is what a Friends group does as a regular part of its annual plan of actions. Some work will be done at specific times of the year (state budget preparation time); some can be scheduled at convenient times during the year.

Fact Sheets

A fact sheet is an essential basic tool, providing factual information about your Friends group in an easy-to-read format. It has many uses:

> as part of advocacy effort
> with publicity documents
> with a fund-raising campaign
> in a membership drive for renewals and new members
> as part of a welcome package for new members
> to recruit board members
> as a historical document

The fact sheet should include pertinent information about the Friends group and its accomplishments, either from its founding or from the past year. It should be updated at least annually and during significant events. It is best if it's printed on one page of letterhead in an attractive layout with the following information (in no particular order):

> summary of major accomplishments or activities from the time of founding or from the preceding year
> fund-raising efforts
> advocacy efforts
> how library and library patrons have benefited from the group
> number of members
> when started
> point of contact (for more information)

A complement to the Friends fact sheet is a fact sheet about the library prepared by the library staff. (See figure 9.) In large library systems, you may want to prepare a fact sheet for systemwide issues and separate fact sheets for each branch library, both for the Friends and for the library, thus taking the information to the community level. This proposal should be discussed locally.

Contact with Elected Officials

It's important to keep the public libraries and their supporters in the minds of elected officials. Regular contact with elected officials is an important part of any advocacy effort. Contact in person, by telephone, or by letter is an opportunity to

Figure 9. *Sample Library Fact Sheet*

The Free Library of Philadelphia—Discussion Points

This past year at the Free Library demonstrated how much Philadelphians value their library:

- The Free Library circulated 6.1 million books in 1992. The last time the library broke the 6 million mark was in 1966. Circulation increased by 10.9 percent for FY '92.

- Approximately 40 percent of Philadelphia's 1.6 million people have library cards compared with 20 percent in 1966 when the population was 2 million.

- There has been a 20 percent increase in library use by children, particularly preschoolers.

- Last summer's innovative reading program "Grand Slam Summer" involved 30,000 children reading and enjoying library services.

- The Free Library has launched a three-year, multimillion dollar fund-raising campaign called the Library Campaign to generate funds from the private sector.

  The Pew Charitable Trusts have provided a three-year enabling grant of $1 million to cover the costs of the campaign.

  In addition, The Pew Charitable Trusts have given the library a $1.5 million challenge grant which the library must match with $7.5 million.

- From July '92 to March '93, there was a 4 percent increase in Access PA borrowers.

show support, as interested citizens, for libraries and the services that they provide the community. It should supplement and complement the information that the library provides through the regular governmental channels.

Writing as a private citizen, expressing your views as a library user, or asking the politicians for their views is one of the inalienable rights we possess. It is always best to use your own words and express your own feelings. Use prewritten materials only as reference. If you use the letterhead of an organization, you have left the rights of a private citizen behind and must follow certain guidelines. Following are some helpful tips when writing legislators.

1. Keep the letter short, rarely more than one page. Type it if possible; otherwise, write clearly.
2. Write it in your own words, and include your own thoughts.
3. Cover only one issue; save other issues for later letters.
4. Show your familiarity with the subject and with the current status of the legislation (mention the bill number if possible). This will indicate that you are serious about the issue, unlike the casual, uninformed correspondents who produce the bulk of constituent mail.
5. Be specific about what you want your representative to do.
6. Give reasons for your position. Cite your own experience and findings if possible. If the bill has a local impact, indicate that fact so that your representative realizes that the bill has a direct effect on his or her district.
7. Ask your representative a direct question about his or her own position on the bill. You want to receive a clear answer, not a form letter. If you are requesting an appointment, give alternate times if possible, and ask for a reply.
8. Don't mention your membership in any organization unless it is directly related to an experience you are describing. The individual citizen's letter is what counts, not the letter choreographed and inspired by an organization.
9. If you can, mention your legislator's vote on a recent issue to show your awareness of his or her record.
10. In general, be helpful rather than threatening. You can best show your genuine concern for the issue by offering to provide further information on the subject. (After all, information management is our business.)
11. When Congress or your state legislature is in session, address all letters to your representatives in Washington or the state capital. At other times, write them in care of their home or local office addresses, if available.
12. Finally, remember: **Any letter is better than no letter!** Postcards are second best.

Contact should be planned with all appropriate elected officials at the local, county, state, and federal levels, when they are first elected and annually thereafter. Remember to contact at-large representatives as well as district representatives. The contacts can be in person by officers of the Friends and/or Friends members and/or paid staff. It is much more effective if one or more of the visitors are constituents of the elected official.

Tracking legislation is a real lesson in how government works, and it requires patience and empathy for the staff people with whom you are in contact. By following the legislative process of a proposed bill, you show your interest and keep informed about how your elected officials are serving you.

1. Familiarize yourself with the proposed legislation or bill. Find out the bill number and name, which legislators are for it as well, and who might be opposing the bill.
2. Contact the sponsors of the bill, or have others in their district do so. Explain your interest in the bill and the impact it will have on the library. Let legislators know how many people are members of the Friends. Establish contact with the legislative aides and secretaries in the sponsors' offices. Get their names and telephone numbers. Whenever practical, visit these offices.
3. Contact chairpersons, staff members, or key people in the legislative committee in which the bill resides.
4. After the session starts, call the sponsors and the committee chairperson on a weekly basis to learn what is happening to the bill, whether it is on the committee agenda yet, when it is likely to be on, etc. Find out if there are questions about the bill or some unresolved conflict.
5. Call the offices of the leadership. Talk to legislative assistants in these offices about the bill, the needs it would or would not fill, the groups backing it, etc.
6. Report back to your Friends group, as things start to happen. As the bill moves from committee to committee or when it is scheduled for a vote, report more often.
7. Visit the city hall or state capital (call ahead) and talk to legislators and staff members. This is the best way to become known to the key people. Explain that you will call to find out when something is scheduled on the bill (don't expect them to contact you).
8. Help to organize support for the bill and contacts on the bill. Set up meetings with committee staff people, legislators, etc. Invite three or four people representing different backgrounds to accompany you.
9. Be alert for any means in which convincing arguments or new approaches can be useful or for ways in which new contacts can be made. If there is a problem, find out why and brainstorm with the appropriate people to solve it if possible.
10. Contact the mayor's or governor's office if the bill passes to see if it will be signed or if there are any problems.
11. Win or lose, thank everybody.

A Friend in Deed: Advocacy

Action Point

Lakewood, California

When the City Council was discussing ways of financing the Lakewood libraries, the Friends filled the council's chamber to capacity. Teenagers, parents of young children, educators, and senior citizens were all present to voice their support for the libraries. The council voted unanimously for the requested library support.

When meeting with elected officials, introduce the Friends, discuss their goals and achievements in the community, and emphasize their willingness to work on behalf of the library. Thank the elected official for his or her support of the library. Provide a copy of your Friends fact sheet and newsletter and library fact sheet, if available. You're building a relationship and letting the official know who you are and what you do. Add the official to mailing lists for newsletters and other announcements.

Social Events

A reception for elected officials and the members of the Friends is another way to build relationships, especially around budget time. You might present a short program and have a recognition ceremony for an outstanding supporter along with the networking and the refreshments. Send a written invitation to elected officials, and follow up with a telephone call from a Friend. If your city or county council issues proclamations to honor groups or individuals, arrange for one to be read by an elected official at the reception. The Friends can assist in its preparation. A local corporation may be willing to sponsor the reception and provide the facilities and refreshments.

Action Point

Stroudsburg, Pennsylvania

A Friends board member was among a delegation to Pennsylvania's Legislative Day in Harrisburg. The Friends newsletter published a full account of her discussions with local legislators, including the legislators' statements on various library issues.

Most statewide Friends sponsor annual state legislative days, inviting local Friends groups to the capital to meet with their state legislators. This is an opportunity to meet legislators and to discuss state funding and other library issues.

Friends of Libraries U.S.A. encourages participation in National Library Week activities held every April in Washington, D.C., sponsored by the American Library Association. It is inspiring to gather with library supporters from each state as they meet to visit their elected representatives and walk the halls of Congress. FOLUSA also presents a Public Service Award to a member of Congress who has supported library legislation.

Testimony at Public Hearings

Advocacy continues when the Friends testify in support of the library at public hearings for the local capital and operating budgets that include the library budgets. Arrange a meeting to testify before the appropriate authorities. Testimony should be prepared in advance to be read at the hearing. Testimony by a Friend should be brief, written on letterhead with a contact name and phone number. Have enough copies to distribute to officials at the hearing before reading it.

Friends should be in the audience when library trustees or staff testify on the library requests. They should wear identifying buttons, hats, etc., or carry identifying signs, if allowed, to demonstrate their support for the library. If appropriate, give the media special notification of this appearance so it can be included in the day's broadcasts or next day's newspapers. (See the next section.)

Send a letter to the elected officials after their vote on the library issue, thanking them for their support or expressing your disappointment if they did not support the issue.

Contacts with the Media

The first step in dealing with the media is to identify your targets. Create and maintain a comprehensive mailing list for media. Search for opportunities to show support for libraries and their patrons and the Friend efforts with the areawide and local media. Introduce the Friends as an important community organization. Find out whom to contact for messages to be published or broadcast and whom to add to mailing lists for newsletters and other announcements. For important issues, recruit Friends to write letters to the editors of both the weekly and daily press.

At major daily newspapers, the editorial staff and columnists covering family, education, government, etc., are the people to contact regarding information about the Friends. Find out about the issues that concern the paper and how you should provide information. Learn how to place editorials on the editorial opinion page. Follow up your contact with a letter and fact sheet.

A Friend in Deed: Advocacy

Weekly community newspapers and weekly free papers are other potential resources for advocacy. An introductory chat with their editors will reveal how they can support the library and your Friends groups with articles, editorial pieces, etc. With smaller publications, the editor may appreciate a draft of an article, thus increasing the chances of your message being published. Find out the requirements for submitting photographs with articles. Chapter 7 provides detailed information on writing news releases.

Business publications, whether weekly newspapers or monthly magazines, may be a source of support for libraries. The proliferation of materials available on-line makes the large and small business dependent on information from the library. Check with the editors or columnists. Follow up with a letter and fact sheet.

Radio, television, and cable television newsroom staff are other potential resources. An introductory chat with the news director, reporters, and producers will reveal how they can support your group and the library. As with any media contact, follow up with a letter and fact sheet. Again, see chapter 7 for greater detail about preparing information for the media.

Community Organizations

Community organizations and informal groups can be sources of support for the library and your Friends group. For example,

senior center members	property owners' meetings
coworkers	community council
Lions Club	preschools
Rotary Club	playground groups
PTA/PTO	AARP
school board meetings	Senior Net
church groups	day-care centers
library events	neighborhood meetings
community bulletin boards	store owners' associations
block associations	

Some of these will allow Friends to speak at their meetings, to post material on bulletin boards, and to include Friends' material with the mailings to their membership. Because the library is one institution that literally belongs to everyone in the community, it caters to the interests of all groups. They all have a stake in it.

OCEAN CITY

FREE PUBLIC LIBRARY
OCEAN CITY, N.J.

Action Point

Haywood County, North Carolina

A Speakers Bureau of Friends members contacted some fifty civic clubs and other groups to solicit support for a building program.

Newsletters

Think of newsletters as an instrument of your advocacy for the library system. Include elected officials, editors in all media, and other community organizations on the mailing list, and get your message out to them at regular intervals. Include the names, addresses, and telephone numbers of elected officials, so your membership knows how to contact them. (See chapter 7 for more information about newsletters.)

Major-Issue Advocacy

Advocacy becomes a critical function for the Friends at times of stress for the library system. These stresses include both cuts and improvements—budget cuts, personnel cuts, funds to expand library services. Friends, as passionate supporters but not employees of the library, can influence the decision makers. In addition to the previously described advocacy actions (use of fact sheets, contact with elected officials, testimony, and communication with other organizations), major issues call for major efforts. Figure 10 summarizes the elements of a major-issue advocacy campaign.

Fact Sheets on an Issue

The influence process starts with gathering accurate information. A fact sheet on the library issue (the budget, the legislative initiative, the construction campaign, the funds for repairs and improvements to library buildings, etc.), prepared in coordination with the library staff, has a number of uses:

> to inform members and others
> as attachment to letters
> as background information for members who wish to prepare their own letters, postcards, calls
> as handouts at meetings or when talking to elected officials, editors, reporters, columnists, library patrons, or the general public

Figure 10. *To-Do List for a Major-Issue Advocacy Campaign*

1. Coordinate with library staff
2. Write a fact sheet on the issue (in addition to the library fact sheet)
3. Write an advocacy alert (provide a sample)
4. Organize
   a. letter-writing campaign
   b. phone campaign
   c. petition drive
5. Set up a schedule for the group to attend public hearings/meetings
   a. prepare testimony
   b. prepare roster of attendance at all hearings
   c. decide on distinctive buttons, signs, etc.
6. Set up a committee for a media blitz
   a. invite reporters to public meetings/rallies called by Friends
   b. write letters to editors
   c. write information for editorials
   d. prepare background briefing for reporters
   e. designate press connection for interviews
7. Organize a rally

This fact sheet does not have to be the same as the library fact sheet on the issue, but it should include the same facts, description, and potential results. Print it on the Friends letterhead, preferably on one side, with a contact name and phone number for the issue. Number and date it to allow for continuing updates as the situation evolves.

Advocacy Alert

An advocacy alert notifies your members and others about a situation that needs their support and suggests actions that they can take. It can be used to inform other individuals and groups that do not regularly receive your mailing, for example, add the Home and School Association or PTA if the issue is a cut in library hours.

An advocacy alert lists the actions required, by whom, when, where, and why. The issue fact sheet and list of elected officials should be included, for example, with a request to contact city council members and the mayor about a cut in funds to the library system. Suggest that the members write letters and make telephone calls using the information in the fact sheet and their own ideas. A personalized

Libraries? **Yes!**

Dear Friend,

As we hope you already know, Citizens for Libraries is seeking voter support for State Question 666 which will appear on the November 8th ballot. It is important to emphasize that SQ 666 is <u>permissive legislation and not a tax increase.</u> It will amend the state constitution to give the residents of every county the <u>option</u> to create a single-county public library system supported by ad valorem funds. It will also allow Tulsans to increase their support of the Library up to 6 mills at a future election. This is the first time in 18 years that there has been a state question pertaining to public libraries.

A Citizens for Libraries committee has formed to promote passage of the question. We are writing to ask for your help with the election campaign. As a friend of the library, you know the value of the quality services provided by Tulsa City-County Library. Please join us in this important effort that is critical to the future of our library. You may volunteer by completing the enclosed form and returning it to:

> Friends of the Tulsa Public Library
> 400 Civic Center
> Tulsa, OK. 74103-3830

As soon as we receive your response, the chairperson of the appropriate committee will contact you. If you have any questions, you may call 596-7962.

As always, thank you for your valuable support.

Sincerely,

Charles Meyers, Jr.
President, Friends of the Tulsa Public Library

Betty Kaiser
Volunteer, Ruth G. Hardman Adult Literacy Service

• •

YES, I want to help campaign for the passage of State Question 666!

Name_____

Address_____ City_____ Zip_____

Phone (Day)_____ (Evening)_____

Branch library I use_____

I would be willing to: (please check one or more of the following)

_____Call voters on precinct lists at a telephone bank

_____Serve on the Speakers' Bureau by making presentations as part of a librarian/volunteer team

_____Recruit people to be listed in an endorsement advertisement

_____Distribute materials such as posters, flyers, bookmarks, etc.

_____Write letters to newspaper editors in support of the library question

_____Recruit other volunteers to help with the campaign

_____"Plant" large yard signs at designated locations

_____Allow "business space" for signs

_____Other _____

_____Yes, I would like my name listed in the endorsement ad in the **Tulsa World** on Monday,

November 7. My contribution of $3.00 or more is enclosed.

Please list my name as (please print):_____

(May be family, individual, organization, or business.) Checks should be made payable to:

Citizens for Libraries.

PLEASE RESPOND IMMEDIATELY
Friends of the Tulsa Public Library
400 Civic Center
Tulsa, OK. 74103-3830

Paid for by Citizens for Libraries • Peter Meinig, Secretary/Treasurer • P.O. Box 2549, Tulsa, OK 74101

A Friend in Deed: Advocacy

letter or phone call is more effective than a form letter. It's a good idea to provide a draft letter with the factual information for people to adapt to their needs.

The Friends can start a petition campaign by gathering signatures in or near the library, in the community, etc. The petition is then presented to the decision makers at a public hearing or another public forum. If possible, invite the media when the petition is presented.

Get your message into the media. Consider letters to the editors from the Friends' leadership and members. Place an article on the editorial opinion page. Provide information to reporters. Submit draft articles for use by editors in smaller publications. (See chapter 7 for details.) Invite reporters to meetings, rallies, etc. Follow up with letters and fact sheets.

Provide information to library patrons that entices them to action. Make available a draft letter to decision makers, a fact sheet, and preprinted, addressed postcards with a message.

FOCUS

The Friends of the Free Library of Philadelphia
Philadelphia, Pennsylvania

Currently, the membership of the Friends of the Free Library of Philadelphia has grown to 9,000 strong including an Alliance of Friends comprising 51 branch Friends groups.

A real success story demonstrating a marshaling of citywide voices, constituents, and concerned citizens by the Friends of the Free Library of Philadelphia occurred in the 1993–1994 budget year of the City of Philadelphia. The city was in financial straits and the new mayor, Ed Rendell, was taking steps to establish financial stability. One target was the budget of the Free Library that was targeted to be cut by $2 million. This would have required the Free Library to close branches, reduce the number of hours of operation, and cut staff significantly. There was a tremendous outcry of protest throughout the city with the catalyst being the Friends of the Free Library. These efforts were crafted, planned, and organized to bring home the message to the council members that you "don't mess with libraries." The project was well orchestrated. The efforts used the newspapers, the TV, letter writing, and neighborhood hearings with thousands of names on petitions. It resulted in significantly reduced proposed budget cuts of $1.3 million or two-thirds. The Free Library was able to maintain its branches, continue to service the neighborhood, and move forward.

Other examples manifesting the advocacy strength of the Friends in Philadelphia include giving testimony at the city council, visiting city council members, holding receptions for city council members, and frequent letter-writing campaigns to ensure that the Free Library and its branches continue to be viewed as vital, important community institutions.

Friends of the Grosse Pointe Public Library Millage Campaign Grosse Pointe, Michigan

(These materials won a special award from the John Cotton Dana Library Public Relations Awards Contest, 1995)

Community Description

The Grosse Pointe Public Library was one of thirty-three Michigan libraries thrown into financial turmoil in 1994 when state finance reform abolished millage support for those public libraries operated by school districts. (Millage refers to the rate of taxation per dollar; a mill = $.001.) The library spun off and formed a district library effective July 1, 1994, and was given one year to generate independent funding by passing a millage.

Because state election law prohibits government entities such as libraries from distributing literature influencing the outcome of an election, the library turned to its Friends group to spearhead the millage campaign. Several community groups worked with the Friends to help mobilize "yes" voters.

The 55,000 residents in the six communities served by the library include a conservative older population thrilled by the tax cut resulting from the canceled millage. These voters typically voted against funding requests and had helped defeat two recent library bond issues.

After voters had defeated two library bond issues to relieve crowding in the libraries, the staff and Friends of the Grosse Pointe Public Library spent several years working together on a number of community relations initiatives that increased the library's visibility, built community partnerships, and generated support for the library. The library initiated joint programming and events with local groups including public and private schools, the Hill Business Association, and the Friends of the Library. These efforts forged successful partnerships and left the library well positioned for a successful millage vote.

Target Audience

The millage committee chose to run an upbeat, positive campaign that virtually ignored negative voters. The campaign slogan was simplicity itself,

"Love Your Library." The logo was a red heart, and the campaign colors were a patriotic red, white, and blue. The target audience included potential "yes" voters in the following categories:

Frequent voters—Analysis of previous school elections indicated that those with a high proportion of "no" votes were those that attracted infrequent voters, usually a millage election or bond issue, rather than a school board election. A list of frequent voters was obtained by manually checking voting records in all six communities.

Library users—The campaign's positive message was aimed at those people who would be expected to support the library—patrons of all three branches, public and private school parents, parents of story time participants, attendees of adult programs, League of Women Voters, Hill Business Association, and members of the Friends of the Grosse Pointe Public Library.

Goal

The goal of the millage campaign was to build on goodwill created through existing community partnerships to secure permanent funding for the new district library.

Objectives

1. Involve at least three existing community partners in promoting both the library and the millage election.
2. Get "yes" voters to the polls.
3. Secure permanent funding for the library by passing a new library millage of 1.7 mills in perpetuity.

Activities

Campaign Development—Create a campaign theme, logo, and materials for all campaign initiatives.

Volunteer Recruitment—Recruit and utilize volunteers to implement the campaign and expand the library's base of support. Groups from which these were recruited: Friends, library staff, volunteer networks from local Parent Teacher Organizations, and library trustees.

Community Involvement—Involve community groups in the campaign to broaden the base of support and to enlarge the library's communication network.

Handwritten notes were added to 7,250 "Vote Yes" postcards; these were signed by 100 volunteers at 5 scheduled signing parties. Other groups also signed and addressed more cards. All were sent first class one week before the election.

Approximately 7,350 "Keep the Doors Open" brochures were sent to frequent voters.

Phone call reminders to vote were made to 2,500 frequent voters on the Sunday before the election.

Polls were monitored to see who had voted. Names of frequent voters were noted, and those that had not voted were called after 4 P.M. by 24 volunteers who made 1,600 reminder calls. All polls reported a "rush" of voters after 5 P.M.

Media Relations—Increase awareness of the library and the election through positive media coverage.

Recognition and Follow-Up—Publicize election results in media, library signage, and letters. Individual thank-you letters and certificates of appreciation were sent to 204 volunteers and staff members.

Creativity

On September 20, 1994, the Grosse Pointe Public Library received a resounding thumbs up from local voters when the library's first independent millage was approved by a 3 to 1 margin. The library succeeded in passing its millage because its campaign focused on those people who had an established history of library support. The campaign made the assumption that those people loved their library and would vote to preserve it, given sufficient information and opportunity.

The "Love Your Library" message was simple, direct, and positive, and an extension of the library's ongoing community relations activities. The campaign committee reflected all the constituencies needed to support the millage and for this reason was able to quickly tap existing networks of library supporters.

The committee viewed recognition and follow-up as one of the most important pieces of the campaign because it affirmed the teamwork and goodwill of the community and reinforced the library's desire for continued cooperation in the future.

Participation

The millage campaign committee, headed by a former Friends board president, included active Friends board members, library staff, library trustees, community library boosters, the library director, the Friends' administrative assistant, and the library's public relations consultant. A group of 204 volunteers, made up of Friends members, school parents, and library staff, carried out the campaign.

Financial Support

Friends promotion and postage budget	$ 2,000
Friends contribution to campaign	3,400
Library public relations and postage budget	4,800
Individual contributions to campaign	1,850
TOTAL	$12,050

Achievements

1. The millage was passed with a 73 percent "yes" vote.
2. The 1.7 mills were voted in perpetuity.
3. Press coverage during the campaign was impressive—local newspapers printed four times the normal number of library-related photos, stories, and editorials.
4. Goodwill generated by the "Love Your Library" campaign set the stage for the Friends group to launch the most successful membership campaign in its history, gaining 120 new members and generating $64,000 during the first three months of the membership campaign.
5. National attention was given to the campaign from the library press.

Action Point

Detroit, Michigan

In the past ten years the Friends have managed and raised funds for four millage campaigns. For this year's campaign the Friends expended $20,000. The funds were used for large ads in three local newspapers and 75 one-minute radio spots on six major stations. It proved to be worth it: The one-mill library tax renewal on the August primary ballot passed by a huge margin of 75 percent to 25 percent.

Public Hearings and Meetings on Major Issues

It's very important that Friends be represented at all public hearings or meetings where a critical library issue is being discussed. Friends' attendance is an important message to the elected officials and the general public.

A Friend in Deed: Advocacy

Testimony at each opportunity is also important. See the previous section in this chapter for general guidelines about testimony. Consider sending a copy of your testimony with a short introductory paragraph to the media for additional publicity.

Friends can call meetings or rallies in their community to get the message to a larger audience. The audience can be elected officials, library patrons, community organizations and businesses, and the general public. Invite reporters and have handouts for them and the whole audience. Take photographs that can be used with newspaper articles and with other advocacy efforts.

After the Campaign

At the end of a special advocacy effort, thank people. Send thank-you letters to elected officials, editors, Friends, etc., including the letters-to-the-editor sections of supporting media. It's important to thank those who gave time to listen, even if the vote didn't come out the way the library wanted. There's always a next time. Plan a thank-you event for Friends who gave their time and make it an evaluation session to determine what worked and what didn't. Records can be turned in at the same time.

As Others See You: Publicity and Public Relations

Peggy Barber

Friends are those rare people who ask how we are, then wait for an answer." This quotation, cited in a library newsletter, says a lot about library Friends—people who really care about the library—and it also sets the tone for this chapter about public relations. The key to effective public relations is the same as the key to friendship—two-way communication. By definition, public relations is a planned and sustained effort to establish mutual understanding between an organization and its public. The organization has something to say, but it also asks questions, listens carefully, and waits for answers.

But you say, "I don't want a 'planned and sustained effort,' I just want a poster and newspaper story that will get people to our book sale." Friends groups exist to bring visibility and support to the library: A planned public relations program is absolutely essential. The poster and newspaper story are publicity tools that will work much better if they are part of an overall plan. Scattershot publicity is a waste of time and money. It doesn't take a Madison Avenue agency to create a public relations plan . . . just some common sense, time, and thought.

There are four basic steps in public relations: research, planning, communication, and evaluation.

Research

In the research step, the group identifies its "publics," or target audience, and assesses their attitudes. These publics include your members, potential members (people who use the library but haven't joined the Friends), the library staff and board, the local media, and library nonusers. For academic library Friends, the faculty, students, administration, and alumni are obvious target audiences.

What trends does your Friends group reflect? Are you gaining or losing members? What percentage of the members are active? Should more be active? Are

you meeting fund-raising goals? Is the community aware of the existence of the Friends? Do you get good media coverage? Does your group represent all local age, income, ethnic, and religious groups? Should it? Is there a positive working relationship with the library staff and library board members and library foundation?

All print materials produced by the Friends should be reviewed. Do they reflect well on the Friends and the library? What is your group's style? Is it elite, friendly, "town and gown," elegant, efficient? What do you want it to be?

Even if you think you know your community, it is helpful to gather all available demographic information: age, income, ethnic background, occupation, religion, interests, community groups, and all other formal or informal data that are available. It's not necessary to hire the Gallup organization, but original research can also be undertaken, from mail questionnaires to telephone surveys to informal meetings with community groups. The goal is constant sensitivity to public opinion. Ask people if they have heard about the Friends and what they think of the group . . . and wait for an answer.

Planning

To achieve your purpose you should make the public relations process an integral part of the total Friends program. After you establish clear target audiences for your public relations efforts based on your community surveys, make sure the library is aware of and in agreement with your efforts. For example, are you promoting the library or the Friends group? What are the library's goals and objectives and how can the Friends help? If your plan is to promote library services, it must be developed in partnership with the library staff or disaster is inevitable.

Be sure to coordinate all plans with the library. How and when do you communicate with the library director and board members? Who has the final approval on all public relations and publicity efforts? Regular channels should be established, and the Friends group should get the information it needs and have a role in the library's planning process.

The beauty of a plan is knowing where you're going and knowing if you get there. For example, your leadership group might decide that membership recruitment is its top priority. Rather than continuing with business as usual—accomplishing a little on many projects—you reach a consensus about focusing on an all-out membership drive. Before launching the campaign, choose the most likely target groups; decide how to reach them (e.g., direct mail, personal visits, telephone calls, presentations at meetings, newspaper stories); select your appeal; and develop a rough budget, volunteer assignments, timetable, and goal. Launch the campaign with a bang (e.g., media event, reception, press conference), and announce your progress and success with equal fanfare. Without a plan, how do you know if you're successful, and how can you brag about it if you're not sure?

The following example shows how a group decided on a project (giving an award) and used it to draw attention to two other projects—an oral history of the community and a written history of its library. The library received media attention as a result.

FOCUS

Port Washington Public Library
Port Washington, New York

During the fall of 1990, the creation of a Friends of the Library Award was briefly discussed at FOL board meetings. A decision was made to create an award and to present it as a part of a January 1991 program that had already been scheduled. The program would introduce the FOL Centennial Oral History Project to the public and explain the library's ongoing commitment to oral history. The first award was presented to the author of a centennial history of the library.

The Friends board decided that the award would be presented

1. to an individual who furthers the mission of the FOL as defined in the bylaws:
   a. to sponsor and support library activities and to initiate special programs
   b. to increase awareness of the role of the library in the community
2. to an individual other than a member of the library staff
3. on an irregular basis as the FOL board sees fit

The award has since been presented twice to outstanding Friends.

Communication

Communication is the part of the public relations program that calls for the outreach, programming, and publicity suggested by your research and planning. The Friends group should build and maintain a media list of publications and broadcast channels, including daily and weekly newspapers, radio, television and cable stations, community group newsletters, school newsletters, and any other media that reach your target audience. If your library has a community relations director or

**Friends of
the Woodbridge
Town
Library**

WOODBRIDGE, N.J.

public relations staff, this press list may already be compiled for you, though the Friends group may want to tailor the special list by adding local opinion leaders, local legislators, and other special people.

Personal contact with people on the press list is especially important. As a nonprofit organization, the Friends group is eligible for free public-service advertising time and space from the media, but it must compete with many good causes. Personal contact can help bring your group to the forefront.

News Releases

The most common way of communicating news to the media is with a news release. For newspapers, find out exactly who handles library or community organization news and send your releases directly to that person. If there is no one assigned to cover the library, suggest to the editor that someone be assigned. In general, you will want to write a separate news release for radio and television. Broadcast media require a tighter style than print. Short words and easily understood sentences are best. Prepare the broadcast release in all capitals, double spaced.

Here are a few tips for preparing a news release taken from *PR Primer*, compiled by the Public Information Office, American Library Association:

Use 8½″ × 11″ white paper.

Double space the lines.

Type only on one side of the paper.

Leave wide margins on the sides, top, and bottom of the page.

Begin typing about twenty lines from the top of the first page; ten lines from the tops of following pages.

Be sure to put your name, address, area code, and telephone number in the upper left-hand corner of the first page. Type either the date for the release ("For release the week of . . .") or "For immediate release."

Make your lead concise and straightforward. If it's confusing or puffy, most editors won't read any farther. Your lead and second paragraph should answer the "five *W*s"—who, what, when, where, and why—and sometimes how.

Write short paragraphs, one thought apiece. Follow the classic "inverted pyramid" by starting with the most important facts and moving to those of lesser significance.

Get a good style book and use it. Be consistent in your spelling, punctuation, grammar, and usage. The *New York Times*, Associated Press, and United Press International all publish style books that are standard references.

As Others See You: Publicity and Public Relations

Type "-30-" at the end of your release. If your news release is more than one page, type "-more-" at the bottom of the first page and subsequent pages until the end. Use an abbreviated version of your headline at the top of each additional page. Instead of numbering pages, label the second page "add one," the third "add two," etc.

Do not hyphenate words at the ends of lines.

Do not use exaggerated or tired adjectives (e.g., "The children's room is awesome").

Don't be cute. You'll end up offending the reporter who has to write the story in news style anyway. Give the facts so the writer can work with the materials as quickly as possible.

Do not depend on an editor, news assignment desk, or reporter to come up with a newsworthy angle. You make the suggestion, no matter how obvious it seems.

These press release guidelines and many other techniques of public relations are comparable to the rules of etiquette, which give you the confidence to choose the right fork. Public relations skills provide the understanding to package Friends and library happenings in a way that can capture public attention. There are many inexpensive and accessible public relations guidebooks that provide more step-by-step instructions. Figure 11 shows a sample news release.

Beyond mass media, Friends can use other publicity tools. These include newsletters, annual reports, posters, special programs, film series, speakers bureaus, and others. Remember, all the print materials you produce reflect on the library as well as your Friends group.

Newsletters

Your newsletter is a vital communications link between you and your members and the community at large. It serves to remind them periodically of both the Friends group and the library. It alerts them to facts about the library and the Friends that make them feel part of a family. In many cases the newsletter is the only membership extra they get in return for their dues.

Through the newsletter, Friends learn about future activities, other members of their organization, and library news. Its features may include recognition of volunteers, donors, and new members; help-wanted ads; and a "wish list."

It is to your benefit to make the newsletter as attractive as possible. No matter what your budget, many aids are available today to help you in this task. Many examples researched for this chapter were created on computers using varying

WATERLOO, IOWA

Figure 11. *Sample News Release*

NEWS RELEASE

Contact: Sandy Dolnick
(215) 790 1674
For Immediate Release

Friends of Libraries U.S.A. Midwinter Programs

Saturday, Feb. 4 Friends from the local area (Mid-Atlantic) as well as conference attendees will *Focus on Friends*. A focus group leader will help Friends identify their problem areas, and groups will do problem solving. Group facilitators will be experienced leaders from FOLUSA's board and the area.

Monday, Feb. 6, Midwinter Author Breakfast Copying the success of the American Bookseller Association's breakfast programs, FOLUSA is presenting four outstanding speakers: Mary Pope Osborne, Random House, author of *Molly and the Prince* and *Moonhorse,* and the Spider Kane series; Christopher Lehmann-Haupt, *NY Times* Literary Critic and author of *A Crooked Man,* Simon & Schuster, a novel about the dark side of Washington politics; Patrice Gaines, Crown, who wil discuss her autobiography *Laughing in the Dark, From Colored Girl to Woman of Color—A Journey from Prison to Power;* and Winston Groom, author of *Forrest Gump,* will discuss a new nonfiction account of the Civil War: *Shrouds of Glory, From Atlanta to Nashville: The Last Great Campaign of the Civil War,* Atlantic Monthly Press. Tickets to the breakfast are $16 each. The breakfast will be held in Lincoln Hall at the historic Union League Club, established in 1862. Attendees will be given the opportunity to visit the club's historic collection of Civil War and Lincoln materials. For tickets send a check or money order to Friends of Libraries U.S.A., 1700 Walnut St., Ste. 715, Philadelphia, PA 19103.

degrees of sophistication. (See chapter 18 for more information on computers.) Computer technology changes so quickly that it would be counterproductive to name software programs, but the following suggestions can help the appearance of any newsletter.

Don't cram everything onto one page. If you want to use only one page, plan what is most important to say.

Two columns are easier to read than a closely printed page.

If your group is a member of Friends of Libraries U.S.A., you can clip information from FOLUSA's quarterly periodical to use as needed.

Use easy-to-read type. Avoid cuteness.

Do not overuse graphics.

Clip art available on disk from the American Library Association covers library-related subjects, and there are many books available with public-domain illustrations.

If you use a computer to prepare your newsletter and do not have access to a letter-quality printer, consider having a "quick-print" store transfer your computer disk to its printer.

Reassess your newsletter periodically. Don't hesitate to consult a professional. This is one reason to have someone with advertising or public relations experience on your board of directors.

Design

There is no substitute for a professional designer when it comes to producing effective print materials. A designer can help you develop a logo and a consistent style for all your materials. The initial investment is very worthwhile.

How do you find a good designer? You can begin by collecting local materials you think are effective. Spend some time comparing the brochures from banks and other businesses. Find out who designed the ones you consider to be the best. Ask the designer if he or she will work for your Friends group. Often fully employed designers will take on a moonlighting assignment for the library, and the Friends group is likely to be a challenging and prestigious account. Don't expect to get good design for free. When you rely on contributed talent it's possible to lose control. It's much easier to ask people to do a job over again if you're paying them (even a token amount) than if they're donating their time and talent. Be very clear about the assignment and discuss costs at your first meeting. To begin your public relations program, your group should consider some basic communication tools including a logo, letterhead and envelopes, fact sheet design, and a membership brochure.

FRIENDS
OF THE
TEANECK
PUBLIC
LIBRARY

TEANECK, N.J.

"Friend to Friend" Library News

From the Friends of the Coeur d'Alene Public Library • Fall 1995
205 E. Harrison Coeur d'Alene • (208) 667-4676

A Light in the Window of Idaho: The History of Idaho's Public Libraries

The National Movement

Ben Franklin started the first subscription library in 1731. However, it was more than 100 years later, in 1845, that Boston Public Library became the nation's first free public library.

The Boston Public Library was the forerunner of what women's clubs, schools and professional groups would identify as a major concern—free libraries for all. These citizens' goal was to promote democracy and education; their objective was to create a "civilized" and well-informed community.

Idaho Libraries

Though Idaho enjoyed few established libraries until the twentieth century, many pioneer civic leaders came from urban Midwestern and Eastern centers where the free library movement already existed. They brought with them similar ideals of the library as a civilizing and educational force in society.

The "State Traveling Library Commission," the precursor to the Idaho State Library, was formed by the Columbian Club of Boise in 1899. With the purchase of 15 cases of books, the library provided services to many of the small towns and mining camps of Idaho. The Idaho Free Library Commission was formed in 1901 with an appropriation of $3000 per year for salaries, transportation and the purchase of books.

The Woman's Columbian Club of Boise also gave the city its first

Idaho Library Exhibit Schedule

"A Light in the Window of Idaho" presents archival photographs detailing the history of Idaho's public libraries. The exhibit will stop at the Coeur d'Alene Public Library September 18–October 13. A slide and lecture presentation about Idaho's library movement is scheduled for September 26 at 6:30 p.m. at the library and will be hosted by the Friends of the Cd'A Public Library.

Madeline Buckendorf, a noted historian, formerly with the Idaho Oral History Program, will be presenting the slide program.

library. The group opened a two-room library in City Hall in 1895. At that time the library operated on a subscription basis, charging $2 per year or 25¢ per month for the use of books off the premises. It wasn't until the Carnegie Library was opened in 1905 that free service was offered to all the residents of Boise.

A Light in the Window

When Judge C.C. Goodwin dedicated the new Carnegie Public Library in Boise on Wednesday, May 3, 1905, he called Boise Public Library "a light in the window of Idaho toward which all her children may turn."

This travelling exhibit explores how all of Idaho's libraries came to fulfill that statement. Attend the exhibit and learn about Idaho's public library heritage and about the backgrounds of the people who shaped Idaho's free library movement.

As Others See You: Publicity and Public Relations

The fact sheet, as described in chapter 6, is a simple one-page description of your group including its name, address, telephone number, officers, purpose, history, and programs. You'll use your newsletter and fact sheet to introduce yourself to the media, funding agencies, etc. The fact sheet should be attractive, up-to-date, and well-organized in easy-to-read copy blocks. Typewritten copy is fine. It doesn't need to be fancy. Chapter 8 includes detailed suggestions about membership recruitment brochures.

Before you hire a designer, have your copy ready for each piece and be able to describe the piece's purpose and audience. If you plan ahead and have letterhead, fact sheet, and brochure copy ready, your initial meeting with a designer will get you started toward a consistent graphic image. In addition to the logo and print pieces, ask the designer to do a "stylebook" with simple layouts showing suggested typefaces, colors, and formats for all printed materials. You can then produce your own flyers and program announcements—even a newsletter—with professional polish.

The quarterly *Friends of Libraries U.S.A. News Update* is a great source of publicity and promotion ideas, and it usually includes a sampling of Friends groups' logos. In addition, this *Sourcebook* contains a wealth of logos throughout its pages.

Consider joining in national library publicity campaigns. National Library Week, sponsored by ALA every April, is a wonderful opportunity for Friends groups to celebrate libraries by staging local events. Every year ALA produces a wealth of promotional materials to help you promote and advocate library support. This cooperative program provides professionally produced materials to libraries and Friends groups at a fraction of their actual cost.

Evaluation

Evaluation, the final step of the public relations process, attempts to find out whether the communications program has met its stated objectives. You can review clips of newspaper coverage, evaluation forms completed by program participants, or surveys. It is often difficult to prove a direct cause-and-effect relationship between a communications program and increased Friends membership or visibility, but you should make an attempt to measure the impact of your public relations investment.

The Friends group should always have its thumb on the pulse of public opinion. Ask "How are you," and wait for an answer . . . as true friends do so well.

CHECK IT OUT
- AT THE LIBRARIES

WORDSEARCH
LIBRARY SERVICES AND RESOURCES

INFORMATION ON INVESTMENT
GARDENING
DESERT PLANTS
BABY NAME
HUNTING FISHING
SPORTS SMALL AND HOMEBASED BUSINESSES
AUTO WIRING
DIAGRAMS CONSUMER COOKBOOKS
HISTORY ART CRAFTS
REFERENCE QUESTIONS ANSWERS
KELLEY BLUE BOOKS
CDS BOOKMOBILE
TAX FORMS
READ A BOOK

AUDIOCASSETTES NEWSPAPERS MAGAZINES VIDEOS
TEST BOOKS MYSTERY NOVELS WESTERNS STORYTIMES
FOR CHILDREN CDROMS WITH CURRENT INFORMATION
ON HEALTH BUSINESS AND MORE PROGRAMS FOR ALL
AGES ONLINE CATALOG CAR REPAIR TALKING BOOKS TOO

```
B O O K N O I T A M R O F N I S T A S T I B
R E D N E W S P A P E R S K O E S I R A H U
P A U D I O C A S S E T T E S N K S E L C S
L T H T I W S N O I T S E U Q I O M W K R I
A B O O K M O B I L E D A E R Z O A S I A N
N A M T O O S M O R D C S E G A B R N E E E
T R E S E D W N Y E L L E K R G T T A G S S
S T B O N F O R M S E E V L B A S B O O K S
C X A T W G N W E S T E R N S M E A K C E C
F I S H I N G A V N H E L P S O T B S U N A
R L E B R B N R E R O M R T M R B Y T R I T
I C D S I I M W O R D R Y A E U E F R L A L
A A L L N S T H I S T O R Y L M D N A E F N L
P R F I G S N F Q E P H E A L T H A R N O O
E F A Y E V U B U S I N E S S E S M C T V G
R N D V K N H I S M A R G O R P R E P A I R
D I N L D I A G R A M S Z B O O K S T R D A
I I N F O R M A T I O N R E F E R E N C E U
G R F O R M E N D L I H C O N S U M E R O T
S T O R Y T I M E S S K O O B N O V E L S O
```

This placemat funded by FRIENDS OF THE YUMA COUNTY LIBRARIES   6/94

YUMA COUNTY LIBRARY DISTRICT
Yuma Headquarters Library
350 Third Avenue
Yuma, AZ 85364
(602) 782-1871
Reference: x23
Youth Services: x26
Administration: x10
Fax: 782-0670

Foothills Branch
11351 Foothills Blvd.
Yuma, AZ 85365
(602) 342-1640

San Luis Branch
23233 First Street
San Luis, AZ 85349
(602) 627-8344

Roll Mini-Branch
Located on the Mohawk Valley
School Grounds
Call Wellton Library (602) 785-9575
for more information

Somerton Branch
240 Canal Street
Somerton, AZ
85350
(602) 627-2149

Wellton Branch
30101 E. Hwy 80
Wellton, AZ 85356
(602) 785-9575

DIAL-A-STORY 329-9828

For Bookmobile Schedule
call 782-1871 x20

A service of the Library District:

**Procurement Assistance Center of the
Yuma Economic Development Corporation**
1600 4th Avenue • P.O. Box 1750
Yuma, AZ 85366 • (602) 783-0193

As Others See You: Publicity and Public Relations

8

Reaching Out: Membership

Sandy Dolnick

The life blood of an organization is its membership. The dues paid are the basis of most budgets. More important are the number of people representing the library and the Friends. Members represent your group, and their attitude contributes to the way the library is perceived by others.

This chapter will help define different ways of membership recruitment, but first, affairs have to be in order. Keep the following principles in mind as you plan your membership recruitment program.

1. *Your mission must be clear.* People have to know why they are joining.
2. *Your group must be attractive to many different segments of your community.* Consider age, income, discretionary time, family responsibility, religion, and ethnic origin. Target a group for membership and measure your results. It will help in future solicitations to learn your strengths and weaknesses.
3. *People have less time to give than in the past.* Your Friends organization can provide them with a chance to help with no further expectation than to pay dues. Keep in mind that programs may not be important to them except for rare events perhaps once or twice during the year, perhaps a large book sale or an unusual speaker. Nevertheless, such people are important to have as members.
4. *NUMBERS ARE IMPORTANT.* The group should have as large a membership list as possible. The degree of involvement of the member is not important. It is important to be able to show that a significant part of the population cares enough to be connected to the library. This is impressive to politicians and corporate donors alike. Set dues with this in mind. Having a low starting fee does not mean that members can't be brought into higher giving circles as they learn more about the Friends.
5. *It is vital to acknowledge receipt of dues quickly.* Let your new members know that you appreciate them.

THE CARNEGIE LIBRARY

FREE TO THE PEOPLE

October 21, 1994

Friends of
The
Carnegie
Library of
Pittsburgh

4400 Forbes Ave.
Pittsburgh, PA
15213

412-622-3102

Dear

Thank you for your generous response to the Friend's appeal for membership. The Friends of The Carnegie Library of Pittsburgh is the largest citizens support organization for libraries in western Pennsylvania. Our memberships demonstrate to legislators the strong grassroots support of the library and help to increase public awareness of the rich resources the Library provides for our community. Friends monetary donations to the library enable projects and acquisitions beyond the scope of the library budget.

Membership in the Friends has grown steadily since 1990 when the organization was begun. In its first year the organization successfully rallied community support during the City and County budget hearings. In 1992 the Friends made a three-year, $60,000 commitment to the Library to institute a plastic library card system. This project benefits patrons and staff by enabling an efficient method of borrowing books and materials.

As a Friends member, you will receive *Friends News*, a quarterly newsletter, as well as notices of other library events and programs. As a Conservator Member, we are pleased to place your name on a bookplate in a new book being added to the library's collection, and to present you with the enclosed brass bookmark.

To become more involved in Friends' activities as a volunteer, or if you have any questions regarding membership in the Friends, please call the Library's Community Relations office at 622-3102.

Again, thank you for your generous membership donation. It is greatly appreciated.

Sincerely,

Lester F. Becker
President

THE CARNEGIE LIBRARY

FREE TO THE PEOPLE

Thank you for your interest and support.
Attached is a Friends membership application.
Please sign the form and return it
with your check made payable to the
Friends of The Carnegie Library of Pittsburgh.

6. *You must make it easy to join.* There should be multiple opportunities to join the Friends of the Library during any given year, no matter what the library habits of an individual.

The rules of membership recruitment are not hard and fast; in fact, it is constantly amazing what inventive means are initiated by dedicated volunteer library lovers to promote and recruit Friends. You must tap into the great well of goodwill toward libraries, often harking back to happy childhood memories.

One caveat to remember for all Friends publicity, including recruiting new members: clear it and time it with your library director. Coordination is supportive; competition is not.

The Basic Membership Tool

Never underestimate the value of word of mouth in interesting individuals in joining the Friends of the Library, but at some point your group will have to communicate with a wider audience. Your basic membership recruitment tool may be a simple friendly letter or a professionally designed and printed brochure. In any case, you should discuss and clear the draft with your librarian, so both of you will know what the Friends group is and where it is heading.

How to Reach Prospective Members

By borrowing member lists from organizations such as the League of Women Voters, the Chamber of Commerce, service organizations, and alumni groups you may find the names of many prospects. Several Friends membership brochures provide space for new members to suggest other names. Many nonprofit arts groups share their lists on a periodic basis or give trial memberships to one another to encourage new members. Investigate this with local art museums and ballet and orchestra groups. In some locales the library reciprocates by sending to its own list of borrowers solicitations for memberships to these organizations.

Some natural friends may not be part of the organization simply because they haven't been approached or made to see how they can benefit from membership. These natural tie-ins include reading clubs that depend on library help. Their members know the importance of libraries, and they might be willing to help the Friends start their own reading circle or help to lead it. Genealogists use the library and always have a wish list for materials to amplify local collections. Parents who teach their children at home (home school) are active users of the library, which may become a classroom of sorts to them. Other special interest groups to cultivate include investment groups, senior groups, horticulturists, and other groups that require specialized reading materials.

Almost any available list will include some library lovers. The whole community, not just the library user, should be targeted.

Bookmarks

Since the most likely new Friends are library users, bookmarks slipped into books as they are checked out is an on-target method of promotion. It acts as a gentle reminder while the books are being read. The bookmark has the added advantage of being economical, requiring no postage and little paper. The bookmark's one disadvantage is that any message needs to be very concise.

Action Point

Houston, Texas

The Friends of the Houston Public Library added a nice touch to their bookmarks by including a tear-off, postage-paid membership form.

Brochures

A bit of publicity may spur an interest in helping the library, but if there is not an easy way to respond to the message, you may lose the opportunity to gain new members. Brochures should be placed at every checkout counter in every library and at every meeting and event. Smaller versions may be printed on other library materials where appropriate. Because book sales are a wonderful opportunity to involve new members, a brochure should be placed in each order of books sold.

JOIN NOW!

Photo by: Anne Day

Become a Friend of The New York Public Library

The New York Public Library

A national treasure in the heart of New York City!

It's more than a great library . . . an archive of civilization . . . and a vast museum. It's a "university" that's open and free for all to use and learn from.

Here you can explore over fifty centuries of human thought and experience in over 3,000 languages and dialects. You can have access to and learn from millions of journals, books, maps, and other items—many of which are found nowhere else. And you can enjoy unusual exhibitions that include rare works from the Library's world-renowned collections.

The New York Public Library is one of the world's five great research libraries. Often called "the Peoples' University," it is the only major research library dependent on private dollars and accessible to all who wish to use it.

It is through the generosity of private citizens, corporations, and foundation benefactors that the Library continues to remain a resource for all. Every individual who makes a donation helps keep it a national treasure for all to enjoy.

Become a Friend of the Library today! You will receive all the benefits detailed on the next page *and* your gift will help the Library:

- **Remain accessible** for everyone who wishes to use it—today and in the future. Your gift will help ensure that the doors remain open and that materials are available for immediate use.

- **Acquire new and important works** for the collections—a critical concern in this age of information.

- **Preserve its priceless collections**— books, maps, films, and all kinds of rare and often one-of-a-kind items.

BECOME A FRIEND AND HELP SUPPORT THE LIBRARY . . .

JOIN TODAY!

Mail Campaigns

Mail campaigns to a broad audience have the chance of being there at the right time—when checks are being written, perhaps at the end of the year. A detailed study of such a program follows. It can be scaled down for any size library.

FOCUS

Friends of the New York Public Library
New York, New York

Donors are acquired in three ways—through cold prospect mailings, distribution of a four-color Friends brochure, and at the Friends desk and library shop at the Center for the Humanities at Fifth Avenue and 42nd Street. In the recent past a donor-acquisition mailing to a targeted group of branch library cardholders has been mailed in the spring, emphasizing donations to the book fund.

Two major cold prospecting packages are mailed each year, totaling more than two million pieces. The first, sent in early fall, is a serious package emphasizing the need for operating support for the Research Libraries. The 1996 package focused on the importance of the library in the technological revolution and the need for the library in the lives of many of its users.

For the past twelve years, the second cold prospecting package has been a raffle mailing whose primary purpose is to get new names to solicit for membership and to obtain an additional gift from current members.

A colorful brochure describing the library and its need for private support along with the benefits of membership in the Friends is sent out to anyone who telephones or writes to the library about making a donation. It is also available in boxes placed around the Center for the Humanities and the New York Public Library for Performing Arts.

Visitors to the library may become Friends by signing up at the Friends desk in Astor Hall at the Center for the Humanities or in the library shop just off Astor Hall. This option is particularly popular during the holiday season, when a shopper can get an immediate 10 percent discount on items purchased by becoming a Friend.

Donors are asked to renew their support of the library by direct mail. All donors receive up to three renewal notices over a five-month period—two months prior to expiration, the month of expiration, and two months after expiration. Contributors who give less than $250 receive a preprinted "Dear Friend" package with variables for those who give $40 or more and under

$40. Donors of $250 to $1,249 receive a standard, personalized word-processed letter with inserts.

In 1986 the library tested the use of a lead letter followed by a telephone call to try to upgrade donors in the $40 to $249 categories when they were due for renewal. The results of the test were quite favorable and the letter and telephone approach is now used to renew all donors of $40 to $249 who can be matched with a telephone number. This use of the telephone has been very carefully integrated into the Friends solicitation efforts and in no way resembles the often "quick and dirty" telemarketing efforts used as a final attempt to get donors to renew their support.

Current donors also receive two other solicitations during the year asking for an additional, nonmembership gift: They are included in the raffle mailing but receive a different cover letter, acknowledging their previous membership support. They also receive either a fiscal year-end or calendar year-end appeal, whichever is farthest from their renewal date.

Contributors who do not renew their support over a fourteen-month period are considered lapsed. Those who were previously $40 to $249 donors and who can be matched with a telephone number are included in a telephone fundraising program six months after they have lapsed. In addition to telephoning lapsed donors, the library contacts donors who make gifts only in response to the raffle mailing. During the call, raffle-only donors are asked to become Friends of the Library. Donors who have given less than $40 within the previous six months are also contacted by phone to upgrade their support to the Friend level. All lapsed donors are included in the two cold prospecting mailings and the fiscal and calendar year-end mailings.

Special Programs for Friends

Each fall and spring a brochure listing all the special programs for members of Friends of the Library is mailed to donors of $40 or more. These programs include members-only previews and VIP openings to major exhibitions, thematic and "meet the author" lecture series, curator's choices featuring behind-the-scenes tours of special collections with library staff, lecture luncheons, and overnight and day trips planned specifically for members.

Recent speakers have included Gerry Trudeau, Ken Burns, John Berendt, and Philip Hamburger. Trip itineraries have taken Friends to Philadelphia, western Massachusetts, Lexington and Concord, and the Hudson River Valley and on literary tours of New York and Brooklyn.

Perhaps the most popular event of the year for Friends is the annual holiday open house at the Center for the Humanities held for four hours on a

Sunday afternoon in early December. Festivities include tours of the closed stacks, tea dancing, choral singing, puppet shows, storytelling, and much, much more.

Other Special Events

The library has a fully staffed special events office that organizes all library benefit events and manages rental of library space. This latter activity generates much-needed earned income for the library. Note, however, that no benefits other than those of the library are held in library space.

The special events office is responsible for the annual Literary Lions Dinner, which honors prominent novelists, playwrights, and poets each November. They also spearhead the annual Gala held in the Center for the Humanities each spring.

The Volunteers of the Research Library organize an annual Literary Luncheon featuring well-known writers and commentators. Panelists at the 1995 sold-out event, entitled "America the Courtroom" featured Floyd Abrams, Linda Fairstein, Terry Moran, and Jeffrey Toobin, with Charles Nesson serving as moderator.

The library also holds a spectacular evening of dinners called "Tables of Contents," described in chapter 14. This biannual event involves the coordination of more than eighty thematic dinners, all held on the same evening, to benefit the library.

Large mailings are expensive. If the mailing list is eligible for bulk-mail rates, the cost is considerably less than for first class. The United States Postal Service (USPS) has finalized its long-awaited version of eligibility restrictions on nonprofit third-class mail in the May 5, 1995, *Federal Register.* The USPS final rule states that a publication must

1. consist of at least 25 percent nonadvertising matter
2. have a title on the front cover in a distinguishable style and size
3. be formed on printed sheets
4. contain an ID statement on one of the first five pages that includes the title, issue date, frequency, name/address of the nonprofit organization, issue number, ISSN or USPS number (if applicable), and subscription price (if applicable)

To use bulk-mail rates, you will need to have a post office number and to print it on each envelope in place of a stamp. (Your library may already have a bulk-mail account and number that you may be able to use.) The addressed envelopes or mailers

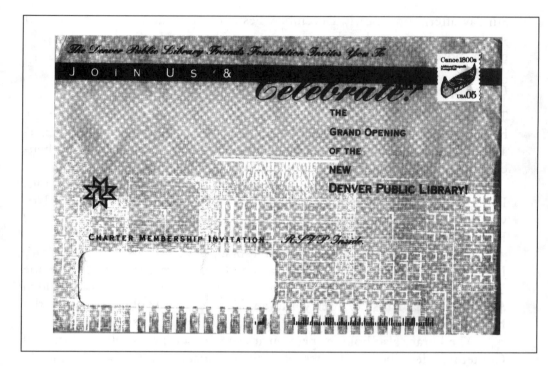

must then be sorted into bundles by ZIP code-plus-four before they are taken to the post office. Each piece in the mailing must also be exactly the same size and weight. Ask at the post office or mailing service about additional ways to save money.

As your membership grows, consider budgeting for a computer to save volunteer time in endless hand-addressing. You'll also accomplish another saving, both in cost of envelopes and the time required to stuff them, if your brochure or flyer is designed as a self-mailer with space on one panel for the address so that no envelope is needed.

If your budget for postage is not as large as you would like, find other distribution means. The Welcome Wagon will often loyally put your information in the hands of new residents. Utilities will also include mention in their mailings.

Action Point

Emporia, Kansas

The Friends of the Emporia Public Library group designed its brochure as a tent card that was placed in restaurants, thus giving diners food for thought.

ITHACA, N.Y.

Questionnaires and Surveys

If one of your goals is to get volunteers to devote time and energy to the library, you may decide to combine the membership appeal with a questionnaire for prospective workers to fill out so that the group can make full use of members' talents. Perhaps a survey of activities, events, or services the respondent would like to see in the library would also be helpful to the library administration as well as the Friends. (See chapter 19 for more on volunteers.)

Incentives for Membership

The majority of Friends groups offer a wide range of incentives. They provide opportunities for volunteer work in the library or interesting activities in which members can participate. They send out monthly calendars, newsletters, and special invitations to events, programs, and exhibit openings. Friends groups offer

---

THE FRIENDS OF THE TOMPKINS COUNTY PUBLIC LIBRARY
312 N. CAYUGA STREET, ITHACA, NY 14850

MEMBERSHIP 199___

Please make checks payable to FRIENDS OF THE LIBRARY and mail to the above address.
Membership and contributions are tax deductible. Your cancelled check is your receipt.
Thank you!

MEMBERSHIP CATEGORIES		AMOUNT ENCLOSED	
❑ Student	$ 3.00		
❑ Individual	5.00	Dues	_____
❑ Family	10.00	General Contribution	_____
❑ Supporter	50.00	Property Buy-out Fund	_____
❑ Sustainer	100.00		
❑ Benefactor	500.00	TOTAL	_____

Mr/Mrs/Miss/Ms _____

Address _____ Zip _____

Telephone _____ Date _____

I would like to help the Friends with:

BOOK SALE	FRIENDS	LIBRARY
❑ Book sorting	❑ Committee work	❑ Shelf reading
❑ Cashier	❑ Serve on board	❑ Answer phone
❑ Telephoning	❑ Publicity	❑ Greeter
❑ Poster delivery		❑ Computer searcher
		❑ Periodicals attendant
OTHER _____		❑ Technical services assistant

Reaching Out: Membership

discounts and free gifts at book sales, book stores, and cooperating restaurants and local businesses. Remember also that one important incentive for membership in all nonprofit Friends groups is that dues are tax deductible.

Action Point

Poquoson, Virginia

Specific books, works by a certain author, or books on a particular subject are located at a members-only Used Book Sale Book Search Service.

Pittsburgh, Pennsylvania

The Friends of the Carnegie Library of Pittsburgh initiated a bookplate benefit for membership donations of $50 or more. The member's name is placed on a bookplate in a new book being added to the library's collection.

Setting Dues and Membership Categories

Since love of libraries crosses all economic barriers, many Friends groups have a graduated dues schedule. Members may give as little as a dollar or as much as a thousand dollars. A growing number of groups have a special schedule for business and corporations.

The fee schedule is almost invariably printed on a blank form that is a part of the printed recruitment piece. The new member then checks off a category of contribution. A good many Friends groups print the fee schedule and membership blank on the reverse side of an envelope, which can then be mailed with the contribution back to the library.

Action Point

South Windsor, Connecticut

Membership in the Friends is now free to seniors, aged 80+.

Newspapers, Radio, and Television

Coordinate your membership drive with releases in the local newspaper, announcements on the local radio station, and even television coverage, if possible. Library pro-

motion on radio and television is usually welcomed, since it helps to fill the station's public-service requirement. Your local newspaper editor might be delighted to write an editorial for you. Many of these people might also be good board members.

If your Friends group is already a going concern, reports of its activities or sponsored events in the newspaper throughout the year help you win recognition when it comes time for your membership drive. If you're just organizing, your group might start off with something newsworthy, such as hosting a first annual picnic, a special author event, or an elegant open house at the library. (See chapter 7 for information on writing news releases.)

You can also "go piggyback" with national advertising and publicity about libraries during National Library Week by making your membership year begin in April. If your budget can be stretched, paid advertisements and spot announcements can be enormously helpful.

Posters and Banners

Posters make a nice complement to a membership drive. They should not be regarded as a prime source for getting new members, however, since they require the prospective member to find a blank membership form, fill it out, and mail or take it to the library. Therefore, if posters are included in your recruitment scheme, make sure they are posted around the entire library and are accompanied by membership blanks.

Banners are a fine reminder to join as one drives past the library. Banners for light poles on main streets also serve that purpose and increase the visibility of the Friends. They are easy to reuse each year and may be underwritten or discounted by a local business.

Welcoming and Working with New Members

Some Friends groups have printed membership cards to issue to new members; some send out a welcoming, grateful letter. You may decide a telephone call would be even better. In any case, make new members feel welcome.

Keep in touch with members throughout the year by sending information about the library in a newsletter inviting them to special events and programs and recognizing volunteers. At the very least, each member should receive an annual report of the group's activities.

Renewals

Having a member join once is good. Having him or her renew on an annual basis is better. It is important to have a renewal program in place so that with each new administration it will be relatively easy to continue the process of mailing without having to start from scratch each year.

The Pensacola type of renewal message works when the group is relatively small. For larger groups a series of letters and phone calls should be instituted.

A periodic evaluation of your present Friends membership can often point up a target area that is rife with potential new members. Look at the membership geographically: Is it all concentrated in one section of town? Is it lopsided economically in upper middles or lower uppers? You can look at it ethnically, or any other way you can think of. If you see an unrepresented area, try a personal call to a community leader. You'll be surprised how that kind of appeal can achieve a continuing neighborhood of library supporters.

Membership Decline

There are bound to be periods when membership figures drop. This is part of life in a volunteer organization. Therefore, it is vital to keep a steady stream of ideas coming to the board of directors. Board rotation helps bring in new points of view and new contacts. Membership in Friends of Libraries U.S.A. guarantees new information on what works well for other Friends of the Library through its quarterly newsletter and other publications.

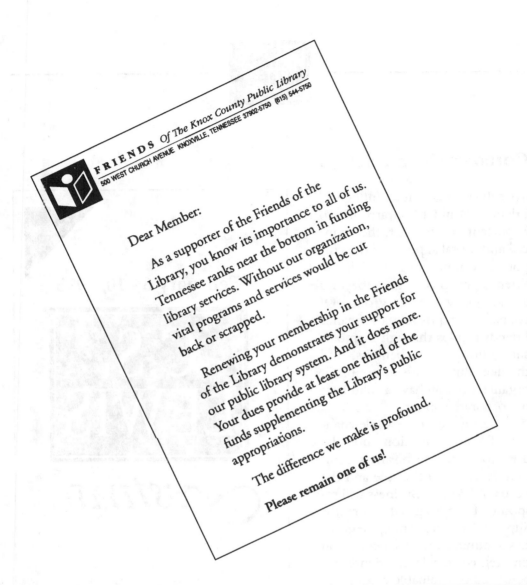

FRIENDS *Of The Knox County Public Library*
500 WEST CHURCH AVENUE KNOXVILLE, TENNESSEE 37902-5750 (615) 544-5750

Dear Member:

As a supporter of the Friends of the Library, you know its importance to all of us. Tennessee ranks near the bottom in funding library services. Without our organization, vital programs and services would be cut back or scrapped.

Renewing your membership in the Friends of the Library demonstrates your support for our public library system. And it does more. Your dues provide at least one third of the funds supplementing the Library's public appropriations.

The difference we make is profound.

Please remain one of us!

Friends

FRIENDS OF THE PUBLIC LIBRARY OF DES MOINES
100 LOCUST STREET DES MOINES, IOWA 50309-1791 (515) 237-1333

Please Renew Today!

To insure proper credit, please return this form with your check payable to: Friends of the Public Library of Des Moines. For credit card information, see below.

Renew my friends' membership at the following level:

☐ $25 Friend   ☐ $100 Collector   ☐ $500 Patron
☐ $50 Book Lover ☐ $250 Sponsor   ☐ $1,000 Benefactor
                                     ☐ Other $ _____

☐ Please bill me quarterly ($100 level and above)
☐ My company has a corporate match program (see back)
☐ Please charge my: ☐ MasterCard ☐ VISA

ACCOUNT NUMBER

SIGNATURE   CARD EXP. DATE

Reaching Out: Membership

Corporate Memberships

To achieve maximum influence, Friends should be aware of two important points. First, the financial and moral support of the corporate community is vital if the Friends group is to grow beyond an ad hoc volunteer group. Of course, it is possible to finance Friends groups through memberships, book sales, benefits, and the like. But successful nonprofit organizations all have a solid base of corporate support.

Second, every possible channel of communication must be used to make the business community aware of the role and the needs of Friends. Business will respond if approached correctly. Support from certain segments of this community may depend upon the degree to which Friends are perceived as a valuable cultural resource. Potential supporters may be interested in activities that make library services available to those who are poor or have disabilities. Literacy and family literacy, technology, and basic education are all of increasing interest to businesses. Corporate contributions policies may advocate support of such specific projects.

A Friends group should think carefully about the nature and type of support it desires from business. For example, the group

February 6 - 10, 1995

C.S. LEWIS

festival

Presented By:
**Friends of the Kingsport
Public Library**

Sponsored By:
**Kingsport Arts Enrichment Program
Indian Path Medical Center
Arts Council of Greater Kingsport
Cultural Services Division of
Kingsport Parks and Recreation
Kingsport City Schools**

may seek funding from a few firms for special projects. Another approach is to develop categories of membership for corporations that will attract substantial annual contributions toward ongoing operating support. The business or corporate membership fee schedule should contain a range that allows small and large firms to participate. The different member categories can be designated as patron, sponsor, benefactor, and the like.

Business firms will be most receptive to a logical appeal that is put into writing. They should be told what the Friends organization does, why it needs money, and how gifts to the Friends will benefit the community. Putting this appeal into writing requires much thought, time, and effort, but it is a necessary prerequisite to corporate support. (See chapter 12 for further information on making business Friends.)

The following rationale was successfully used by one Friends group to train persons who solicit corporate and foundation contributions. The general approach of this organization can be adapted to fit the requirements of almost any Friends group.

1. The library is a basic educational resource for all citizens. It is of increasing importance since people need more and more information to cope with the complexities of urban society.
2. As a public agency, with its income derived primarily from local property taxes, the library is chronically short of the funds needed to maintain high standards of community service.
3. Municipal budget cutting has resulted in a gradual erosion of services with fewer books, shorter hours, and a smaller staff.
4. Friends help the public library to maintain and improve its services by supplementing tax appropriations with private funds and by providing volunteer labor.
5. As the volunteer arm of the library, the Friends group has increased its contributions. As budgets tighten, the needs of the library and the Friends group will increase.
6. The Friends group has been building the financial and organizational base that will enable it to meet the growing needs for library support services.
7. Over the past few years, many business firms have become annual members of the Friends, providing funds for improvement of office operations and programs.
8. Membership categories have been established at annual rates of $25, $50, and $100. Several firms have contributed additional sums, the highest being $1,000. The Friends hope to increase their supporting membership while inviting higher contributions.

A Friends group should plan to solicit at least 50 percent of its membership income from the business community. It follows from this that the business community is an important library constituency. Business participation in Friends must be accompanied by recognition that the business community has great needs for library and information services; the library should meet these to the best of its ability.

As a general rule, business people, like other members of the public, do not know of the many resources that the library has available for them. Therefore, develop a long-range informational program designed for the business community as a basis for its future financial support. It is important that corporate Friends know that they have an advocate working to make the library of maximum value to them.

When eminent historian Barbara Tuchman was asked for a statement for the Friends of the Greenwich Library's membership brochure, she wrote: "Friendship for libraries is enlightened self-interest." That should serve as the last word.

9

Friends in
Academic Libraries

Joan Hood

A library is the heart of an educational institution, whether the institution is public or private, large or small. Library Friends organizations have existed for decades to assist libraries by providing additional sources of revenue, increasing visibility, and working as advocates.

The first university library Friends organization was founded at Harvard in 1925. By 1930 there were other library Friends groups at eastern private colleges. In analyzing the growth of Friends groups from the 1930s to the present, the number increased during periods of financial constraint and decreased during ample funding. The golden age for higher education in this country was the 1950s and part of the 1960s. A downturn in funding began in the 1970s and accelerated in the 1980s. True to form, there has been an explosion of Friends organization development activities in academic libraries in the past fifteen years and in public universities during the past decade. Trend spotters predicted that the first priority of higher educational institutions in the 1990s would be adequate funding. Libraries are in the midst of this quest for additional revenue sources.

Historically at academic libraries, Friends groups were formed to support special collections, rare books, or a narrowly defined interest such as fine printing. While this support and interest remains a valid and vital one at most colleges and universities, it has become essential for many Friends groups to broaden the base of their support, especially if one of their major purposes is fund-raising. Library Friends can play multiple roles in assisting an academic library. A Friends organization can help by increasing visibility through publications and programs; identifying and soliciting individuals, corporations, and foundations for financial contributions and gifts-in-kind; and lobbying for an increase in the tax base for a public institution.

Organization

The library Friends organization at an academic institution can be a separate not-for-profit or 501(c)(3) organization, or it can be part of a university or college foundation if one exists. The Friends board of directors establishes the policy for the organization. It must be very clear that the group does not establish policy for the library.

Many acceptable types of organization can be tailored to the needs of a particular college or university. Despite the structure, it is important to achieve a good balance of community, faculty, and alumni representation. It is always a good idea to include a lawyer on the board. The bylaws should specify rotation of board members to foster the development of new ideas for the organization.

A committee structure should be established, although the actual committees may vary according to the activities of the organization. Examples of committees in Friends organizations are

development	program
membership	volunteer services

Many Friends organizations have a five-year planning committee that develops with the library faculty and staff a written plan containing goals and objectives. This document provides the necessary framework to formulate, administer, and later analyze agreed-upon plans.

For a Friends group to be successful a library director must make a total commitment to the effort. That commitment must include a personal involvement of time and energy. In addition, a specific library employee should be the liaison with the Friends board of directors. The designee should have sufficient authority to make decisions and commitments on behalf of the library.

The stated purposes and functions of Friends of academic libraries can be infinitely varied, but certain basic goals are usually found among established groups:

encourage better understanding, appreciation, and support of the library

provide opportunities for people interested in the library to meet together

promote commitment to the belief of the value of libraries' collections, services, and programs

develop the resources of the library by encouraging gifts and bequests of library materials within the established library gift policy

foster a favorable climate for improving public, private, and institutional support of the library

The following Focus briefly describes a program that won an annual award from FOLUSA because of its implementation and success in mobilizing its members to benefit the library.

FRIENDS OF THE SMU LIBRARIES

DALLAS, TEX.

FOCUS

Friends of Lovejoy Library, Southern Illinois University Edwardsville, Illinois

The Friends special project was to expand their fund-raising and establish a development committee. They began a major gifts program for the library, the first need being better access to the online catalog because there were only six public terminals for 11,500 students, faculty, and staff. The Friends needed to purchase twenty-five additional computer terminals and furniture. Their goal was $37,500 over two years, and they raised $40,775 in one year by using personal solicitation, mail campaigns, and personalized letters to prospects. The mail campaigns provided 49 percent of the goal. A diverse group of donors were involved and were recognized by the library at special events. The program also served to personally introduce people in the community to the collections programs at the library. An outgrowth was the creation of a public relations committee to continue the outreach begun by the development committee.

Programs

Most academic Friends organizations sponsor a major program each semester for their members. Activities successfully carried out throughout the country include

presentations by noted authors and speakers

programs linked to other institutional and community activities

student book-collecting or essay contests

receptions for faculty authors and displays of their publications

special exhibitions of library materials

poetry readings

literary landmarks programs recognizing literary figures, an author's birthplace, or his or her principal place of writing

trips to literary sites or other libraries

Library programming offers an excellent opportunity to cooperate with many university units because the library encompasses all academic disciplines and units of a university. The possibilities for cooperative ventures are endless.

Communication

Most library Friends organizations sponsor a variety of publications, among the most vital being a regular newsletter. However, an annual publication can highlight the library's collections, services, and personnel in greater depth than is possible in a newsletter. A financial statement of the Friends organization should be presented in addition to pertinent library financial information. In addition, an important segment of the annual report is a list by giving categories of all donors to library Friends during the fiscal year.

Many Friends groups support the publication of exhibition catalogs developed in conjunction with exhibits to which Friends are invited. Individual major donors to publications as well as general funds donated in a pool by library Friends can be recognized within the publication.

Fund-Raising

The foremost purpose of most academic library Friends groups is to raise money for the library. Because of the growing reliance on private support at most universities and colleges, sophisticated decentralized, yet coordinated, systems of development are in place. Although many current examples of tensions exist between library Friends groups and the library's development office, this tension or working at cross-purposes can be eliminated by careful planning and cooperation.

The University of Illinois at Urbana–Champaign Library successfully expanded its development effort by, in effect, turning its Friends of the Library group into a level of annual giving, much like the Friends of the New York Public Library. The Friends are still the Friends; they are just seen as one part of the whole development plan.

THE RUTGERS UNIVERSITY LIBRARIES

utgers, The State University of New Jersey, founded in 1766, is the eighth oldest institution of higher learning in the United States. As Rutgers has evolved into a major research university, its library system has grown into one of the top research libraries in the country. Today, the university's 18 libraries serve the needs of more than 50,000 students, faculty, and staff on three campuses, supporting academic course work and statewide research.

The system's largest divisions are the Archibald S. Alexander Library on the College Avenue campus in New Brunswick and the Library of Science and Medicine on the Busch campus in Piscataway. These collections are supplemented by the collections held in the libraries on the Cook, Douglass, Kilmer, Newark, and Camden campuses.

Special research libraries provide additional scope and diversity. Some are scientific, such as the Chemistry, Herbarium, Mathematical Sciences, Microbiology, Entomology, Physics, and Center of Alcohol Studies libraries. A number are business or law oriented such as the Institute for Management and Labor Relations Library and the law libraries in Camden and Newark. Others contain rare collections or focus on unique topics, such as art (Art Library), music (Blanche and

Irving Laurie Music Library), jazz (Institute of Jazz Studies), East Asian studies (East Asian Library), and urban policy (Center for Urban Policy Research).

The holdings of Special Collections and Archives, in Alexander Library, include unique manuscript and rare book collections which focus on New Jersey, Westerners in the Orient, women's history, twentieth-century Latin American politics, the Age of Discovery, and British and American political and literary works.

THE FRIENDS

The Friends of the Rutgers University Libraries are composed of alumni, friends of the Rutgers community, and current and retired faculty and staff.

A diverse group of people who have a mutual interest in the growth and future of the Libraries, the Friends sponsor activities that make the collections and services of the Libraries better known to the university, to the scholarly community, and to the general public. In addition, the Friends encourage gifts of books, manuscripts, publications, and other library materials. The members also assist the university librarian in organizing book and library-related activities for the benefit of the Friends and the library community.

FOCUS

University of Illinois Library Friends
Urbana–Champaign, Illinois

The library of the University of Illinois at Urbana–Champaign successfully moved a narrowly defined local Friends support group interested solely in special collections into a national Friends organization that supports the entire library system. This broad support is vital for the long-term growth of the library. The library established an office of development and public affairs staffed by a full-time director. The goals of the office are to promote private financial growth through the addition of a major donor program and the development of a network of nationwide support. Library Friends established the annual funds program, and the group plays a vital role in the library's total long-range development program. The public affairs component of the Friends complements the development responsibility, because greater visibility increases public awareness of the library and concomitantly increases private support.

In examining successful library fund-raising efforts, four elements are important: positioning, access, partnerships, and patience.

Positioning

The library must work hard to establish a central position for itself within the university structure to ensure that it derives concrete benefits from its central role. It must be included in any capital campaign or special fund-raising project mounted on the campus. Campus administrators and leaders should be given many opportunities to interact with the library to learn about its functions and resources and to appreciate the importance of its collections and services to the entire campus community.

Access

The library has no graduates of its own. However, virtually all graduates and faculty derive benefits from library resources and services. Therefore, many will be willing to donate money designated for the library. Friends of the library should push for access to the university's central donor base and make sure that this access is granted at the highest possible university level. Access will allow the Friends to identify, cultivate relations with, and solicit funds from alumni and other donors.

An argument often made against library fund-raising campaigns is that the library's efforts will act merely to redistribute funds that would otherwise be ear-

marked for another unit within the university. On the contrary, statistics indicate that fund-raising for the library expands the pool of donors to the university.

Partnerships

The function of the campus library cuts across all disciplines; it supports all academic and research programs throughout the university. Hence, the library should develop this mutuality into fund-raising partnerships with academic departments or colleges within a university.

Patience

Keep in mind that the development of an academic library fund-raising program is a long process carried out over years and even decades, so patience is a key attribute for Friends and the library involved in the campaign. The library should take a long view of the program, seeing it as a critical investment for the future rather than a quick fix for current library budget woes. Fund-raising activities require commitment and continuity of effort, and a good program will yield steady progress. Planned giving and endowments are a part of the total picture.

Networking

Useful information about academic Friends groups can be found in the quarterly newsletter of Friends of Libraries U.S.A. In addition, FOLUSA sponsors conference programs at the American Library Association Annual Meeting. The Library Administration and Management Association, a division of the ALA, holds fund-raising discussion groups and programs within its structure. Two library development membership groups, Development Officers of Academic Research Libraries (DORAL) and Academic Library Advancement and Development Network (ALADN), sponsor computer listservs.

Summary

In all types of academic library fund-raising and promotion efforts, Friends are invaluable. Because they have no vested interests in the library's operation, Friends can publicize the strengths of the library through their wider circle of acquaintances and influence far more credibly than anyone who works for the library. Friends are the core of the academic library's development program.

Development is a process carried out over years and decades and should not be regarded as a short-term project. Sometimes the annual contributions of a Friends group scarcely justify its existence in the beginning. However, over time the annual fund grows to support not only its own program but also to become the critical factor in the longer term investment of bequests, significant donations of gifts-in-kind, capital programs, and the building of endowment funds. By carefully cultivating a variety of sources, Friends groups have helped academic libraries gain better collections, support, and service for patrons.

10

Friends in School Libraries and Junior Friends

Dale Buboltz

School Friends

In some areas of the country school-library and media-center librarians are in a fight for survival and are presiding over collections of outdated materials that no longer have relevance for the students. Declining budgets, shrinking and consolidating school systems, changes in staffing, and poor morale have had negative impacts upon one of the most important areas in a school system. New ways have to be found to address these problems, and a growing number of school librarians have turned to organizing Friends of School Libraries.

Organization

There are several ways of organizing a school group. The librarian always has to be involved, but the central participants may be parents, students, or the administration. The variety of activities chosen will depend on the way the mission of the group is defined. Following are some examples of what can be accomplished.

Advocacy—having parents and children speak out to funding bodies about the need for current materials and adequate staffing

Fund-raising—raising money to use for nonbudgeted items

Reading promotion and development—making reading exciting and promoting reading as a life-long pleasure

Community involvement—helping the community realize that a good library in the school will enrich children's education and expand their interests

The library media center director (librarian) sets the tone of the Friends of the Library. A director or librarian interested in organizing a Friends group in a school library may want to consider the following suggestions. Give your decisions enough time to work, but don't be afraid to give up an idea or change things that don't seem to work for you. Above all else, keep your perspective. What fails or succeeds today can always be evaluated and improved tomorrow.

Think of ways to give the hard-working officers of the group status and recognition.

Make every effort to let the officers communicate with administrators, especially the principal.

Make sure teachers and administrators are invited to important Friends activities.

Avoid making the student Friends group a "pets of the librarian club."

Actively seek recognition of the student Friends group as an equal among the extracurricular activities of the school.

Have the student Friends work with other school leadership groups such as student council and student scholarship organizations.

Be careful to give status to students doing repetitive, boring library tasks. Student aren't slaves. Burnout will result from overwork.

Set high standards, but be flexible and ready to forgive.

Recognize and encourage activities to meet the social needs of students.

Always insist that meetings have a written agenda submitted by the morning of the meeting. (It should be typed and duplicated for everyone attending the meeting.) These agendas form an important, though abbreviated, record of the work of the Friends.

Examples of these activities are included in the following Focus sections. The first study shows how easy it is to form a group if the right person (the librarian, in this case) happens to ask just the right group for help. Desperation may have driven her to it, but the results are lasting and, indeed, have since grown beyond this school to others in the area.

FOCUS

Friends of the Library, Denton High School West
Denton, Texas

When a second high school was opened in Denton, resources were lacking for the school library. Parents and community leaders were encouraged to help provide the materials necessary to open the school, and a group of approximately fifty fathers met with the principal to offer their commitment and support.

FARMINGTON HILLS, MICH.

An outgrowth of that first meeting was a group of fathers, now called "Dad's Roundup," who wanted to help the school library get additional resources. The initial group included two college professors (including the dean of the School of Library and Information Science at Texas Women's University), a city administrator, and two businessmen and the school superintendent, principal, and librarian. The Dad's Roundup has provided parental support that has been crucial to the success of opening a new high school.

Their activities included

accepting book donations and computer peripherals

substituting for librarians

introducing district librarians to multimedia technology

securing information about library grants

Their involvement and support were instrumental in getting substantial funding from the school district for the coming school year. What has evolved is a group of men who have spearheaded an organization that will lend support to all the libraries in the district: two high schools, two middle schools, nine elementary schools, and other specialty programs. They are committed to adding new members as new grades are added to the school.

What should be noticed in the following study is that the activity is generated by the children in the school. Although they are guided by adults, it is the children's energy and interest that keeps the group vital. It is especially noteworthy that the Friends group reaches beyond the school "family" into the community for some of their programs.

FOCUS

Wadsworth Elementary School Library Friends
Palm Coast, Florida

The Friends program is made up of three groups: parents, community, and students. All groups have the following goals:

improve all aspects of the library media program

increase community awareness

provide an opportunity for parents and community members to become involved

increase student feelings of "ownership" of their library media center

The parents group and the community group each meet three times a year. They contribute volunteer hours assisting librarians, presenting programs, and assisting the student group with their projects.

The student Friends group meets once a month after school. Those students who cannot stay after school can take part in the activities set up by the core group. The activities during Library Media Month have included button day for teachers, bookmark making day, book character day with a character parade, guessing the number of books in a large pyramid 6 feet square at the base, door decorating contest, a readover for all third grade students planned by the fourth and fifth grades, and voting for the Florida State Sunshine Young Readers Book. The students also worked on developing reading lists for each grade, which they put on illustrated bookmarks and distributed to the classes.

Other student Friend activities included reading shelves and getting them ready for scanning with the bar wand, orienting new students, assisting teachers with equipment and materials, staging a membership drive during open house, working at the book fair, developing the Color Corps and a float in the Columbus Day Parade with more than 100 members marching behind, creating a display for Veterans Day and a reception for area veterans, and presenting a parade entry for Arbor Day.

Student Friends also held a book swap that was expanded to collect books for students who had lost their own books in Hurricane Andrew. They collected books and inspected them and decided whether the book should go to the Florida City Elementary School media center or to an individual student. If the book went to the school, students filled out a form to assist the school media staff in processing the book. All of the students agreed that this was one of the most worthwhile tasks they had done and that it taught them how books make their way to their shelves.

The students get to decide how the money they earn from their ways-and-means projects will be spent. In the past they have supported the school's "Living Library" of birds, fish, gerbils, a cat, and a rabbit. They have decided to purchase concrete benches to put outside the media center to have a place to read. They also support the planting and upkeep of one of the flower beds beside the media center. They have made contributions to the schoolwide reward program and have purchased the items needed for the Color Corps. Other projects they have supported were promoting the Veterans Day program, paying for a storyteller, and purchasing special promotional materials for the media center.

The organizing force behind this group was the parents, motivated by a desire to bring improvements to their children's library. They were willing to use their personal resources as well as a great deal of time and physical effort. Motivation of parents to provide a better learning environment for their children makes the formation of these groups relatively easy, resulting in a less time-consuming role for the school library media specialist.

West School Parent Teacher Council
New Canaan, Connecticut

The West School Parent Teacher Council (PTC) made a major effort beginning in 1991 to improve and enhance both the physical facilities and the program offerings of the library.

West School is a public elementary school, grades K–5, in a Fairfield County suburban community. The enrollment is approximately 400 students with 32 administration/certified staff.

Total proceeds from the 1991 Spring Fair, a fund-raiser earning profits in excess of $8,000, were earmarked for the refurbishing and expansion of the library or Learning Resource Center (LRC). A committee was formed consisting of the principal, the district library supervisor, the school library media specialist, and several parents. Because of the parents' strong commitment to ongoing improvement of the school LRC, the PTC voted to become a member of FOLUSA so that it might avail itself of the pertinent information offered by that organization. In the first calendar year of the PTC effort, significant strides were made toward the goal, with the recognition that the effort would be ongoing and continuous.

With the consensus of the library committee, funds were spent in the following manner. After the diligent effort of parent volunteers to inventory and box books (approximately 1,200 volumes) and other materials, the LRC was painted in bright primary colors and was reorganized into three separate rooms. The computer room, located to allow for a research/whole-class instruction area, was equipped with a computerized *Compton's Encyclopedia* and a printer. The central room houses the nonfiction and circulation areas, and the third room is for picture books and the fiction collection. This latter area was attractively decorated with comfortable upholstered chairs and a cozy, separately carpeted story-reading area with bright sit-upons for the young listeners. New staff desks and plants were added, and fourteen frames were donated by a parent to provide a rotating display of children's artwork. Provisions were made for the construction of a display area in the corridor outside the LRC. Additionally, funds were used to purchase two TV/VCRs, an extensive collection of videos (including numerous *National Geographic* titles), reference books, two paperback racks, and software, including BookWhiz.

The town's First Selectman, members of the Board of Education, and the Superintendent were invited to a ribbon-cutting ceremony. Students demonstrated some of the new additions to the LRC. The following day, the library media specialist hosted a kick-off luncheon meeting for parent volunteers. At that time, the volunteer coordinator distributed a handout delineating numerous ways in which volunteers could help the LRC. (Volunteers help on a daily basis with shelving and circulation activities.)

In addition to the financial and material contributions, the PTC suggested and supported efforts to enhance program offerings. A lunchtime story hour hosted by an LRC staff member began during the holiday season. Due to the enthusiastic response of the audience, the program will be continued on a year-long basis. Parent volunteers also assisted with small-group library skills instruction for some classes. A wish list was provided at the Fall Book Fair so that parents could buy selected books at the Fair and donate them to the library. Nameplates noting the donors were inserted into the books. This wish list program will be a part of the Spring Book Fair as well.

The LMS initiated a Carmen San Diego Club that meets weekly and involves approximately twenty children. They presented their own show, and a parent arranged a wonderful prize for the winning team—a trip to a taping of the Carmen San Diego television show.

Medieval Merriment is the popular new theme of this year's Spring Fair. A major component of the planning for the Fair has been in the area of the schoolwide educational enrichment program at the Metropolitan Museum in New York City on the subject of arms and armament. As a result of the training and further individual research on the part of our library media specialist, the LRC will be very much involved in the educational enrichment aspect of the Fair through appropriate displays, a bibliography of publications dealing with the period, and an exciting program designed to entice students to read about the Middle Ages.

Among plans for future PTC involvement are the following:

site visits by parents to other school libraries

continued periodic meetings of our library support group with emphasis on definition of our goals and objectives

sponsorship of an authors'/illustrators' day

increased participation of parents and senior citizens as volunteers in the LRC

invitations to working parents to schedule a time to come in to read to their children's classes

periodic entries in the PTC weekly newsletter regarding new LRC acquisitions

the implementation of a birthday book program in which a child could donate a book to the LRC on his or her birthday

periodic requests in the PTC newsletter for parents to come in to share their special interests or talents with students (for example, the library media specialist might advise the PTC that a certain grade was studying electricity and that would be noted in the newsletter)

sponsorship of a turn-off-the-TV program

the use of parent volunteers to help individual students with research projects (coordinated through the library media specialist and individual classroom teachers)

The junior high Friends in the following Focus have made a school club that has prestige equivalent to a sports team. Making the club available only to those willing to take a library test is unusual, but it makes the students achieve a goal that will benefit them throughout their lives.

FOCUS

South Gate Junior High School Friends of the Library
Los Angeles, California

There's something very reassuring about being a friend. Students at the middle-grade level, just beginning those shaky teen years, feel the need for all the friends they can find. Parenthetically, it's not inappropriate for them to learn to be or sharpen the skills of being a friend. A student Friends of the Library group can meet some of the middle school students' needs as well as a very real need of the active library program.

The Friends of the Library in South Gate Junior High has changed over the years because much of the character of the group depends on the student leaders who emerge. It is one of the most influential clubs on the South Gate campus. Over the years it has developed outstanding students, who have gone on to become high school leaders. The club serves students and teachers.

South Gate Junior High School Library

CARD STOCK

FRIENDS of the LIBRARY

_____is a member
in good standing of Friends of the Library
Club. He/She has agreed to use this card
only to go to the library. If the card is not
being used correctly, any staff member
may take the card away.

Date	Librarian

Students Name _____ agrees to follow the rules of
Friends of the Library at all times.

1. The membership card will be used only to go to the
library at lunch and/or nutrition.
2. The membership card will never be used to go to his/her locker.
3. The membership card will never be given to another student to use
in any way.
4. Student's Address:

Student's Phone (____) _____

Student's HR Code Number _____ Grade _____ Track _____

FRIENDS OF THE LIBRARY CARD

- Each year the color of the card is changed.
- Each year students are required to re-check their library skills by taking a test. This gives us an opportunity to include new library policies.
- The date of isse is used along with the librarian's signature.
- The large section (3×5) is kept on file.
- Selected students administer the library test and issue the cards.
- Since the librarians seldom work at the circulation desk, signing the cards in person is a good opportunity to learn names.

Dale Buboltz, Librarian
Ruby Ling-Louie, Librarian
South Gate Junior High School
4100 Firestone Boulevard

Most important for the librarian, the members have made significant contributions to the very active program of the library.

South Gate Junior High School has about 4,000 students that attend school year round. The Friends group has about 2,800 members. The library media center has two librarians—one works eleven months a year and the other

works three days a week throughout the school year. There are also six other full-time employees and one who works part-time.

The Test

A student must pass a fifty-question multiple-choice test of library skills with a score of 90 percent or higher to become a member.

The Friends of the Library test grew out of suggestions during a regular Friends meeting. The Library Test Factory by the Library Bureau of Investigation (a computer program) is used because it is possible to generate "new" tests with the push of a button. This program rearranges the database of questions or multiple-choice answers and provides an attractive test format.

Every effort is made so that students wanting to take the test learn the material needed to pass. A student never takes the test without having a Friend review the answers individually with him or her. After a student's third attempt without passing, a Friend reads the test, and the student answers on the answer sheet. A student's problem in passing the test is also a good indicator of potential reading problems. Special classes review the materials and take the test, though the testing takes longer. There is also a Spanish version of the test.

English teachers are encouraged to have every student tested. The teacher helps the students review the questions in class. (This ensures that teachers learn the proper use of the library.) The test is always given in the library, and the scores are returned to teachers so they can record them in their roll book.

At the suggestion of students and teachers, a four-page *Learning about Your Library* information sheet was developed that gives all the answers to the Friends test and other important facts. It is a good starting place for new-teacher orientations to the library. Copies are kept on the circulation desk in notebooks for students who want a quick review or who are new to the school.

The test is machine scored to make the correcting process easier. The Friends handle much of the testing and scoring of the test as well as the individual instruction of students. Once a member of Friends of the Library, a student may use the membership card to gain access to the library at nutrition time (twenty minutes) and at lunch time (thirty-five minutes).

Activities

Contests and special events are conducted by Friends for Friends. The Friends of the Library is a critical factor in the school's successful book fairs. The members help keep the "store" in order and provide the best security force that could ever be found. Other important tasks include helping with the schoolwide campus beautification projects, selecting some of the library materials, and checking passes or Friends membership cards at the door during nutrition and lunch times. The Friends have often started and refined activities only to have the responsibilities in the library assigned to a paid staff member.

Constitution

The South Gate Friends of the Library Constitution is on a computer disk and is similar to the U.S. Constitution, which may be helpful to students as they study that document. To keep the Friends constitution a living document, it is dated. The most-recent version is the law for the club.

Administrators and librarians will find that the well-planned efforts of students and parents can bring needed resources the library media program needs. Students make people at the decision-making levels of the district aware of immediate needs, often cutting through red tape. They have strong potential for being lifetime library advocates. We can never underestimate the early training of Friends!

Junior Friends of the Library

Leslie Langley, Elizabeth Neff, and Elaine Jackson

Many libraries have found it worthwhile to devote time and attention to nurturing a Junior Friends of the Library or a Young Adult Friends of the Library. These programs are really dependent on the devotion and energy of the librarians who work with these groups and their ability to find a core of youngsters (and parents) willing to take on the task. The ages of those involved will depend on the availability of the programs.

Many of these programs take place after school and have come about because of the increased number of children using the library as a place to go for an after-school program. Librarians can enrich the children's knowledge of the library by helping them use library resources for completing homework and can use young people's opinions as a basis for selecting materials. During the summer, these same children may take on a special role in the library's summer reading program.

In some cities, grown Friends of the Library come in to help with the homework coaching and with story times for young children. Many middle schools and high schools have a community service requirement that is met by serving the library. Young Friends learn about how the library functions and how to use online materials. Many of the jobs they perform help them develop skills in organization and leadership. These skills are often amplified in later years in the students' résumés. Following are some descriptions of successful programs.

Georgia O'Keeffe
Friends of the Library

April 4, 1994

Dear "local star";

Help extinguish illiteracy by being a "star" at the Georgia O'Keeffe Elementary School Night of A Thousand Stars

Wednesday, April 20, will be a very special night at our school. On that night, during National Library Week, we will join libraries across the nation to "*keep the lights on*" for an evening of family read-alouds with celebrity guest readers.

Known as the "*Night of a Thousand Stars*," this event will focus national attention on family literacy and the importance of families reading together. Our "*light*" will join 1000 other libraries across the nation.

Who will be the celebrity guest readers? Our "*stars*" will be local New Mexico celebrities. We are writing to you to invite your participation as a celebrity reader. As one of our community's most respected citizens, you are in position to make a powerful statement about your concern for children and a more literate nation.

As a special guest reader, we ask that you read aloud from a favorite children's book on the evening of *April 20* at *Georgia O'Keeffe School Library* between 6:30-8:30 pm.. We would also appreciate your sharing your concern for literacy or an anecdote from your reading memories. Each total time slot will be not more that 1/2 hour though it may be shorter if you choose.

We are very excited about this event and hope that you will share our enthusiasm. Your participation will guarantee a "*****four star*****" production.

Thank you for your consideration. Please fill out the reply letter and return it in the self-addressed envelope as soon as possible. We hope you can help make this event a success.

Action Point

Teaneck, New Jersey

The Teaneck Friends sponsor a Junior Friends organization for sixth–eighth graders. The Junior Friends help out with library and Friends programs including the spring book sale. They benefit by learning the inner workings of the library, meeting new friends who share their interest in books and stories, and enjoying refreshments at their monthly meetings. In this competitive age, they are also honing leadership skills.

Friends in School Libraries and Junior Friends

FOCUS

Junior Friends of Norton Public Library
Norton, Massachusetts

At the Norton Public Library in Massachusetts, the Junior Friends are in grades 4 through 6. They have two fund-raisers each year, a penny sale in February and a flea market in the summer. With the money they earn they choose programs that they sponsor for other children at the library. In the past they have funded magic shows, live animal exhibits, musical programs, and craft workshops for children their own age and younger.

During the summer the Junior Friends help with the record keeping for the summer reading program. They put up bulletin boards in the children's room, and each member has adopted a shelf that he or she must keep in order. At the weekly meetings they learn about the library and occasionally prepare crafts for small children to make at a drop-in craft session. Every year they have a sleepover at the library.

Junior Friends of Buckley Library
Poteau, Oklahoma

Junior Friends of the Library is an organization that is based on the principles of Friends of the Library. Middle and high school age young adults are eligible for membership and must meet the following basic requirements:

> be in middle school or high school
>
> own a current library card and be a patron in good standing
>
> attend or assist in providing library-sponsored juvenile and young adult programs and activities
>
> perform 100 hours of service to the library

Junior Friends are awarded a T-shirt with the library logo and "Junior Friends of the Library" printed on it for meeting all of the eligibility requirements.

Service to the Library

Junior Friends provide a variety of services to the library, including

> shelving juvenile easy books, juvenile and young adult paperback books, and adult paperback books
>
> straightening and storing newspapers and magazines

dusting shelves in the main body of the library

cleaning and maintaining the aquarium

watering and general caring for plants

sweeping the front and rear steps and keeping the grounds litter free

changing the messages on the exterior sign on a regular basis

maintaining the Campbell's Soup label file

assisting the children's librarian with bulletin boards and cut-color-paste projects

setting up and removing tables and chairs in the library auditorium

Basic Operations

Junior Friends sign in each day they perform service to the library. They are allowed no more than two hours of service after school and may not accrue hours when the children's librarian is away from the library.

A card file holds a card for each Junior Friend. The secretary of Junior Friends transfers the number of hours of service to the card file daily and totals the number of hours weekly. Hours are announced at the regular meetings.

Meetings are held as per the bylaws and jobs are announced and assigned at this time. Several jobs are assigned on a long-term basis to an individual Junior Friend.

A media event is planned when one or more Junior Friends reach the 100-hour mark and T-shirts are awarded at this time. Additional awards for years of service are in the planning stage.

Junior Friends are the future of libraries in this state. As individuals, they benefit greatly from this organization. The young adults are performing community service and at the same time improving not only their library skills but their reading skills as well. Junior Friends are encouraged to remain in the organization throughout their tenure in middle and high school and to participate in a Friends of the Library group when they reach adulthood. They are also encouraged to become lifetime community volunteers based on their experiences with this organization.

The Library Staff Recommends

Favorite Books from the Dallas Public Library Staff

Friends of the Dallas Public Library, Inc.

11

Friends in Branch Libraries

Sara Oates

Libraries across the country are finding out that branch libraries are a major factor in the health of the library system as a whole. A new excitement and interest in Friends of Branch Libraries has developed. Their necessity became obvious as city budget crunchers looked for new victims.

The branch Friends are a potent ally when library funding is threatened. Their branch is of vital importance to them and their families. They have the most to say about who represents them in the local elections and can influence their neighbors. They have pride in their neighborhood strengths, and the library is part of that image.

This chapter will show how some cities organize and work with branch Friends. This chapter also gives examples of how Friends groups can organize branches to become part of a larger group. The larger group may just provide a means of communication and resource to the branches, which are formed separately from the main group and become part of a geographic council of Friends. Or the branches can be part of a large umbrella organization that helps them perform their functions as part of the whole (as described in the Focus section on San Diego). A third scenario (as exemplified by the Focus section on Pittsburgh) follows.

The Pittsburgh Friends of the Library had the difficult task of organizing branch Friends, including some groups that were already in existence and had been organized previously. It was a delicate task to make all parties happy about the new structure.

FOCUS

The Friends of the Carnegie Library of Pittsburgh and Branch Library Friends Groups
Pittsburgh, Pennsylvania

SARA OATES, head, Community Relations

Relationship Models

The Carnegie Library of Pittsburgh (CLP) includes the main library, eighteen branch libraries, the Martin Luther King Jr. Reading Center, two bookmobiles, and the Library for the Blind and Physically Handicapped. The Friends of the Carnegie Library of Pittsburgh is a charitable membership association of people interested in the support of the total library system. The purpose of the citywide Friends association is to receive and encourage gifts, endowments, and bequests to the library and to support and cooperate with the library in developing library services and facilities for the community through focusing public attention on the resources and services of the total library system.

The Branch and Music Department Library Friends are charitable membership organizations of people who support a neighborhood Carnegie Library or the music department of the main library. The purpose of each branch/department organization is to promote the branch/department library's service and resources within the neighborhood community and to raise funds for branch/department programs and services.

While the citywide CLP Friends organization supports the library system in its totality and the branch/department Friends organizations support individual branch libraries or departments, they share a concern for the health and vitality of the Carnegie Library of Pittsburgh. It is to the advantage of the total library system that the Friends groups work together on advocacy efforts and present a united voice to the community and to local, county, and state funding sources. It is in this spirit that we propose to work together, supporting, encouraging, and learning from one another. We recognize that this is a developing partnership, and while it is important to establish a communication mechanism at first, we also recognize that other areas of effort will emerge.

Membership

The citywide Friends organization has seven categories of membership, with provision for corporate and group memberships. Every branch Friends group with active status will be considered as a group member of the citywide Friends organization. (Active status is defined as any group that has met two times during the year and contributed $50 or more to the branch library during the year.)

Members of branch Friends groups may take individual memberships in the citywide organization and be entitled to such membership privileges as are given other individual members.

Council

The council is composed of one representative from each of the branch/department Friends groups and one member from the CLP Friends board of directors who is also active in a branch Friends group and who will serve as chairperson of the council. The council will meet at least three times a year.

BE A FRIEND

Friends provide vital support for the Library by:

- ■ bringing crucial library issues to the attention of the community and elected officials

- ■ promoting public knowledge of library resources, services and programs

- ■ raising much-needed funds through book and bake sales and other events for the purchase of new books and other important materials.

Support your local library. Ask your branch librarian for details on becoming a Friend.

- -

Yes, I want to join the Friends at _____

Branch Library

Name_____

Address_____

_____ Zip Code _____

Telephone_____

The purpose of the council is to provide a mechanism for communication, mutual support, and sharing of ideas and to encourage coordination of activities among the Friends groups. Branch Friends groups will be responsible for selecting their council representatives. Council membership provides

a forum for sharing ideas, materials, promotional efforts

a voice in the citywide Friends organization

registration as a 501(c)(3) organization

registration as a state charitable organization

participation in Friends recognition events

ten copies of the quarterly Friends newsletter

bulk-mailing permit

Other support services may develop as needed. These might include sample materials (forms, membership cards, etc.) and workshops on record keeping, fund-raising, and membership recruitment.

Fiscal Issues

Monies raised by the CLP Friends shall be managed by the Friends board of directors and, in consultation with the director of the Carnegie Library of Pittsburgh, used to support programs and projects of the library that are of benefit to the entire library system. Monies raised by branch/department Friends groups for the support of their local branch or department shall be kept in separate bank accounts and managed by the local branch or department Friends group. Monies raised by any joint efforts of the citywide organization and branch/department Friends groups shall be collected, managed, and distributed by equitable division agreements made at the onset of each individual project.

Action Point

Kansas City, Missouri

Barnes & Noble teamed up with the library to help collect books for the new Southeast Branch. Throughout the month of April, patrons could pick up a wish list of books for the new library. After making a selection, books were taken to the checkout counter where the purchaser received a 15 percent discount on the price of the gift. The generosity was also recorded on the Honor Roll of Donors and posted at the Southeast Branch when the doors opened. Each gift was also recognized by a letter confirming the tax-deductible donation.

Friends of the San Diego Public Library show how successful well-established groups work together. Almost autonomous in most instances, they are still part of a larger mechanism that helps them in their efforts and takes care of the administrative details that slow down volunteer efforts.

FOCUS

Friends of the San Diego Public Library
San Diego, California

BETTY SHERMAN

The Friends (also referred to as FSDPL—Friends of the San Diego Public Library) is a 501(c)(3) public-benefit, tax-exempt corporation. The organization reports annually to the IRS and to the State Franchise Tax Board both the income and contributions from all affiliated Friends chapters made to the San Diego Public Library. The FSDPL group is dedicated to support the central library and all affiliated branch libraries. For 1995 there are thirty branch chapters of the Friends. All activities are conducted 100 percent by volunteers. A directory lists the elected officers of the corporation and the branch chapter groups' presidents.

Headquarters activities are primarily concerned with management. Monthly book sales are held throughout the year at the headquarters.

A plaque is annually given to a chapter to hang in its branch for a year, and a check is given to matching funds for $100. This meets with enthusiastic local response and increases its membership and donations to the branch.

A typical agenda for forming a new branch group follows.

1. Introductions—President of the Friends of the San Diego Public Library
2. City Council member from Branch District
3. Invitation to create a chapter of the FSDPL

Policy Statement—Executive Director and Corporate Secretary

Goals of the Parent Tax-Exempt Corporation

Goal I.   To serve as the communication link between all chapters in the entire city of San Diego
To provide service, some governance, and tax-exempt information to all affiliated chapters
To network with other allied groups

Goal II. To serve as community advocate for the San Diego Public Library

Goal III. To provide financial support to the library

To increase and unifiy membership citywide

To promote the FSDPL Endowment Fund held at the San Diego Community Foundation

To encourage fund-raising (publicity and information covered in the FSDPL Operations Guide) through book sales, memorial gifts, bequests (special fund-raisers need prior approval and special attention to IRS nonprofit rules)

To ensure proper financial accountability from each chapter (each responding annually with a balanced financial statement)

Goal IV. To support the HUB concept of a new main library

To recognize the main library as a necessary hub for citywide library services: administration, information support, and technical services and as the principal reference resource center with the largest book collection in two counties

Goal V. To preserve our status as a tax-exempt corporation

4. Closing statements: public comments, opportunites to obtain individual membership, consideration of Volunteers to form and operate a chapter, selections of officers, and banking arrangements

Chapters

Within reason, all branch chapters are quite autonomous. Each chapter holds book sales (our principal activity for fund-raising) at times convenient to the chapter. Such sales may be ongoing daily sales during the hours the library is open or may be especially large one- or two-day sales held in the library. (Special liability insurance is not needed for these sales as the city would be responsible for matters happening *within* city libraries. Occasionally, these sales have been held at off-library sites. This creates a need for liability insurance. FSDPL headquarters can help chapters apply for this insurance.)

Several Friends chapters have undertaken special fund-raising activities when new library buildings are built. FSDPL has developed guidelines for the special fund-raisers. The guidelines were primarily made to comply with the recent IRS regulations concerned with fund-raising being related to the purpose of our organization. This has changed from the old concept: "If the money raised was given to the library, it was OK." Now every activity must be

FRIEND OF BOYDEN LIBRARY

FOXBORO, MASS.

related to our "purpose." Consequently, policies were developed to cover these new circumstances.

FSDPL as a total group has been contributing more than $250,000 annually to the San Diego Public Library system, a result of basic fund-raising.

Workshops

The FSDPL has frequent workshops for the chapters. The most needed is for the July closing of the chapter books. The August board meeting is a workshop for treasurers to help them close out their books, balance them with bank statements, and turn them in for an audit before the tax return is prepared.

The Broward County Friends represent a heterogeneous group of branches. Their ability to work together is due to an ongoing commitment to the importance of the vital library system they support and to the organizational attention to detail for each branch.

FOCUS

Broward County Friends of the Library
Broward County, Florida

Organization

Each chapter has a vote in the business of the central board. Local Friends groups operate by the policies and procedures of the Friends of Broward County Library and are covered by the Friends of Broward County bylaws and letters of incorporation. In addition to the regular board members, the director of the library system, the Broward Public Library Foundation, and the library advisory board are represented as ex-officio members.

Goals of the Umbrella Friends

At its inception, systemwide roles and goals were established for the Friends by its board in cooperation with the director of the library system. Generally, the Friends are dedicated to the support of the library system and its mission: to strengthen and expand available services and to respond to the needs of the community.

Goals of the Local Friends

The branch librarian, in partnership with the local Friends group, designs the goals for the branch Friends group. It is understood that roles and goals of the local group may change to meet changes in the economy or political climate or to meet special needs of its own community. Generally, there are several basic reasons for establishing and maintaining a Friends group:

Advocacy—An informed, active citizen lobby can be the most effective voice the library has. A Friends group has the ability to react quickly to events in the community. For example, the Friends of the Coral Springs Library were effective lobbyists for an expanded parking lot for their facility.

Public Relations—Each Friend is a walking public relations vehicle for the library. Often, in a social situation, Friends are called upon to explain or discuss library policies and procedures. Friends increase the public's awareness of library programs, projects, and relevant issues. For example, Friends of the South Regional Library sponsor special programs and events, such as the annual Star Trek adventure, and regularly organize events to recognize the efforts of its many loyal volunteers.

Community Involvement—An organized Friends group is living proof of the library's value to the community. For example, participation of Friends in local Chambers of Commerce provides a high-visibility platform from which to create new relationships. Membership of the Friends of the Davie/Cooper City Library in the local Chamber of Commerce forged ties with local nurseries. These new relationships resulted in a plan to improve and beautify the library grounds. The improvements were made, the Friends and other participants received recognition in local newspapers, and a valuable network was created.

Programs—Friends organize programs and events that serve to emphasize the roles they have selected for themselves. For example, annually, the Friends of the Broward County Library donate new children's books to kindergartners in county schools.

Money—Friends traditionally raise funds for projects, equipment, or acquisitions not provided for in the library's budget. For example, local Friends of the Library groups such as Fort Lauderdale, South Regional, West Regional, and Lauderdale Lakes regularly fund staff-development projects and continuing-education opportunities for library staff. The Friends of Broward County Library fund speakers and programs for staff in-service training.

Relationships

The relationship between the branch librarian and the Friends group should be characterized by a basic understanding and acceptance of the goals and objectives of the library and the Friends and mutual respect and appreciation of each other's individual potential for achievement. It is essential for all parties to understand their respective roles.

Responsibility for the relationship between the Friends and the library is one aspect of the librarian's overall responsibility for good public relations. In order to ensure success, the librarian must believe in the benefits of having a Friends group and arrange for time to work with the group. Continuous communication, information, and encouragement are necessary to sustain interest. Time must be provided to attend all Friends meetings, whether they be executive committee, board, or membership gatherings. The librarian serves as an ex-officio member of the Friends board. (At no time will the librarian or any other member of the staff serve as signatory on Friends checks or bank accounts.) The librarian must convey to the Friends the importance of working in tandem on all projects. Friends must be made to feel that the branch librarian is an important and indispensable part of their endeavors, but the relationship should also cultivate leadership by the Friends and not dependence on the librarian. The branch librarian also must provide leadership in helping Friends to formulate long-term goals and to think and plan ahead. To do this, the librarian must provide guidance in assisting the Friends to understand the legal and organizational structures of the library and how they fit into the organization. He or she must provide praise and publicity for the achievements of the group and realize that his/her performance can and should inspire faith in the library program and inspire the Friends' willingness to work for the program.

Starting a Branch Friends Group

Boards can meet and make policy decisions, but to make branch Friends a viable institution it takes hard, hands-on work at the local level to involve the community. The following points come from successful branch officers of the Philadelphia Alliance of Library Friends for those who wish to start a new program.

> Contact area advocates in neighborhood activities to see if they would like to be part of the steering committee. Also contact school principals and reading specialists.

Friends in Branch Libraries

Alliance of Friends Fact Sheet

- 51 Branch Friends Groups

- 4,000 Branch Friends Citywide

- First and Largest Branch Friends Group: *Friends of Chestnut Library, established 1971; current membership of approximately 800 people*

- Newest Branch Friends Group: *Friends of Nicetown-Tioga Library*

- Approximately 500 volunteers working approximately 3,000 hours per month make Saturday hours possible for the first time in 20 years at 10 branch libraries, tend gardens, catalog archives, and assist in the summer reading program

- A+ for Advocacy

    Participation in Pennsylvania Library Legislative Day in Harrisburg

    City Budget Mobilization - 1993 during a five-month period Branch Friends: met with City Council members • testified at City Council Hearings • conducted branch library budget meetings • wrote letters to local newspapers and to elected officials • circulated petitions • rallied in front of Central Library • convinced the Mayor and City Council to restore 66% of proposed cuts to the Free Library FY94 Operating Budget

- Gifts to Branch Libraries
    bookcases • magazine racks • new meeting room • large print books • carpeting • signage • honoraria for guest speakers • audiocassettes • children's books • stencil maker • draperies • computers, printers, laser scanner, computer hardware and software • graffiti cleaning brush and supplies • gardening tools • magazine subscriptions • banners for children's department • window blinds • bookcart • slide projector • interior painting • plants • chairs • extra telephone line • patio umbrellas • vacuum cleaner • postage meter • tape recorder • upholstery • map table • bulletin board • toys for children's department • funding for summer reading program prizes • funding for buses to Phillies Games for children in summer reading program

The idea of a coalition of citywide Branch Friends Groups was conceived in 1979. For the past twelve years the Alliance, comprised of the presidents/co-chairs of Branch Friends Groups, has provided a forum for these grass-roots volunteers to exchange ideas and to plan strategies to keep the Free Library strong. This Fact Sheet covers their activities and contributions between 1991-1994. For more information contact the Friends of the Free Library of Philadelphia, 1901 Vine Street, Philadelphia, PA 19103-1189, telephone (215) 567-4562, FAX (215) 263-7323.

Contact area banks and merchants for seed money.

Approach merchants in the branch location and request a 10 percent discount on their goods to members of your Friends group.

Ask the local paper for help in advertising meetings.

Develop a good relationship with branch head and staff.

Have regular steering committee meetings.

Keep focused on advocacy.

Set up membership files.

Set dues, and have steering committee pay first.

Discuss fund-raising ideas.

Distribute membership flyers to patrons.

Set a date for "Friends Day" during which patrons will meet the board. Invite officials from Central Friends along with other local dignitaries.

12

Making Business Friends

Jane Turner

Friends of the Library groups have had to become more aggressive in finding community partnerships to sustain their growth and enhance the library's development. As a result, local business contacts are a necessity. Three ways to promote these partnerships are discussed here: cause-related marketing, in-kind support, and grants.

Cause-Related Marketing

As businesses seek to enhance their corporate images and add new energy to their marketing efforts, many are looking to causes as the starting point for ideas and programs. Corporations see an opportunity to cut through the clutter of media messages and connect with their customers by "borrowing" the emotional bond a cause enjoys with the public. Sometimes called "cause-related marketing," these partnerships differ from foundation grants since they are designed to achieve marketing objectives for both partners. A donation is made to the Friends by the corporation in return for using the name of the group in a promotional effort.

Among the causes corporations could choose as partners, libraries offer the benefits of being inclusive in their positive impact across a wide spectrum of the public as well as being relatively free of the controversy that comes with more politically charged causes. While individuals are still the greatest source of continuing support for Friends groups, corporations can deliver a major commitment of dollars or other resources to make a "big idea" possible.

The First Steps in Reaching out to Business

What do you want?

Know your objectives and what you'll need from your business partner to accomplish your objectives. Know from the outset what success for your program

would look like. Greater awareness of the library and its role in the community? Funding for a specific project? More participation from a particular constituency of your library—children, parents, or seniors, for example? Once you've visualized the outcome, you can begin to decide how a corporation might provide the needed resources to get you there.

What's in it for the corporation?

Businesses may become your partner for a variety of reasons. The more you're able to put yourself in their shoes as you create your proposal, the more likely you are to get a "yes" and a program that will renew for the future. A business might partner with you to

> increase positive awareness of its name
>
> enhance its image as a good citizen in your community
>
> increase traffic at its retail locations
>
> give its employees a vehicle for being known as "good guys" in the community
>
> increase sales through all of the above

Deciding which businesses to approach is part fact finding, part instinct. As with individuals, those corporations that already see value in giving are most likely to give more. You already know the good corporate citizens in your area, and they should be at the top of your list.

Your group should develop a policy about the type of business with which you do *not* want to be allied. This is useful in saving the time of both parties. While tobacco- and alcohol-related businesses are sometimes excluded from consideration, this depends wholly on the community in which the group exists.

If a national corporation has its headquarters or one of its major divisions in your

BYBLOS and FIRST UNION *present*

Day of Literary Lectures

Short talks by some of the most impressive authors ever assembled under one roof in Fort Lauderdale

Saturday, March 11, 1995
9:30 A.M. to 5:00 P.M.

Broward County Main Library Auditorium
100 South Andrews Avenue • Fort Lauderdale

FREE ADMISSION WITH TICKET

Sponsored by AT&T

Night of Literary Feasts

Invitation-only Reception and Dinner with Author of your Choice.
Saturday, March 11, 1995 • 7:00 P.M. • $125/person
Benefits Broward Public Library Foundation. Call: 357-6371

SPONSORS
UMBRELLA SPONSOR: First Union National Bank
NOVEL DAY FOR STUDENTS: JM Family Enterprises, Inc.
DAY OF LITERARY LECTURES: AT&T
MAJOR SPONSORS: American Airlines • The Herald
Mayhue Corporation • WLRN Public Radio
SUPPORTERS: American Express • Bank of North America
Blockbuster Entertainment Corporation • Citibank
Deloitte & Touche • Marquis George MacDonald Foundation

Arranged by
Broward Public Library Foundation,
and the Florida Center for the Book
at Broward County Main Library

community, it's likely to be a good prospect. Many major corporations recognize the benefit of supporting local educational and cultural institutions in the areas where their employees work and live. You might take a look at the company's annual report to get an idea of how it likes to think about itself and who its key customers are. If a company stresses its global image, for example, a program that expands your community's global awareness or focuses on multiculturalism could be a good fit. If a pharmaceutical company is based in your area, it might want to support a special program you've envisioned for seniors. A food company that markets to families might be interested in funding a children's program. In short, try to make your proposal the answer to a question they're already asking.

FOCUS

Project JumpStart, Friends of Libraries U.S.A.

JumpStart was a national program in conjunction with Friends of Libraries U.S.A. to promote library card sign-up and reading among children. The Prudential Company was approached to fund materials for more than two million families, to provide a college grant as a grand prize, and to make a significant financial contribution to FOLUSA.

Why did Prudential say yes? The audience matched Prudential's customer base: parents of first-, second-, and third-graders (the focus of JumpStart) are at a "lifepoint" when they're likely to be giving serious thought to the future, including financial responsibilities. The cause fit Prudential's corporate values: community, education, focus on the future. The program offered opportunities for both the company and local management to put their best foot forward and enhanced Prudential's ability to make new contacts and retain customers. A Prudential spokesperson summed it up:

> Building relationships is important to any business, but it's critical in the insurance business. Our customers don't view insurance as just a policy on a piece of paper but as something that involves hopes and dreams. We want to make the company as approachable and warm as possible. That's why we believe in cause-related marketing.

You don't have to have a national corporation in your community to develop a business partnership. Other naturals as corporate partners include local and regional banks and car dealerships. These companies recognize that while they are selling specific goods and services, a large part of their success comes from being

Here's How
You Can Participate

ONE Take your child to your public library. Show your librarian your "sign-up" card (below). Your librarian will help you complete any additional form that might be necessary to receive an official library card in your child's name.

Two Fill out the other side of the card for a chance to win the $50,000 Grand Prize or one of many other great prizes. Cards must be complete and legible to win. Everyone who returns the card receives our follow-up summer reading issue of JumpStart free.

Three When children return to class and show their official library cards, they get to "sign in" on a JumpStart poster in their classroom and receive an "I Got a JumpStart at the Library" sticker from their teacher.

Sign-up

Show this card to your public librarian.
YES, sign me up for my own library card

_____
Child's Name

Complete the other side for a chance
to win $50,000 for college
or other great prizes.

I got a JumpStart At The Library

Friends
of
Libraries
U.S.A.

known and trusted in the community. And, of course, that's what partnering with you should offer.

Although smaller, local businesses don't have the financial and staff resources of major corporations, they can be the source of opportunity. Look, for example, at how business friends helped one library in the following summary.

Action Point

Ridgefield, Connecticut

The Friends of the Library in Ridgefield, Connecticut, worked with a group of restaurants in town to raise money for the library by encouraging more people to eat out on traditionally slow weeknights. During the program's period, any diners who showed their library card on a weeknight had a percentage of their dinner bill contributed in their name to the Ridgefield Friends group. The program delivered additional funding and publicity for the library while addressing a classic problem in the local restaurant business.

Making Your Proposal

Once you've clarified your objectives and you've decided on companies you plan to approach, the next step is presenting your case to the right person. Depending upon the content of your program, your contact could be the head of public affairs, a marketing executive, or even the owner of the company. The key is to know your audience. The simple rule is that your proposal and that person's role in the company should be in sync. You won't always find your champion within a company on the first call, but each conversation should get you closer to the right person or to knowing whether the company is a viable partner.

Your proposal should include the following elements:

1. A brief overview of your library as a community resource
2. An outline of the program you have in mind, why it matters, and whom it will reach
3. A clear description of the link between the program and the company's business and constituency
4. A specific list of what you want from them
5. Timing and next steps for moving forward

Make it easy for your business contact to make a decision by presenting a fully formed idea. That doesn't mean that you won't work together to add new wrinkles or tinker around the edges. However, if you leave too many loose options on the

table, you're asking your prospective partner to devote time and thought sorting through possibilities. Most businesses (just like libraries) are lean these days, and a decision on your program could be postponed forever for lack of time to give it extensive thought.

FOCUS

Atlanta–Fulton County Friends Group
Atlanta, Georgia

When the Atlanta Friends decided to create the Atlanta International Book Festival, they envisioned a three-day celebration as a gift to the city of Atlanta to heighten awareness of the library, the Friends group, and an image of Atlanta as "a reading city." Plans included bringing one hundred authors to Atlanta for talks and book signings, staging live performances based on books, and showcasing storytellers.

Successful execution of the festival demanded extensive resources: goods, services, talent, and money. The business community rallied round, providing such necessities as rooms for visiting authors (Ritz Carlton), refreshments (Coca-Cola), "zillions of shopping bags" (Rich's Department Store), and publicity (*Atlanta Journal Constitution* and local radio stations). Seemingly daunting logistical problems such as receiving and storing signing copies for the one hundred participating authors were managed by the loading dock personnel of Rich's Department Store. Supporting financial contributions were also part of many corporate commitments.

The festival was a resounding success with more than 10,000 enthusiastic attendees, new relationships for the library and the Friends group, and extensive publicity for all participants. The event had all the elements of an effective partnership with business: clear objectives, well-planned execution of the event itself, and publicity highlighting all partners.

The Value of Publicity

While many of the benefits you offer a corporate partner are rooted in goodwill and may be hard to express numerically, getting a company's name in front of customers has real media value that businesses are used to paying for. Although 10,000 people might attend the Atlanta International Book Festival, for example, hundreds of thousands are likely to see a photo in *Atlanta Journal Constitution* of a smiling mother and daughter holding Rich's shopping bags as they listen to a favorite children's author. These kinds of images have tangible value for corporate sponsors.

Set yourself up to get lucky. It is worth your time and energy to prepare releases for news media and arrange for photos that include your corporate sponsors. You might include a quote from the president of your sponsor company explaining why the company believes in investing in the community. The publicity book that you can put together after the event will give you concrete evidence of success for current partners as well as a showpiece for prospective partners for future events. (See chapter 7 for further information on publicity.)

Keeping Them Sold

It's much easier to renew or increase the contribution of a current corporate partner than to find a new one. After a program is completed, take the time to thank sponsors by reviewing the success of the program. This is also a good time to begin planting the seeds of growth of the program for the next time around. If anything didn't go as expected, you'll have the opportunity to listen to your partner and discuss improvements for the next effort.

And don't forget why businesses teamed up with you in the first place. While it's important to approach your partnership with business in a businesslike way with clear, rational measurements of success, it doesn't hurt to secure the emotional bond as well. You are valuable to business because there is value *and magic* in your relationship with the community. Let your partner get the feeling firsthand. Pass along a copy of that crayon-scrawled thank-you note from a children's program. Invite your business friends to events that showcase the everyday magic happening in your library. A partnership that serves both the head and the heart is more likely to survive the threat of budget cuts and continue to grow over time.

In-Kind Support

Discover Total Resources, a pamphlet distributed by the Mellon Bank Corporation for nonprofit groups, includes the major topics money, people, and goods and services as examples of in-kind support. From the very smallest to the largest Friends group, this type of support is invaluable, making benefits available to your group that would not be financially possible in any other way.

Corporate philosophy can encourage involvement in nonprofit causes to enhance a company's public image and to give its young executives an opportunity to become active in the community. Take advantage of their expertise as board members or advisers.

Friends groups frequently approach local businesses to ask for memberships, donations, and ticket purchases. However, a business leader can often give far more in support and business acumen by serving on the Friends board of directors than by simply giving company money.

Encourage volunteerism among business associates with expertise in

accounting and budgeting
communication and marketing
technology
personnel and administration
long-range planning

Tie the Friends' cause to the company's public relations and marketing programs. Ask for their help to

donate products, space, and equipment
become sponsors and underwrite fund-raising campaigns
buy tickets to the group's functions to use as employee benefits and business entertainment
promote and publicize the group's events as a company policy

Other examples of in-kind support include

stores donating percentages of cash register tapes on a special day
stores printing "Join Friends of the Library" on grocery bags
banks and stores allowing donated books to be dropped off for later pickup
restaurants including a $1 donation for each meal sold on a particular day
utility companies including a Friends message in their bills
businesses donating used furniture and equipment
businesses donating phone banks for special efforts
businesses donating printing, layout, and design help
businesses underwriting book collections and magazine subscriptions in pertinent subject areas
accounting and legal firms offering pro bono help
advertising agencies donating logo design and media help with promotional spots
media figures acting as guest hosts
corporations and businesses cosponsoring special events

Bookstores

One type of business has a special affinity for libraries—the bookstore. Many communities find excellent cooperation between the Friends and bookstore owners. Bookstores may

> provide discounts to customers presenting a special offer or membership card
>
> sell books for book and author events and give a percentage of sales to the Friends
>
> cross-promote author appearances
>
> buy and remove books left after a book sale (used bookstore)
>
> cosponsor Banned Book Week
>
> jointly promote mystery nights, book discussion groups, and Children's Book Week

Applying for a Corporate Grant

Community or public affairs offices maintained by banks, utilities, manufacturers, and developers are good sources for corporate underwriting of projects to benefit a library. Heads of smaller companies can be interested in giving, especially if a larger company has set an example of corporate giving in the community to which the Friends group can point when making its approach.

The Friends group should work closely with library community relations people to put together a proposal for corporate sponsorship of a program. (See figure 12.) The Friends group is actually providing the business a means to enhance its image in the community by publicly allying itself with a cultural, educational institution with a social component. The business may not see an immediate obvious return on its monetary investment, but the public relations value is extremely important. Stress the importance of the program to the library's target audience and the ability of the Friends group to carry out its responsibilities. Match these points with benefits to the company, including prestige for the company and wider visibility leading to increased sales. Steps in making a proposal, based on the experience of the Broward County Public Library Foundation, follow. (See also chapter 15 for additional tips on grantsmanship.)

1. A board member makes a connection with the chief executive officer.
2. The chief executive officer recommends contacting the official responsible for coordinating contributions, often the vice president for corporate affairs.

VERMILLION PUBLIC
LIBRARY
VERMILLION, S. DAK.

3. The executive director or volunteer head of the Friends group contacts the official and makes an appointment. (It is important that accurate and detailed records are kept of every contact and that the history of previous gifts is known.)

Figure 12. *Outline for a Corporate Proposal*

1. A brief cover letter from the Friends leader, expressing appreciation for the opportunity of submitting a proposal, gives thanks for any previous support and offers to meet to answer any questions.

2. A general information page about the proposal
   a. requesting organization, address, and telephone number
   b. contact person, title, and telephone number
   c. project title
   d. amount requested

3. Project description page
   a. project summary, including what is special or necessary about the project
   b. detailed description of each activity to be undertaken, target groups to be served, needs addressed, timetable, and how its success can be measured

4. Project budget detail page

5. Benefits to the corporation
   Examples: Publicity and promotion associated with the project: name on bookmarks, recognition at a special event for corporate sponsors held during the project, feature article in newsletter, named as a Founder or similar permanent honor, corporate membership for one year, name added to a list (enclosed) with the proposals of past corporate contributors at their level

6. Friends fact sheet
   Background of the Friends group, its latest accomplishments, a list of the board of directors, and a library service or project it supports

7. Attachments
   The Friends 501(c)(3) tax-exempt notification letter from the Internal Revenue Service, a letter from the library director or trustee chairperson acknowledging and reinforcing the Friends' proposal, a Friends newsletter, a copy of the Friends' annual budget, the most recent audited financial statement, and an annual report, if available

4. During this appointment, discussion covers not only various possibilities for helping the library but also the corporate goals for giving, the company's market, and basically "what interests them." The library director sets up a date to give the official a tour of the library and describes the library's strengths and needs.
5. The Friends group prepares and presents a proposal in a cordial setting. They follow up until they ascertain firm interest.
6. The Friends group makes any required adjustments to the proposal. If the final proposal doesn't fit the goals or field of interest of the institution, the Friends representative expresses appreciation for the opportunity given and suggests returning in the future with another concept, thus keeping the door open.

Resources

Opportunities abound for Friends to gain corporate fund-raising expertise. State libraries and library associations, educational institutions, and community service agencies offer workshops and seminars. Libraries have access to books, reports, newsletters, and other reference material. Friends of Libraries U.S.A. provides ideas and inspiration through its newsletter and publications. Materials and advice are available from the American Library Association and other publishers in the library field, the Foundation Center, Independent Sector, the Taft Group, and similar sources.

Summary

Many Friends of the Library groups enjoy the challenge of pursuing sophisticated methods of fund-raising in the private sector. Help is available from a variety of sources, especially through library channels. Approaches to business require serious attention to analysis, preparation, and personal contact. The rewards go far beyond monetary support, bringing greater public awareness and political support for the library and growth in prestige, membership, and programs for the Friends.

13

Event Planning

Sandy Dolnick

Of all the elements that go into a successful Friends of the Library group, one area is most visible for the public to judge—the public programs. The Friends' public events—advocacy, authors, book sales, booths at street fairs—provide those outside the immediate library circle opportunities to learn about the library and make judgments about it.

There are many examples of successful programs given in this book, and the *Friends of Libraries U.S.A. News Update* always has many ideas garnered from groups across the country and the world. For example, Australia contributed a contest to see how far a romance novel could be thrown (on Valentine's Day). A list of program possiblilities from A to Z is shown in figure 13.

Many of these specific functions are covered in other chapters (public relations, advocacy, book sales, fund-raising). The purpose of this chapter is to provide the planning foundation that is necessary for any type of program to be successful.

Program Purpose

The purpose for the program and its expected outcome should be determined prior to all other planning. Reasons for programs usually fall into one or more of these categories:

    raising money

    educating the community about library resources

    educating the corporate or political community about the needs and resources
        of the library

    creating goodwill/recognition

Figure 13. *A–Z Activities of Friends Groups*

Advocacy	Organization—how to organize desks, closets, lives, suitcases
Books—authors, reading clubs, how to write them	Phonathon for new members
Children's programs—with or without parents	Quotes—reporters or community experts on hot topics
Dinners—tables of content, restaurant nights	Recognition
Executive education to bring in business	Storytelling
	Travel
Fairs—community booths, art, antiques	Understand your community—representatives of different organizations
Garden tours	
Homework helpers	Value—how to shop, good buys, consumer information
Investment information	
Junk—flea market sale	Walkathon
Kin—genealogy programs	X-rated—banned books program
Literacy tutoring	Youth power
Mystery nights	Zany—do something not expected, just have fun
Natural foods, not natural foods, eating trends, cookbooks	

Logistics

Some programs are by invitation only; some are open to the general public. Once the target audience is decided, a site for the program can be chosen. Although the library would be the first choice, that is not always feasible. It may be necessary to locate an alternate free space or rent a facility.

If contracts are involved, they should be carefully scrutinized to make sure there are no hidden charges or guarantees. What is the financial responsibility for the Friends? For example, if a specific number of people must be guaranteed for food orders, find out how many extra plates will need to be set. Determine the cutoff date for guaranteed places. Find out if a tip and tax are included in the price. If the tax is included, this is the time to use the state tax-exempt certificate. If renting a hall, find out what is included. Try to have as many items as possible given gratis by making use of the goodwill for a nonprofit organization and the free publicity given the site through your audience and your newsletter.

Event Planning

SAINT PAUL, MINN.

Hospitality

Every program given by the Friends should always include two activities: building friendships and circulating membership applications. Hospitality, whether through offering refreshments or just providing a chance for socialization, is a necessary component if you wish to increase the impact of the group. Someone should be present to greet and welcome people as they enter and to answer questions. The introduction to the program should include a pitch for the Friends. At the conclusion of the event, a Friend's representative should thank the audience for coming.

Offering hospitality to or cosponsorship with another organization will provide a larger audience and new membership opportunities and will maximize the success of an event. If the speaker has a subject that would appeal to a specific business group or arts group, make sure they are alerted in plenty of time to notify their membership or trade association.

Planning for a Guest Speaker

Certain steps must be taken to stage any successful program, many of which are covered here. The following steps deal with planning a program with a guest speaker.

Identify the authors or other speakers for the event by researching or by getting recommendations from trusted sources. *Library Journal, Publisher's Weekly, Booklist,* and other magazines for the book trade that list books months before they are published are excellent resources. The library gets many of these as well as publisher's catalogs

The Friends of the Orange County Library System invite you to

BOOKED FOR SUPPER

A dinner with authors to celebrate books and reading

Saturday, November 12. Orlando Expo Center. Reception 6:00 pm. Dinner 7:00 pm.

The Featured Authors

Roy Blount, Jr.

His New Book: *Roy Blount's Book of Southern Humor*

"Roy Blount's stuff makes me laugh so hard sometimes I have to go sit in a room and shut the door." — GARRISON KEILLOR

Dennis McFarland

His New Book: *School for the Blind*

"This is an honest, uplifting book, the most affecting and satisfying work of fiction we have read this year."
— MIAMI HERALD

Judith Rossner

Her New Book: *Olivia, or The Weight of the Past*

"Few writers are better than Judith Rossner at describing the agonized ties between mothers and daughters ..."
— THE NEW YORK TIMES

Please look inside for more about these fine writers.

Menu

that are not circulated. It is also a good idea to check with local bookstores or colleges to see what speakers they have scheduled. It is likely that your audience would not be the same, and a bookstore can help you sell the books.

A publisher's publicity department is another resource that will help you find the right speaker. They can tell you what authors will be promoting a new book in the area. In a recent development, many publishers have hired specialists who work with the library market; their names will be listed in *Literary Market Place*. The Friends of Libraries U.S.A. office also will help you get in touch with publishers.

You will need to work closely with a publisher or local bookseller to find the right person for the program. If the speaker is unknown, trust the judgment of the publisher. While few publicists would tell you that someone is a poor speaker, they may gently discourage a choice. Marcia Purcell, director of library promotion for Random House, offers these tips for an author appearance:

1. Plan as far in advance as possible; six months is reasonable.
2. Put the request in writing, and give all known details: name of the sponsoring organization, location of event, date, time, anticipated size/age/makeup of audience, name of contact person.
3. State the exact nature of the event and the author's participation: book and author event, school classes, conference address, panel, multiauthor event. Discuss the length of presentation and its theme or topic.
4. Do **not** ask for the most famous author of the moment! Because popular authors have high profiles and can draw an audience, everyone wants them. Your chance of getting a Toni Morrison or John Grisham is about the same as winning the lottery. Many authors who are not as well known will charm and delight an audience.
5. Request several authors in order of preference. Of course, make sure they are published by the company from which you've requested them.
6. Be up-front about expenses you can cover: speaker's fees, transportation, hotel, and meal costs. Much of this is already covered if you can take advantage of an author's publicity tour.
7. Tell your contact if you will have an autographing opportunity or will sell books, and state who will handle this. Find out how to get the books from the publisher or wholesaler. Books should be on hand well in advance of the event. Find out how returns of unsold books will be handled.
8. Once the author has said "yes," confirm all arrangements and agreements with a follow-through letter.
9. Make the trip as worthwhile as possible from the author's and publisher's point of view. Get the library staff informed and involved. Publicize the

event, and try to set up other appearances at the local bookstore, radio, TV, newspaper. Be sure to give the publisher credit in all publicity.

10. After your successful event, follow up with a thank you and report to the author or publisher. If something went wrong, state your suggestions or plans for improvement.

To Be Avoided Like the Plague

The FOLUSA office often hears author visit/event horror stories from Friends and publishers.

A board chair from a large library system made a convincing case about sending a well-known author to his library. Two were sent, and when they arrived there were no signs or posters announcing their appearance, no staff greeted them, the person at the checkout desk didn't have a clue and didn't care, and only twenty-five people were waiting in the auditorium when 300 had been promised.

I would say that less than half the time do I get any sort of response after providing an author. This is not good.

Honesty is extremely important. It's fine to glamorize your event in an effort to lure the author; however, if he or she is expecting to see a ballroom filled with people and your space holds only sixty, this is a problem. If proper groundwork is laid, a small, interested group is not a drawback.

Money is a topic that everyone likes to dance around. Be up front. Frankness here can save everyone concerned a lot of time. Also, by going through the publisher you may just be able to have most of the expenses covered.

It helps to have everything in writing so that there are no unpleasant surprises. This is a valuable exercise to make sure that all details are covered . . . You mean the author needs a place to stay?

Organization and Evaluation

Once the speaker and site have been obtained, the publicity wheels can begin rolling and the invitation prepared. Consult the checklists in figure 14 for details that should be considered. Figure 15 is a sample report to be completed after the event that will help you evaluate how well you met your goals. It will also provide a valu-

Figure 14. *Event Checklist*

Facilities
- ☐ Meeting room open and staffed
- ☐ Seating style as requested
- ☐ Cooling/heating operating
- ☐ Sound system operating
- ☐ Lectern in place, light operating
- ☐ Ice water and glasses at speaker's table
- ☐ AV equipment operable
- ☐ Decorations
- ☐ Lighting in place
- ☐ Photographer present
- ☐ Signage outside
- ☐ Evaluation sheets on chairs
- ☐ Registration table in place
- ☐ Money for change available
- ☐ Gift or token for speaker (optional)

Immediately after the Event
- ☐ Collect evaluation sheets
- ☐ Total money and deposit
- ☐ Pay bills for event
- ☐ Write thank-you letters

Follow-up
- ☐ Committee meeting for evaluation and recommendations
- ☐ Summary of audience evaluation sheets
- ☐ Thank all who helped
- ☐ Finalize and file report

able history for those who stage similar events in the future. Figure 16 is a sample evaluation form that the audience completes at the conclusion of an event. Such feedback can influence planning for future events.

Many items go into making a successful event, and a good committee can make it relatively easy to do. The key is good record keeping and follow-up as well as learning from past events. Having sufficient help is vital. This can be provided by members who may not be on the board but who enjoy working on something special once a year. Break down tasks so that no one feels overburdened, and all will have an enjoyable time.

NEPTUNE BEACH, FLA.

Figure 15. *Sample Report Sheet for Event Evaluation*

Event Title   Date

Location   Chairperson

Purpose

Description of event

Friends staffing

Library staff involvement

Publicity (attach)

Facilities and equipment used

Proposed and Actual Budget totals (attach actual budget)

Materials needed and cost

Source of materials if unusual

Number of books (or other items) sold

Problems

Recommendations

Additional comments

Event Planning

Figure 16. *Program Evaluation Sheet*

Our program committee will use your responses to guide future decisions. Please rate each of the following items. Choices range from 1 (poor) to 5 (excellent).

	Poor	→			Excellent
1. Content of program	1	2	3	4	5
2. Effectiveness of speaker/speakers	1	2	3	4	5
3. Handouts (if applicable)	1	2	3	4	5
4. Room arrangement	1	2	3	4	5
5. Time of day	1	2	3	4	5
6. Day of week	1	2	3	4	5
7. Food service (if applicable)	1	2	3	4	5

I would like you to consider having more programs about _____

_____

I would like membership forms sent to these friends who would have enjoyed being here. (Please give name as found in phone book and street if possible.)

_____

_____

_____

Other comments

_____

_____

_____

If you would like to volunteer to help the Friends or would like to have someone call you about a special concern, please write your name and phone number here.

_____

Please leave on chair, or hand to a hostess on your way out. Thank you.

Summary

Experience mixed judiciously with experimentation is the basis for the correct programming formula for each Friends group. Outside influences, over which programmers have no control, can make a disaster out of a potential success. Bad weather, local crises, and economic conditions all have to be taken into consideration up to

a point. Remember that in spite of careful planning, no one date is perfect and no program is exciting to all; once the decision is made to go ahead, the best the program chairperson can do is plan carefully for all contingencies and hope for the best.

The Friends of the Chicago Public Library request the pleasure of your company at the

16th Literary Arts Awards Dinner

presenting the
1994 Carl Sandburg
Literary Arts Award
for Fiction, Nonfiction, Poetry, and
Children's Literature

Friday, October 28, 1994
The Arts Club
109 East Ontario
Chicago

Reception 6:30
Presentation 7:30
Dinner 8

Black Tie

The North Kingstown Arts Council and
The Friends of the North Kingstown Free Library
Present

Sunday Musicales

AT THE LIBRARY

1995 Concert Season
10th Anniversary Celebration
"Artists in Residence"

North Kingstown Free Library
Sundays at 3p.m.

Partially Funded by
The Rhode Island State Council on the Arts

14

Basic Fund-Raising

Sandy Dolnick

Fund-raising has become such a necessary part of Friends of Libraries activities that it is almost synonymous with the name. It has changed the image of Friends from introverted book circles to that of a force for community outreach. Fund-raising is labor intensive and a labor of love. The means used have had to become more sophisticated as needs of libraries have increased. Today, the cash counted at the end of the book sale is only a small part of the funds generated by Friends. This chapter considers more-traditional methods. Chapter 15 discusses less-hands-on, more-technical information regarding grants, planned giving, and annual solicitations. Chapter 16 deals with library foundations. Another chapter, 17, focuses specifically on book sales and library shops.

Fund-raising provides money for items that can galvanize a community. It satisfies the library staff's need for special nonbudgeted items and raises money so that children feel comfortable and develop a life-long love for the library. As suggested in figure 13 in the previous chapter, activities to raise money are so diverse they almost defy categorizing. Following are several examples.

Action Point

Mazomanie, Wisconsin

The Mazomanie Friends came into existence specifically to promote building a new library for their village. The old library had 935 square feet, one functional electric outlet, and no bathroom. The Friends, library board, and Historical Society joined forces to plan, fund, and build a twenty-first–century library in a nineteenth-century, wooden frame train depot.

The Friends accepted the challenge of raising $110,000 to complete the project and succeeded—no small task in a library service area of only 1,600 people. A major fund-raiser was "Cabin

Fever Reliever," a locally written and produced show featuring song parodies commissioned by local businesses for fees ranging from $50 to $800. Ticket sales, in-kind donations, grants, and sales of everything from food to personalized bricks finally put them over the top.

Community involvement makes a tremendous difference in the type of projects that can be undertaken. It is not uncommon for cities to fund buildings, leaving the rest up to the library. In Taos, the library was fortunate to have ambitious Friends.

Action Point

Taos, New Mexico

The Friends of the Harwood Library embarked on a $400,000 fund-raising drive to provide furnishings, landscaping, and other finishing details for their new library. Their first project was a series of four raffles: a pickup truck; an arts package of seven items, ranging from jewelry to paintings to lithographs; a gourmet package offering dinners at various restaurants; and a sports package including a bicycle, a raft trip, and more.

The following project won a prize from FOLUSA and caught on as an idea across the country, where many libraries were also able to raise money with this innovative fund-raising technique.

Action Points

Washoe County, Nevada

Friends of the Washoe County Library raised $10,000 at their first "A Tisket, A Tasket, A Literary Basket" auction. This was a library fund-raiser of the most organic kind: One that raises money by celebrating books and reading. Auction attendees were offered plenty of food, drink, and entertainment during the bidding for nearly 100 literary baskets. Individuals and community groups created and donated the baskets or other containers, each built around the theme of a particular book or author. For example, *The Complete Adventures of Peter Rabbit* was packed in a large watering can with a stuffed rabbit, gardening tools, camomile tea, and a hand-painted garden sign.

A TISKET...

A TASKET,
a literary basket

A Tisket, A Tasket
A Literary Basket

October 24, 1992
Reno Central Library

A Novel Event
sponsored by
Friends of Washoe County Library

O 10   Summer of '49 by David Halberstam
This basket is a baseball collector's dream. It contains a mint condition 1958 Los Angeles Dodgers Year Book (the first year the team was on the West Coast, valued at $150), a Reggie Jackson signed baseball, a Silver Sox crying towel and baseball cap and the "book on cassettte" of the Halberstam title. All donated by Jack Patton of the Reno Silver Sox and packaged in a basket donated by First Class Baskets. Value: $180

O 11   Night Before Christmas by Clement C. Moore
Create a holiday (or other party) to remember with 2 hours live violin music donated by Mickey Lufkin/ violin for a Christmas party, Christmasberry honey and Santa bear donated by Moonshine Trading Company. Zunini's Floral Treasures have contributed a large basket, miniature Christmas tree and a wooden church. Christmas tea packages from Davidson's.
Value: $175

O 12   Howard's End by E.M. Forster
Everything you need for a Victorian Christmas with this basket donated by Sharon and Jon Davidson. A wicker serving tray contains a teapot, Victorian tea cozy and matching tea napkins, 4 teabag caddies, 3 fabric bags filled with teas, a tape of Beethoven's 5th Symphony and a Christmas ornament that looks a bit like the house Howard's End!
Value: $100

CHAPEL HILL, N.C.

Saxonburg, Pennsylvania

In Saxonburg, the Friends sponsor an annual Read-a-Thon for children ages 6 to 18. In 1994, the participating children read a total of 1,181 books and collected a total of $3,300 in pledges to be used to purchase books and materials for the juvenile and young adult departments of the library.

As would be expected, more-sedate fund-raising projects are used by academic libraries.

Action Points

Colorado Springs, Colorado

The University of Colorado Libraries benefit from the sales of a very popular item, *The Colorado Cookbook,* a hardbound, professionally printed book with color photographs.

College Station, Texas

Friends of the Sterling Evans Library at Texas A&M sell notecards featuring squares from a quilt that was raffled in 1993 to benefit the library.

Books, manuals, and articles abound with suggestions, instructions, and ideas for fund-raising. All agree that the most important ingredient for successful fund-raising is a commitment to the cause for which money is being raised. In addition to commitment, the organization needs up-to-the-task energy and up-to-date tax-exempt status under provisions of 501(c)(3) of the IRS Code. The American Library Association also cautions that fund-raising projects must be conducted by individuals who are knowledgeable about the library, the purposes of the Friends groups, and the uses to which the money will be applied. Furthermore, all fund-raising projects must be planned in consultation with the library director.

Choosing the Project

Although membership dues and donations are usually the first source of income for Friends, used book sales are often the first real money-raising project. Beyond these, sales of all kinds, adopt-a-book and adopt-a-magazine projects, and raffles and auctions of donated items are popular sources of income.

Many Friends groups organize special programs and charge admission. Book-and antique-appraisal sessions are popular. Meet-the-author events provide an additional source of income: Friends can arrange to sell copies of the author's books for an autograph session. (See chapter 13 for planning suggestions.) Local authors are potential guest stars for coffees, luncheons, teas, dinners, and talks. Even small towns are sometimes able to arrange for visits from writers who are nationally known.

Raising money for building projects offers many possibilities. Often groups will sell artifacts from the old building as souvenirs or make it possible for people to "buy" parts of the new one—for instance, to have their names inscribed on bricks in the foyer for a donation of a certain amount.

Action Point

Bluffton, Indiana

When Bluffton built a new library to replace its beloved old Carnegie building, the Friends sold book bags with a drawing of the old library on one side and the new building on the other.

Special events held in the library itself may have the added benefit of bringing more attention and publicity to the library. "Dinner in the stacks" is a popular theme for Friends events. Sometimes local restaurants or caterers will donate specialties so that all the proceeds from ticket costs can benefit the library. Mystery events, with an audience-participation drama and dinner or dessert, have provided entertainment and profit for many libraries.

Other fund-raising ideas may arise from a look at the individual Friends group's talents and situation.

Action Points

West Allis, Wisconsin

The West Allis Friends make and sell Polish Star Christmas ornaments.

Speedway, Indiana

Speedway Friends earn money every year by parking cars in the library's lot during the Indianapolis 500.

Waterloo, Iowa

Friends of the Waterloo Library have republished a pictorial history of Waterloo, a book long out of print and much in demand.

However unlikely they seem, unusual events have also raised funds for libraries. House tours, theater parties, art auctions, bridge marathons, fishing tournaments, sailing regattas, walking or running marathons, and a roster of other programs have been successful. Most of these projects are "hands-on" types that involve committees and a broad community involvement that may go beyond the membership. It is labor intensive in most cases, but the project fosters teamwork and a real feeling of accomplishment that is an additional plus. People who have invested time and energy have identified with the organization, and that may be as important as the money raised.

Partnerships with businesses and other groups may result in fund-raising possibilities. Some bookstores and other merchants have developed share-the-profit programs in which the library receives a rebate from purchases by Friends or purchases on a designated day. Local theater groups may agree to let the Friends sponsor a performance and share the profits on ticket sales. Golf courses, restaurants, and movie theaters might be interested in creating partnerships.

Planning

All fund-raising events or programs must be planned with great care. The Friends group should begin by setting a dollar goal for a specific purpose. It should appraise its assets realistically. (See chapter 4.) If the group has only a few working members, it cannot expect to carry out a complicated program.

Friends with much free time and the willingness to donate it are assets. So are members with experience in fund-raising events. The Friends must estimate how much seed money will be needed to set up the event and when these funds must be available. It must also attempt to predict the potential audience or public participation in the event or program. Case studies of library-related programs and events that can serve to raise money are reported quarterly in *Friends of Libraries U.S.A. News Update*. The following Focus section, by Fran Tschinkel, manager of public affairs for the New York Public Library, points out the importance of planning and coordination.

FOCUS

The New York Public Library
New York, New York

Every other year, for the past fourteen years, the New York Public Library has been fortunate to have had a team of volunteers produce a wonderful party aptly called "Tables of Content." The *New York Times* called the first party "one of the most ambitious and far-ranging benefits in the City's history." The basic idea is to hold many parties around the city on the same evening for the benefit of the library.

It is an ambitious undertaking. It takes more than a year to put together, and it is the work of a very active group of volunteers under the supervision of the library's special events department. The cochairpersons are members of the volunteer executive council. They asked prominent food specialists (cookbook authors, caterers, food writers, etc.) to be advisers.

This committee's members began the work of getting at least one hundred people to host dinners. They asked friends, acquaintances, and business associates. The hosts who obliged included celebrity chefs, businesspeople, socialites, restaurateurs, authors, and executives. The parties were held in private houses and apartments, clubs, hotels, and boardrooms. This phase of the event planning required a great deal of personal contact and letter writing. Forms and an elaborate file system was developed for the prospective hosts.

The committee and the hosts also provided the invitation lists. Because many of the parties were being held in private homes, the committee felt that each of the 6,000 individuals on the invitation list had to be known to someone on the committee. A great deal of work was involved in culling the lists to eliminate duplicate names.

The hosts provided the themes for their dinners. The themes have been literary, historical, or unabashedly culinary—as was Marcella Hazan's, "Bologna the Fat." One past dinner was a "Surrealist" dinner called "Peggy: The Wayward Guggenheim—A Voluptuous Feast." In 1995, dinners included "The Best of Gourmet," given in the magazine's boardroom by Gail Zweigenthal, and "A Romance of Two Cities," hosted by Peter Marino in "an elegant setting." For more than a touch of the fashionable there were dinners by Bill Blass and Carolyn Roehm and by Isaac Mizrahi. Mary Higgins Clark was an honored guest at a dinner entitled "Sumptuous Sleuthing in Soho." Henry Grunwald's "A Roman Feast . . . Americans in Rome," featured guests John Guare and Adele Chatfield Taylor.

The event calls for a very unusual invitation. Each year it has taken the look of a small, tasteful book, often with a lively, original drawing. The pages list the dinners with a brief description of each. The invitations, as well as a reply envelope and an elaborate reply form, are mailed eight weeks in advance of the event. To meet the mailing deadline of October 1, the following schedule is used:

December   The committee and its advisers are formed.

January   Letters and telephone calls are made to prospective hosts.

The New York Public Library

100 Dinners

for the Library's 100th Birthday

Tables of Content
Chapter VII
December 6, 1995

SCHUBERT AND FRIENDS

Enjoy a *gemütlich* dinner and a chamber music concert hosted by Charles Michener, music critic and author.

To be held at the home of Carolyne Roehm
For 9 guests • 7:30 p.m. • cocktail dress and dark suit

A NIGHT IN THE GARDEN OF GOOD AND EVIL

Spend a Savanna evening with bestselling author John Berendt. Guest chef Eileen Weinberg, owner of "Good and Plenty," will prepare the Southern repast mentioned in Mr. Berendt's book, *Midnight in the Garden of Good and Evil*.

For 20 guests • 8:00 p.m. • Southern Comfort dress

MAD ABOUT KING GEORGE

They could write a book about antiques, but the owners of Kentshire Galleries would rather talk about them over a special dinner created by David Bouley, New York's leading chef.

For 12 guests • 7:30 p.m. • festive dress

REMEMBRANCE OF THINGS PROUST

A Proustian repast in elegant 18-century-style surroundings is followed by a lively discussion of Proust with Olivier Bernier, distinguished lecturer and author of many books on French history and culture, and William Howard Adams, historian and author of *A Proust Souvenir*. Each guest will receive a copy of *Dining with Proust*.

For 12 guests • 7:30 p.m. • soigné dress

Basic Fund-Raising

March Confirmation letters or telephone calls and thank-you letters are sent to each host.

June Hosts are in place.

July–August All dinner information is assembled, and the invitation copy is written, edited, and approved by hosts. All mailing lists have been gathered and invitations are designed.

August Lists are purged.

September Envelopes are hand-addressed; invitations are collated and stuffed.

October Invitations are mailed.

Once the reservations start to come in, six volunteers work at least twenty hours a week until the parties take place. The requests are handled on a first come, first served basis. Each response card has space for the prospective guests to list their preferences in order from first choice to sixth choice.

The volunteers assign the guest to the various parties. This time-consuming chore—matching some 2,000 guests with 100 parties—would be a very expensive operation without a great volunteer staff. Many telephone calls are involved in this process—between hosts, guests, and volunteers. Another important element in this phase of the planning is space. Because making assignments is so complicated, undisturbed space is needed. Also, several telephone lines exclusively for making party arrangements are needed.

The expenses for the event are the invitations, the postage, a part-time event coordinator, stationery, and a souvenir booklet as well as telephones and office equipment. The hosts provide the dinners at their own expense.

There is no doubt that the money raised from labor-intensive events is not as great as money raised by advocacy or grants. However, event participation has something equally significant to offer: the obvious choice of the members to make a commitment of time and energy to the library. This is a dramatic way to demonstrate that the community cares. An event can generate press coverage and human interest stories. It can bring in local businesses to work with you and provide help. All of these elements need to be brought together over time, and a schedule is essential.

Any time that you are dealing with fund-raising, there has to be a definite arrangement for keeping track of the money. Checks have to be acknowledged and quickly deposited. Contracts and arrangements have to be agreed upon. There should be no hidden surprises except for the weather and acts of God.

Book Endowments

A Friends book-endowment project, or memorial program, can be as simple or as complex as the group wishes to make it. It can be handled entirely by volunteers or with the support of library staff. Book endowment is one more good way to enable the community to show its support and appreciation of the library. Because of its tangible connection to books, it will appeal on many levels to many types of donors. Books can be given to commemorate births, deaths, birthdays, graduations, promotions, anniversaries, or any event worth celebrating, such as the installation of new officers in a club or to honor an outgoing president. It is up to the Friends and the library to spread the word to the rest of the community about this easy-to-use gift that benefits everyone.

Give a gift of lasting value
THE GIFT OF A BOOK

A contribution to the Gift Book Fund of The Carnegie Library of Pittsburgh is a special way . . .

- to provide a lasting memorial
- to celebrate a birth, anniversary, graduation, or other special event
- to say thank you to someone special
- for organizations to honor individuals
- for holiday gift-giving

Acknowledgements will be sent to the honoree or the family of the person memorialized and to the donor. A bookplate will be placed in each book for a donation of $25.00 or more.

The Gift Book Program is a cooperative project of the Friends groups of The Carnegie Library of Pittsburgh.

FOCUS

Friends of the Orange County Library System Orlando, Florida

The Friends of the Orange County Library System established a Book Endowment Fund to provide a channel for sizable donations and to accommodate the desire of people to participate in the growth of the library.

The Friends invite donations of $150 to establish a book endowment that provides each year in perpetuity a worthwhile book in memory or in honor of a person. (The $150 is invested, and the interest earned buys a book each year.) A letter from the president of the Friends of the Library is sent to the person honored or the family of the person memorialized as designated by the donor(s). A bookplate is placed in each book each year giving the name of the person honored and the name of the donor.

The endowment can be established in the full amount of $150, in three $50 installments, or by family groups, friends, or organization members who have accumulated a total of $150. The donor receives a letter of acknowledgment that also acts as a receipt for the tax-deductible contribution.

To start the endowment project, the Friends incorporated the Friends of the Library Book Endowment, Inc., with the same officers as the Friends of the Orange County Library System. They opened one savings account to receive the $150 donations; checks are made out to the Friends of the Library Book Endowment. At the end of each fiscal year, the Friends turn over to the library's book budget all of the interest that has accumulated that year. The principal ($150) from each donation remains permanently in the savings account (or another investment account earning more interest).

A library staff member in the Friends of the Library office handles most of the correspondence for the Friends and keeps records of donations and book selections.

Donors are invited to designate an interest area from which books should be chosen for each endowment each year; some endowments are directed toward travel or local history or antiques. Most are left open to the discretion of the person making the selection. As each endowment matures in its anniversary month, a library staff person chooses an attractive volume from the available new books on their way to the shelves. In other communities, a volunteer could handle this job.

It is rarely necessary to order a special book to fill an endowment. A beautiful book already chosen by the library receives the bookplate, and the endowment is filled each year with worthwhile books that are needed in the collection. The endowment income pays for that book and boosts the book budget by that amount.

Usually the purchase price of the selected book is more than the $9 or $10 interest actually earned by the invested endowment. The library simply absorbs the difference in cost in its regular book budget. (It is possible that the library discount price that comes from quantity buying is near the amount of interest earned.) The public relations value of having such attractive books for endowment selections is obvious; otherwise, the bookkeeping necessary to

charge the discounted price against the endowment records would be too time-consuming and unproductive.

A file on each endowment records the name of the donor and the person honored or memorialized; the names, addresses, and contributions of the contributors; additional information such as a subject area toward which the endowment is applied; and a list of the titles and the authors of the books purchased with the endowment. In the first year or two of the project, the Friends sent the notice of the book chosen to each donor. This practice has been discontinued for several reasons: the costs in time and postage, the difficulty of maintaining an updated address for donors, and the irrelevance of such a gesture after a few years. However, any donor(s) can contact the Friends of the Library office for a listing of all books purchased that year with endowment funds.

Donor Recognition

Whatever method is used to raise funds, there is one ironclad rule: *Always recognize the donor!* Whether a donor gives one dollar or ten thousand, the sum represents a portion of the donor's income. Whether the donor is named on a brass plaque, listed in a book on permanent display in the library, recognized in the Friends annual report or newsletter, or just thanked with a personal note from the president, something is needed to make the donor aware of the importance of his or her gift. Many organizations want that dollar, and it is common sense to thank people for favors received.

15

Advanced Fund-Raising

Peter Pearson

The mission statement of every Friends group in the country will differ significantly in the details of the types of activities in which it is involved. However, the one underlying theme in every Friends of the Library mission statement is its intent to support the library. You don't need to look far from your hometown to find libraries that have closed branches, reduced hours, and curtailed materials budgets for lack of public funding. The outlook for all types of public funding (federal, state, and local) is bleak at best. It seems as though all libraries are being asked to do more and meet increasing circulation needs with less money.

With this dose of reality as the backdrop for most public libraries today, the need for a Friends group to support the library financially is more evident than ever. Libraries now need private funding to sustain the efforts that public funding provided in the past. Many would say that private fund-raising is among the most important jobs that a Friends organization can do for a library. Fund-raising can no longer be looked at as one of the necessary evils in which a Friends group must be involved; it must be the substance of a comprehensive program of support that the Friends group provides for its library.

The Friends group, itself, also has a need to raise some basic funding to support its activities. The problem arises when a Friends group raises money strictly for its own operation: The extra funding raised by the Friends group usually does not assist the library. The use of private funds for the operation of the Friends versus the use of private funds for supporting the library is an issue that must be dealt with at the local level. There certainly are successful Friends organizations whose private fund-raising efforts are strictly for their own operation. In these cases, the activities that the Friends group conducts are deemed by the library to be so significant that the lack of private funds for the library itself is not a significant issue. However, typically the need for private funds will be significant on the library's part, and the Friends group should certainly consider part of its mission to be the provision of those funds to the library.

Another option that will be discussed in chapter 16 is the creation of an additional support organization for the library whose sole purpose is private fund-raising. This type of organization, usually referred to as a library foundation, is found more frequently in large, urban areas and has become more prevalent within the past five years. There are very successful models of Friends groups and library foundations working side-by-side in complementary roles. However, when the decision is made to create a fund-raising organization outside the Friends, a great deal of thought and consideration must be given to clarifying the roles and responsibilities of both organizations.

Fund-Raising for the Operations of Friends Organizations

Friends groups fit a variety of structures. Some work solely through volunteer efforts of individuals in the community; other Friends groups are staffed with anywhere from a part-time position to ten full-time staff positions. Another model allows a library staff person to play a significant staffing role for a Friends group. With any of these structures, a Friends group will need some private funding for its own operations. Even a fully volunteer structure has a need for some operating expenses for postage for mailings to members; printing costs for newsletters, brochures, and other informational pieces; and funds to pay for author and special programs held at the library.

One logical source for the funding necessary to operate a Friends organization is through membership dues. Most Friends groups offer memberships for individuals, households, students, senior citizens, and life members. Membership dues may range anywhere from $1 to $500 or more based on the category and the type of community. Any solicitation for membership should make it very clear that funding operations is the purpose of the dues collected. This will make it possible to approach members at a later date for an annual contribution that should be over and above their membership fee.

Other Friends groups pay operational costs through an annual book sale. In some cases, proceeds from the book sale are kept by the Friends group for their own purposes. In other situations, the revenue from book sales reverts back immediately to the library for book purchases and library projects.

A third way to support a Friends operational budget would be through endowed funds. Frequently, library and Friends' supporters may leave a bequest to the Friends organization for undesignated purposes. When these endowed funds are not restricted or dedicated to a specific purpose, the interest may be used for Friends operational support.

Whenever possible, Friends operational support should be limited to the income from the three types of activities described in this section. All other fund-raising activities described in the next section are most appropriate for the support of the library.

Fund-Raising for the Library

Organizational Readiness

Before any organization can begin private fund-raising, a number of steps must be taken. First, an organization must have a well-thought-out mission statement. The mission statement describes exactly why the organization exists, what it hopes to accomplish, and through what means it will accomplish this. A mission statement should clearly distinguish an organization from any other similar organization in the community or in the country. Once a clear mission statement and purpose of the organization are established, the next step is to identify the need. Fund-raising activities should be the natural response to a library's need for financial assistance. Some fortunate libraries in the country still receive adequate public funding for all of their operational needs, so the library and Friends group may decide that there is no need for private fund-raising. Therefore, a Friends organization would better spend its time in the areas of public awareness, programming, and advocacy. However, where a strong need exists for private fund-raising, the needs must be clarified, defined, and prioritized. This will give the Friends group and the community a clear idea of the purpose for which funds are to be raised.

Second, a case statement is typically developed. The case statement is usually a written document that describes the library and its current needs. Some case statements are presented in a simple, written format similar to a proposal describing organizational background, needs, and objectives. Other case statements for more complicated fund-raising efforts are done in booklet form that includes pictures, charts, and graphs as well as information about the organization and the need. You may not need to include all of the following items, but it may be easier than you think to put together and to help you define the way you wish to present your group.

> introduction—brief two-paragraph history of the organization and its importance and role in the community
>
> mission
>
> goal
>
> major milestones and achievements

community needs
name and purpose of campaign
giving levels
recognition methods
list of needs

The third step in conducting a fund-raising effort is to identify the prospects in the community. Typically, Friends groups look for people who have already indicated a strong interest in the library. These may be people who serve as library trustees, library staff members, members of Friends organizations, or community volunteers with a strong interest in reading, literacy, and libraries. Also included in a prospect list should be corporations and foundations in the local community that have formalized giving programs and an interest in libraries and education.

Next, one of the most critical aspects of private fund-raising is to identify volunteers in the community who are willing to take the lead for the Friends organization in raising money. Often, this consists of people who wish to serve on the Friends organization's board of directors. However, sometimes an individual may be committed to raising money for the organization as a volunteer but does not want the responsibility of sitting on a board of directors. Both types of volunteer leadership are necessary in effective fund-raising. The importance of the leadership in fund-raising is summed up most appropriately: "People do not give to causes; people give to people who care passionately about an issue." Selecting the volunteer leadership for fund-raising is, without a doubt, the most important aspect of fund-raising. Without the right volunteers spreading your story in the community, your fund-raising efforts will be far less successful than they should be.

After volunteer leadership is enlisted, one or more individuals must be identified to be the chief contacts for fund-raising. Often, this is a library staff person, especially in Friends organizations without sufficient funding to hire staff. On the other hand, a volunteer who is extremely committed to the cause and willing to commit many hours per week would be an appropriate person to serve in this capacity. Ultimately, one person will have to organize the fund-raising activities and all the written materials and files that accompany them.

Organizations interested in fund-raising need to be conscious of several housekeeping items. All nonprofit fund-raising organizations must maintain a tax-exempt status. This tax-exempt status, known as $501(c)(3)$ status, assures contributors that the organization is tax-exempt and is registered as such with the Internal Revenue Service. (See chapter 5 for more information on tax exemption.)

Finally, another activity that fund-raising organizations must attend to is financial record keeping. Typically, organizations that raise large amounts of money must conduct an organizational audit on an annual basis. If an audit is not necessary, careful financial record keeping is essential to show accountability to donors. Fund-raising requests that are submitted to donors need to include evidence of an organization's tax-exempt status, evidence of an audit or financial accounting, and a listing of the organization's board of directors. With these background pieces in place, an organization should be ready to begin fund-raising.

Types of Fund-Raising Activities

Event Fund-Raising

Successful event fund-raising takes place in thousands of Friends groups across the country. A large core of volunteers is always necessary to plan and coordinate events. Examples of successful events are discussed in chapter 14. Many fund-raisers state that event fund-raising is often the most time-intensive activity engaged in and often results in the smallest net profits. In some cases, event fund-raising is more useful for raising public awareness than for raising private funds. The most successful events are those that have a large core of volunteers and that have been repeated on an annual basis. Therefore, members of the community come to anticipate these events and respond willingly.

Book Sales

Income derived from book sales can be quite significant. Many Friends groups report annual book sale revenue in excess of $100,000. The use of this revenue is determined by the library and Friends group at the local level. Sometimes these funds revert immediately to the library to supplement the book budget; other times these funds go directly to a Friends organization for the variety of services and activities it provides to the community and the library. Chapter 17 deals with the specifics involved in successful book sales.

Annual Solicitation

At some point during the year members and other individual supporters in the community are asked to make an annual contribution to support a library special project. Timing for this annual solicitation is critical because it should not be closely tied to the membership schedule (when members pay their dues to support the

organization itself). The membership request and the annual solicitation should be separated by at least six or seven months in the organization's fiscal year.

One important aspect of the annual solicitation is an effort to upgrade an individual's giving category in successive years. Provide opportunities for an increase in giving for members. Many organizations feel that they get the best response to individual solicitations when they are hand addressed and use stamps rather than postage meters—the personal touch. Response cards and self-addressed return envelopes also increase responses. November and December are excellent times to conduct this annual solicitation because individuals are giving consideration to their year-end giving and its tax ramifications.

An annual solicitation also can be conducted targeting small local businesses and small family foundations that do not have a dedicated staff to review such requests. Such requests, typically for $100 to $1,000, may support a variety of Friends projects rather than one special project.

Corporate and Foundation Grants

The next level in difficulty for fund-raising is to submit formal grant requests for large projects to major foundations and corporations in a community. Most foundations will not accept proposals requesting general operating support, such as the type of support received in annual solicitations. While this type of fund-raising has far greater benefits to the organization in terms of size of grants, the effort in terms of grant writing is far greater. The size of these foundation grants can vary anywhere from several thousand dollars to several hundred thousand dollars to even several million dollars. As outlined in figure 12, chapter 12, such funding proposals can be anywhere from five to fifteen pages long. This type of fund-raising is usually governed by a foundation's guidelines, which must be requested by phone or through a letter. Also, the timelines for submitting these proposals must be closely watched. Another factor to consider is that special-project funding from private sources is typically for a limited number of years. Private foundations may choose to fund a project for only one to three years. At the end of that time, the foundation funders expect that the project will be fully implemented or supported from other sources of revenue. This does not, however, exclude the possibility of approaching the same foundation for a different project after several years. Accurate record keeping is also extremely important in this type of fund-raising. Most foundations will request interim and final reports on the use of these funds. Strict accounting procedures must also be employed in monitoring the use of these funds.

Whether applying for a grant or soliciting the local bank for a donation, the support materials from the proposal are necessary and important fund-raising tools. Make copies available to members for any type of solicitation, by person or mail. Remember to add persuasive touches to the fund-raising material, such as the number of an industrial firm's employees who would use a new wing or service or how many employees' families would be served by a bookmobile. Researching and compiling data for "Friendly" persuasion can be a rewarding project in itself.

Government Grants

Government funding is decreasing for libraries, yet at times specific government grants become available for special library projects. For example, the federal government in past years has had several special titles within the Library Services and Construction Act that are available to libraries. These typically require writing a special grant directly to the U.S. Department of Education—a task most libraries are not staffed to handle. A Friends group or other volunteers can be of help in writing these government grant requests. Individuals who are familiar with writing foundation grant requests could readily transfer those skills to writing government grant requests since many of the requirements for information are the same.

Planned Giving

Planned giving is probably the most sophisticated form of fund-raising for any organization. It is not an immediate gift but one that is planned for a future time. Planned giving includes bequests and other types of trust instruments such as a charitable remainder trust. For this type of fund-raising to be successful, a dedicated staff and volunteer structure is essential. Also important is readily available legal counsel for individuals who are interested in making a planned gift.

Many organizations are not aware that they are already involved in planned giving. For example, a Friends group member or supporter may have included the organization in his or her will without notifying the Friends. Often, the receipt of an initial planned gift can be the impetus to begin a more formalized planned giving program.

One necessary step in continuing a planned giving effort is to create a donor recognition society. This donor recognition society should have a special event each year recognizing the fact that these individuals have made a permanent commitment to the Friends organization. Once such an organization has been publicized broadly in the community, the number of members increases dramatically.

THE DENVER PUBLIC
LIBRARY

A Money Management Guide
For a Secure Retirement

All of us face important financial decisions both before and after we retire. It is important that you begin your financial planning for retirement well before that eventful day—particularly as it applies to your short- and long-term investments. You must consider your retirement goals, the lifestyle you'd like to have, and the many options you can pursue to reach your goals.

You should also be prepared to answer many questions upon your retirement. The booklet titled *Retirement: How to Make Your Dollars Last* will help you answer such questions as

- What's the best way to take distributions from my pension accounts?
- Who should manage my retirement funds?
- How should I invest for retirement?
- How can I minimize income taxes?
- How can I boost my retirement income?

We believe this booklet can help make your retirement more pleasant and fulfilling by providing suggestions for putting your financial house in order. To receive your <u>free</u> copy, simply <u>complete the reply portion below and return it to us</u>. There is no obligation.

Sincerely

John Kivimaki

John Kivimaki
Director of Development

(Cut along line.)

☐ Please provide me with the free booklet, *Retirement: How to Make Your Dollars Last.*
☐ I have made a provision for your organization through
    ☐ my will   ☐ a life insurance policy   ☐ a trust arrangement.
☐ I am considering making a provision for your organization. Please call.

_____   _____
Name   Telephone

_____   _____
Address   City, State, Zip
This information is strictly confidential.

Advanced Fund-Raising

Action Point

St. Paul, Minnesota

In 1972 the Friends of the Saint Paul Public Library became the recipient of a $2 million bequest left from a strong but silent friend, Dr. John Briggs. The Friends of the Saint Paul Public Library started a donor society in 1991 with thirty-six members. Three years later that number had doubled because of regular publicizing of the donor society and annual events to recognize its members.

Memorials

Many libraries raise funds on an ongoing basis through a memorial program or book endowment. As discussed in chapter 14, donors may contribute money for the purchase of books at the library in memory or in honor of a loved one. In one approach, all monies contributed are used for immediate purchases of books. Another approach takes all funds contributed and puts them into a permanent endowment fund, and the interest from this fund is used each year for the purchase of new books.

Capital and Endowment Campaigns

Once an organization has had a track record of fund-raising, it may wish to embark on capital and endowment campaign fund-raising. The Friends group and library typically identify a number of special projects that are needed over a period of several years. The projects are put together under one theme and described with a case statement to the community to indicate the dollars needed for funding these special projects and the results intended from these projects. These campaigns can create endowment funds where none exist or increase existing endowment funds. This type of fund-raising is also successfully used for building projects and larger dollar special projects.

A typical capital and endowment campaign has a goal of several million dollars and runs for three years. The capital campaign combines individual and small-business solicitations as well as corporate and foundation grants and planned gifts. As in all fund-raising, adequate volunteer leadership is necessary for these campaigns to be successful. It is also common for at least one paid staff member to oversee the campaign.

Rules for All Fund-Raising Activities

A comprehensive program of fund-raising can often be overwhelming. The first step is just to begin. An organization that has no history of fund-raising can begin with an annual solicitation of its members. Several years of success in this area might lead to the annual corporate or foundation solicitation. From there, success is usually built and organizations gradually move into grantsmanship with major foundations and planned giving. Again, need is the primary factor in determining the level of involvement in fund-raising.

A few simple rules need to govern your internal procedures for all fund-raising efforts. Accounting is extremely important. If a contribution has been given for a specific purpose, it is critical that the purpose be identified and that separate-fund accounting tracks the expenditure. You should also have a permanent record of individual contributions in written form or, preferably, in a computer database. Foundation and corporate giving must have separate, cumulative files for each foundation or corporation so that a history of the giving from each can be tracked readily.

One of the most important things in fund-raising is to acknowledge and thank the donor for every contribution. The sooner this acknowledgment is done, the better—certainly within a week of receipt. And finally, don't forget to ask. Very few organizations receive unsolicited contributions. Explain the need for donors' on-going support. And every time they choose to contribute, make sure that the thank you or acknowledgment follows immediately.

16

Library Foundations

Kay Harvey

The traditional financial underpinnings of most libraries were shaken during the past decade. Suddenly budgets were being scrutinized and, most often, cut. Organizations downsized, with fewer people doing more work. Interest rates declined, depleting income from investments and trusts. Stocks considered blue-chips suddenly were no longer productive investments. Tax laws changed. Private income was affected by these same factors, making charitable giving a budget item to be carefully considered.

The pressure these changes put on the income needed to supplement library budgets forced more libraries than ever to look for ways to increase their endowments or to start one. Foundations, trusts, and endowments suddenly occupied much of the energy of administrators. Some libraries added development offices to help acquire funds. In many cases, Friends of the Library were in place in the library and had been functioning as the fund-raising arm. They were often asked to change their function and leave the bigger donors to other departments and continue with annual giving below a preset, agreed-upon amount.

This chapter provides ideas for Friends contemplating the formation of a foundation or looking for ways to cooperate with an existing library foundation. A fine example of an event proposal will show many ways in which Friends can help.

Areas of Responsibility

The creation of a library foundation can cause difficulties for an existing Friends group when the existing Friends group has been involved in fund-raising also. Frequently, the library develops a foundation when the level of fund-raising that the Friends has participated in is not adequate to meet the demands that the library has for its private funding. The difficulty arises when two organizations representing the same library are raising private funds separately within a community, thus

resulting in confusion and overlap for those who are being solicited. When a Friends group that has been conducting successful fund-raising efforts exists, the library administration or trustees should first approach that group when it is obvious that additional private funds are needed. If the Friends group indicates an unwillingness or inability to expand its fund-raising efforts to meet the library's newly identified needs, then it is clear that a new structure will be necessary.

It is important that the roles of each organization be clearly defined at the outset if the new structure is developed on top of an existing Friends group. For instance, a Friends group may focus its efforts on volunteers, book sales, advocacy efforts, and author programs. The foundation, working side by side with the Friends group, may then choose to focus all of its efforts on corporate and foundation fund-raising and fund-raising events. Friends and foundations working side by side should have one or two members of each board sitting on the other organization's board to allow for ongoing communication between the two groups.

Another model that has worked successfully in some settings is a combination Friends-and-foundation group. This model has worked successfully for the Denver Public Library and the Saint Paul Public Library. In these groups, one board of directors serves in an oversight capacity for typical Friends operations as well as fund-raising activities.

FOCUS

Wilbraham Public Library
Wilbraham, Massachusetts

The Wilbraham Public Library has two groups that exist solely to benefit the library: the Friends of the Library and the Library Memorial and Endowment Fund.

The Friends provide enhancements to the library. The lean town budget provides the basics for staff and materials—and the Friends provide many embellishments. For instance, Friends purchased all the videos in the adult and children collections; they purchased a computer in the public area as well as software. They also purchased most of the audio cassettes, compact discs, and books-on-tape for the library and sponsor almost all of the numerous children's programs, such as puppet shows, ventriloquists, and presentations on Egypt and India. In addition, the Friends sponsor the adult programs, such as a health series, the Bellringers, and a book discussion group.

The Friends raise money through their annual membership drive, twice-a-year used book sales, and fines for overdue videos. All money raised is used to benefit the library on an ongoing basis.

The Wilbraham Library Memorial and Endowment Fund was established in 1979 to provide long-term supplemental funds for the library. The Fund differs from the Friends in that all donations to the Fund are invested, and only the income—or interest—is spent for books, such as encyclopedia sets or other reference books, and accessories pertinent to the use and purpose of public libraries. As the fund continues to grow, it will be there for future needs.

There have been difficult adjustments for Friends, as a result of their change in roles, but as earlier described, Friends have many functions. As long as the community sees them as an accessible linkage to the library, Friends will always play an important role as advocates. They form the basis of neighborhood society; therefore, they can naturally be the part of the library that stages many of the social events, many times in conjunction with the foundation. It is sometimes difficult to change roles, but since all groups are working on behalf of the library, there should be respect and accommodation on all sides.

Friends can help in gathering donations that result in a foundation. Some ways are listed below.

gifts of cash

gifts of property

gifts of books, art, or other
   nonprint materials

gifts of stocks or bonds

memorial gifts honoring friends or
   relatives

gifts through a corporation

gifts of capital gains

gifts of insurance policies or
   dividends

bequests in wills

Recommended Steps in Forming a Foundation

Suggestions from the Broward County Library Foundation for forming a foundation include the following steps.

1. Form an organizational committee of a minimum of four volunteers to serve as interim president, vice president, secretary, and treasurer. Include a lawyer in the group, if possible.
2. Establish first year "getting started" goals.
3. Formulate the Articles of Incorporation and file it with the Secretary of State's office.
4. Establish a nominating committee to appoint a board of directors.

5. File a 1023 "Application for Recognition of Exemption" with IRS. If the foundation is to have employees, apply for a Federal Employer Identification Number (FEIN) on IRS Form SS-4. (IRS Publication 557 provides general information that will be helpful to you.)

6 Apply for registration as a charitable organization to your state, if required.

7. Form standing committees using traditional fund-raising disciplines.

8. Establish a three-year strategic plan and prepare a case statement in brochure form.

9. Begin a public relations campaign to create public awareness.

10. Begin a membership drive to establish a constituency.

Forming a Foundation

11. Begin a special gifts campaign.

12. Set up an honorial/memorial program.

13. Have at least one high-visibility fund-raising event the first year.

14. Begin work on planned gifts and endowment program.

In other words, *have a plan!* A good year-round fund-raising plan is essential. It is critical to *let people know* you are asking for private funding—and why. Put up a sign and tent cards in the library. Put brochures in prominent places. For example, the Broward Public Library Foundation sets its purpose before the public with the following message.

Fine libraries everywhere exist with public funds, but it is through private gifts that they flourish. The Broward Public Library Foundation was incorporated in 1982 to provide books and materials that go beyond what is available through traditional tax-base funding. The nonprofit Foundation is the catalyst in sparking private funding and endowments to ensure that a state of excellence is achieved throughout the Broward County Library system.

Sample Foundation Event

The Broward Public Library Foundation has sponsored several community based events that are unique in their scope. They have generously shared their materials to explain the way the foundation is able to appeal to sections of the community by positioning their events and sponsors. One of their events is described below. A second, a wonderful Children's Reading Festival, is in appendix D.

The Night of Literary Feasts began as a very special author event, but it has blossomed into an educational program for the whole community. The authors appear in the public schools, at a private dinner, and speak at the library in open forums.

FOCUS

Broward County Public Library Foundation
Broward County, Florida

8TH ANNUAL
NIGHT OF LITERARY FEASTS
AND
DAY OF LITERARY LECTURES

March 9, 1996, will mark the 8th annual Night of Literary Feasts and Day of Literary Lectures. All proceeds benefit the Broward Public Library Foundation in its efforts to provide books and services not otherwise available to the Broward Public Library System.

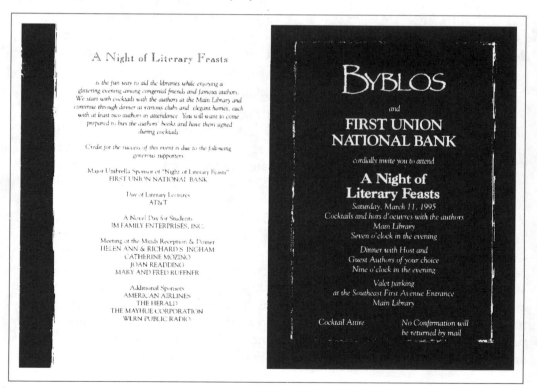

FREE PUBLIC LIBRARY
OCEAN CITY, N.J.

Recognized as one of the premier literary and cultural events in South Florida, The Night of Literary Feasts and Day of Literary Lectures presents authors from around the world to our community. Authors have included Russell Banks, Barbara Taylor Bradford, Jimmy Breslin, Robin Cook, Frank Deford, Robert Fulghum, Winston Groom, Carl Hiaasen, Elmore Leonard, Esmeralda Santiago, Susan Stamberg, Gay Talese, Stuart Woods, and many more.

The event offers a unique and distinctive mix of literary, social, and educational elements. Event includes:

A Novel Day for Students
Friday, March 8

The authors participate in a very special educational outreach program. Each author's works have been incorporated into the curriculum for the Broward County schools. Their books are provided to the students of selected schools and the authors visit the schools to meet with the students and discuss their work.

To encourage our own young writers, students may enter a short story writing contest judged by the authors and representatives of the school board and BYBLOS.

Meeting of the Minds
Friday, March 8

A special by-invitation-only welcome reception and dinner for the authors and BYBLOS supporters. Hosted at the home of one of the Foundation's major supporters.

Day of Literary Lectures
Saturday, March 9

The Day of Literary Lectures is held in the main library where the authors are presented in a day-long series of panel discussions, talks, and book signings in which thousands of readers and students have the opportunity to see and meet many of today's noted authors.

Night of Literary Feasts
Saturday, March 9

The Night of Literary Feasts begins with a V.I.P. reception and book signing in the main library followed by a series of dinners with authors as the honored guests held in private homes and clubs around Broward County.

Library Foundations

Prologue to a Party
January 1996

This special reception provides a special preview of the upcoming Night of Literary Feasts. Guests and supporters will have the opportunity to receive advance invitations and purchase Feasts' books. A special surprise literary guest will also be on hand.

As one of the finest literary events in South Florida, this special weekend recognizes and celebrates writers and their reading public all in support of our greater purpose—that of working with the Library Foundation to make a good library great.

The weekend has become one of the premier events in South Florida, receiving more coverage as a social and literary news story than any other Broward nonprofit event.

Our umbrella corporate sponsor is First Union National Bank. Support for A Novel Day for Students is provided through a major grant from JM Family Enterprises, Inc. The Day of Literary Lectures is sponsored by AT&T. Promotional support is provided by the *Herald* and American Airlines.

Sponsorship Categories
Night of Literary Feasts

Sponsorship Opportunities

Event Sponsorship	$10,000
Event Co-sponsorship	$ 5,000

Prologue to a Party
January 1996

Meeting of Minds Reception and Dinner
Friday, March 8, 1996

Day of Literary Lectures
Saturday, March 9, 1996

Night of Literary Feasts
Saturday, March 9, 1996

Promotion Sponsorship	$ 3,000
Supporter	$ 2,000
Author Sponsor	$ 1,500
Dinner Hosts	$ 2,500

"NLF" Promotion Sponsor

Sponsorship of selected printing and promotion of "NLF" including

Invitations	Flyers	Tickets
Postage	Bookmarks	Posters
Programs		

Sponsor receives:

- Sponsor name acknowledged in selected "NLF" promotional items:
  - 5,000 invitations   20,000 bookmarks
  - 5,000 programs   2,000 tickets
  - 20,000 flyers   100 posters
- Sponsor recognition in all press kits and press releases sent to local and national media
- Recognition in Foundation newsletter with 6,000 distribution to Foundation supporters, civic/educational/cultural organizations
- Recognition in library calendar with 25,000 distribution
- Signage and recognition at events

Sponsor also receives:

- Guest tickets for two to "Night of Literary Feasts" reception and dinners to follow
- Six reserved tickets to the "Day of Literary Lectures"
- Framed memento of sponsorship featuring signatures of participating authors
- An autographed book by author of your choice

Promotion sponsorship: $3,000
Selected items: $1,500

"NLF" Author Sponsor

Sponsorship of an author of your choice to help underwrite travel and hospitality costs.

Sponsor receives:

- Sponsor name on "NLF" print promotional pieces distributed to all library branches, Foundation supporters, civic and cultural institutions, including
  - 5,000 Programs   20,000 Flyers   100 Posters

- Sponsor recognized in all press kits and press releases sent to local and national media
- Sponsor recognized in feature article in Foundation newsletter with distribution of 6,000
- Sponsor recognized in feature article in library calendar with distribution of 25,000
- Recognition at "NLF" events
- Guest tickets for two to Night of Literary Feasts reception and dinners to follow
- Guest tickets for four for Day of Literary Lectures
- An autographed book by your chosen author
- Author's book(s) purchased for the library with bookplate commemorating your gift

Author sponsor: $1,500

"NLF" Dinner Hosts

Sponsorship of "Night of Literary Feasts" dinner with two authors
Your support provides you with

- Sponsorship acknowledged in "NLF" invitations sent to 5,000 Foundation supporters and Sponsor guest lists
- Sponsorship acknowledged in 5,000 "NLF" programs
- Two guest invitations to "Meeting of the Minds" reception and dinner
- Guest tickets for two to "Night of Literary Feasts" reception and dinners
- Four reserved tickets to the "Day of Literary Lectures"
- An autographed book by the author of your choice
- Your authors' books purchased for the library with bookplates commemorating your gift
- Framed and signed memento photo of sponsor with guest authors

Approximate cost: $2,500

Supporter

We seek the support of organizations whose customers, clients and employees will benefit from this wonderful community event.

As one of the premier cultural events in South Florida, it involves many of the area's noted business, cultural, and civic leaders. Your support would provide your employees, clients, and customers an opportunity to meet many of Broward County's leaders as well as provide your organization with positive exposure throughout our community.

Your support would entitle your organization to

- Guest tickets for ten at Night of Literary Feasts reception and dinners
- Four reserved tickets to the Day of Literary Lectures
- Recognition in print promotion, including
    25,000 flyers distributed through all 32 libraries
    5,000 programs distributed at Day of Literary Lectures and Night of
        Literary Feasts

Supporter: $2,000

17

Books and More
for Sale

Carolyn McReynolds, Christy Connelly

Book sales are fun, hectic, exhausting, and rewarding. They are undoubtedly the most popular form of fund-raising for Friends groups. This is apropos since it corresponds with the purpose and mission of the Friends to encourage reading. Projects that align well with the group's mission statement are successful in two ways: They raise funds for the group, and in doing so they satisfy the accomplishment of the group's purpose.

Book sales vary from small to large and from an annual one-time event to a year-round project. While each requires unique attention to details, the similarities in organization, preparation, and volunteer help remain constant. Putting on a successful book sale can focus publicity on both the Friends and the library. Getting books into the community at a reduced cost is also very rewarding.

Whether you are a novice or an experienced hand at holding a book sale, remember that planning and preparation are crucial to success. Following are ten suggestions for those planning a first book sale.

1. Ask yourself if you really need a book sale. Why? How will you use the proceeds? When you've answered these questions you should develop a statement of purpose for the book sale.
2. Start early. Preplanning and good organization are important. Prepare a draft budget, even if it's small, and include provisions for contingencies. Choose the date and place. Rough out a calendar of planning deadlines and responsibilities.
3. Involve as much of the community as possible through book donations, sorting, and working at the sale. Use many routes for publicity: TV, radio, and newspapers. Good publicity is a key factor in success.
4. Provide recognition for volunteers before, during, and after the sale.
5. Keep the initial book sale small and simple until you learn the amount of work and money involved in larger sales.

6. Keep detailed records, including written end-of-project evaluation reports.
7. Include training opportunities for volunteers so they can assume expanded responsibilities in the next book sale.
8. Focus on good public relations: Remember the library and Friends are in the limelight with their events in and for the community.
9. Be flexible. *Don't* expect perfection, and *do* expect change in the least likely quarters at the most inconvenient times.
10. Through it all, have fun! You're raising funds for worthwhile programs.

All of the suggestions can be expanded as the book sale grows through the years. Reevaluate as the sale evolves from a simple undertaking to a major community event. Engineering an annual book sale can require year-long preparation and a large contingent of volunteers.

Figure 17 shows the organizational chart for a greatly enlarged book sale that is in its seventeenth year. The book sale committee consists of 25 chairs and co-chairs including the two coordinators. In excess of 600 volunteers work at the actual three-day affair while another 30 work year-round sorting and pricing books for sale. Of course, not all book sales are this large or require such an intense labor force.

Collecting

Sale books, magazines, audiotapes, videotapes, records, and art prints are public donations or library discards. Donations are solicited throughout the year by various means; it is important to make it as easy as possible for the public to contribute. Collection sites should be available at libraries. If there is a sorting site, provide information about the location and times of operation. Give high priority to publicity about donations as well as about the book sale itself. Donations of books can be solicited in various ways:

1. Place printed or photocopied notices at the checkout desks of all branches of the library.
2. Send news releases to area newspapers and public service announcements to local radio and TV stations.
3. Arrange to have notices included in the city's water bill mailing or with monthly statements from banks.
4. Place posters in grocery stores, schools, libraries, used-book stores, and other public places.
5. Write an article for the Friends newsletter requesting donations.

Books and More for Sale

Figure 17. *Organization Chart for Friends Book Sale*

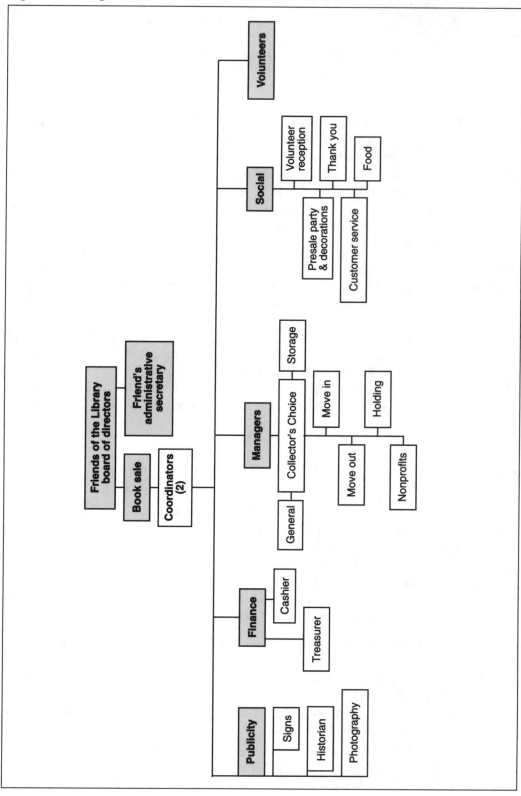

Arrange for either volunteers or library staff to transport donations to a site for sorting, pricing, boxing, and storing until the time of the sale. Collect books all year long and process them as they come in so that the work does not pile up and become overwhelming.

Some communities do not allow the library to donate its deaccessioned books to the Friends, but the library could sell them for a token amount ($1) to the Friends In the worst cases, the books are destroyed because of antiquated city codes. The Friends can push to have these old statutes dropped and new language incorporated to allow for these discards. Once the public and the media find out that books bought with their tax monies are being destroyed, it makes it easier to pass the necessary legislation.

Sorting, Pricing, and Boxing

Sorting and pricing can be done by volunteers in library space for a small sale, but a large sale requires a work area with either shelf space or table space to divide books into categories. The categories should be diversified enough to provide easy customer selection but not so numerous as to cause confusion at the sale. At the sale, categories should be clearly marked by signs or numbers for easy identification. Another idea is to use different colored balloons to indicate different categories. A selection of sample categories to choose among includes

Biography/Autobiography	Medical/Law
Business/Computers	Mystery
Children	Nonfiction
Education	Paperbacks
Family Living/Home	Psychology/Sociology
Fiction	Records/Tapes/Videos
Fine Arts	Reference
Foreign Language	Religion
History/Politics	Science
Humor	Science Fiction
Literature	Senior Citizen/Large Print
Magazines	Sports/Hobbies
Math/Engineering	Travel/Geography

Volunteers should sort the books into categories as they come in. If the book sale includes both a general area where books are sold for the same price and a special area where books are priced individually, then sorting for the two areas should be the first step. Books for the general area can then be sorted by category and boxed immediately. As soon as a box is full, it should be closed and marked by number or colored dot to indicate its category. Books for the special area should be sorted and placed on shelves.

Volunteers who sort or price books should be alert for rare, old, first edition, or expensive books. Handle these separately and have someone with special knowledge price them. They may be displayed on a special collector's table at the sale or sold by silent auction during the sale. Pricing guides can help determine the value of these special books, but it is imperative that someone with knowledge and expertise be on the lookout for them.

Pricing books can be difficult because it is subjective, but volunteers should be as consistent as possible throughout the year. Prices should be reasonable so that customers will feel they got a bargain and will want to come back to the next sale. Take into account the condition, scarcity, and popularity of the books; the number and quality of illustrations; and their original retail prices when pricing them. Encyclopedia sets, usually good sellers, should be judged according to their age, quality, condition, and completeness. Magazines should be priced low or not handled at all. A good rule of thumb for magazines is to balance how much time and effort are expended versus how much profit is to be made. Sorting magazines into bundles of a whole year's issues is a time-consuming job, and it may be more feasible to sort by year into boxes and let the customers make up their own bundles. *Reader's Digest Condensed Books* are usually very plentiful and bring in little profit. It might be better to donate them to local hotels, motels, rest homes, or hospitals than to price and sell them.

It is a good idea to evaluate what sells and what doesn't. What takes up a lot of space and brings in small profits? What is too labor-intensive for the return it brings? Adjust your pricing and collecting accordingly.

After books have been sorted into categories and shelved, experienced volunteers should price them. Take care in marking prices on the books. Marking prices with ink is permanent and damaging, but it solves the problem of prices being erased at the sale. Colored pencil, using a new color each year, is hard to erase but less damaging than ink. *Prices should be marked in the same*

place on each book to speed up checkout during the sale. Lines are held up when a book gets to the checkout area without a price, so books should be double-checked for prices while being boxed.

All books from both general and special areas should be marked by category, counted, and recorded before being stored. This count will help determine the number of tables that will be needed at the sale.

Organizing the Sale

Publicity

Once the material to be sold has been collected, priced, and boxed, the publicity chair must publicize the sale. Send announcements to local radio and TV stations and notices to local parent teacher associations, senior citizens groups, bibliophile clubs, teacher organizations, and bookstores. Promote the sale in the Friends newsletter. Distribute posters throughout the community including the branch libraries. Hang banners outside the libraries as well as in the sale location. If possible, keep the same location for all subsequent book sales so that patrons get accustomed to a particular site. Return customers are an important element of a successful book sale, so make it easy for them to locate the sale.

Action Point

Atlanta, Georgia

Atlanta is blanketed with one-of-a-kind posters prior to the Friends of the Atlanta-Fulton Public Library annual book sale. Thousands of posters are printed with the dates, times, and location at the top and bottom. The center area is left open to be completed by students of all ages, kindergarten through high school. Within two or three weeks of distribution to the schools, approximately 8,000 posters are returned to the Friends office at the central library. Each poster includes the student's name, school, and grade. The posters are distributed to supermarkets, laundromats, shops, schools, downtown office buildings, law firms, and any place that has a window, lobby, or waiting area in which to display a poster. Every library in the system has posters on every level and in every department. The remaining posters decorate the sale site itself, hung three rows high all around the sale room.

Legalities

Coordinators should make certain that permits, if needed, are obtained and that sales tax forms are submitted after the sale. To make it easier to charge sales tax, simply include it in the base price. Then you can forgo all the tax charts and figuring at the time of the sale. For example, instead of charging 50 cents per book, charge 60 cents including tax. Then the only tax figuring at the time of sale would be to subtract the amount of tax for tax-exempt customers.

Finances

Finance chairs should obtain coin wrappers, bank deposit slips, stamps designating the library or Friends group as payee for the front of checks and "for deposit only" for the back of checks, and currency and coins for change for the cashiers during the sale. They should also have in place volunteers helping to count the money if the sale is large. Deposits should be made every day if the event is longer than a day.

Volunteers

A chairperson or designated volunteer must schedule workers to transport the boxes of books to the sale site, set up the tables of books, work during the sale, and clear out the site following the sale. Depending on the size of the sale, this could number from a few to many hundreds of volunteers. The volunteer chair must solicit volunteers by sending form letters to past volunteers, to other nonprofit groups or companies in the area, and to library staff. In addition, notices calling for volunteers could be given in the Friends newsletter and through announcements on local radio and TV stations. Make charts of work shifts along with workers' phone numbers, and send confirmation notes to volunteers so they show up at the proper time. Overlap shift times to allow for a smooth transfer of responsibilities and the possibility of late arrivals. Local Girl Scout and Boy Scout troops, social sororities or fraternities, and high school National Honor students can be very helpful during this time; they are often required to do community social service work. Take care to avoid very young volunteers. Some book sale committees limit the age to sixteen for volunteers.

Arrangements

Chairpersons must arrange for the room or hall where the sale will be held and plan for tables or shelves to display the books. They must provide signs showing cate-

gories of books and any other signs. They will need calculators, extra batteries, cash boxes, and boxes and bags for the customers' books. Have on hand at each check-out station price lists showing prices on categories of items for sale. Include a stamp with the organization's name at each checkout site to use on checks. Miscellaneous supplies such as pencils, pens, scissors, tape, staplers, and paper clips should be on hand. Include name tags and coffee for volunteers. To have a book sale run smoothly, the chairpersons should think through procedures carefully and try to anticipate what will be needed. Once the sale begins, the pace will be frantic.

Members' Presale

Friends can be admitted to a special presale before the sale opens to the public. The first night of the sale is often for Friends members only. Memberships should be available at the door, and many people will come early to join at that time. Chairpersons must make arrangements to have a membership table set up and to accept new members as well as renewals. Have a list of current members on hand as well.

During the Sale

During the sale, one way to handle the money is to have one or more of the volunteers totaling the prices of customers' books and one cashier taking the money. Having a volunteer runner who tracks down prices can also speed things up. One of the chairpersons should remove extra cash from the cash boxes as soon as it increases beyond a minimum amount needed by the cashiers. Take this cash to an extremely secure place for

counting and recording on a record sheet to get a running total of sales. If the sale involves a large sum of money, it may be advisable to hire or get as volunteers off-duty police officers to provide security.

Add books to the tables as books are sold and space is available. As the sale progresses, prices can be reduced at the discretion of the chairperson, for example, prices can be cut in half the last day or hours of the sale. Perhaps you could promote selling a bag or box of books for one dollar to help clear out the remaining books. Often, a local store will donate the bags with its name on them. Remaining books can be sorted, and those of good quality can be donated to nursing homes or veterans homes. One sale invites nonprofit organizations, by letter, to attend at the close of the sale and choose books for their organizations at no charge. This helps to reduce leftover books without additional labor by the book sale committee. Also, used-book sellers will take sale leftovers.

Library Involvement

One of the most important elements of a successful sale is the full support of and good communication with the library director. Without it, a sale can be a point of contention or even detrimental to both groups.

In an ideal relationship, library staff members work very closely with the Friends in development of the book sale and other programs throughout the year. Their help is valuable in all phases of preparation for the book sale and during the sale itself. Discards from the library can be an important part of the inventory of a book sale, and volunteers should work closely with staff members in processing these books. The library may benefit too: many times it can fill in gaps in the collection from donated books.

Depending on the size of your library or library system, library staff are sometimes needed for the heavy work connected with a sale, such as collecting the donated books from branch libraries and transporting them to a central location for volunteers to sort. The library's facilities may be needed to help produce and distribute flyers and posters. During the sale, the cooperation of the library's staff is vital, as volunteers will need assistance in a variety of ways. The presence and support of staff members at the book sale and other programs serve as great sources of encouragement to the Friends, and the camaraderie enjoyed is an important bonus.

Proceeds from the book sale can benefit the library greatly. The Friends group may have been working toward a goal previously established with information provided by the library director, or it may use the money in any number of ways. A "wish list" could be submitted from branches of the library system to the head librarian or executive director of the library and the money granted for requests. If a gift is purchased with the money, it should be marked "Gift of the Friends of the Library," in honor of the many hours of volunteer time that make up a successful book sale.

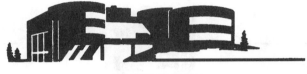

Friends Stores in Libraries

Christy Connelly

Many of our library retail stores are extensions of used-book-sales operations. These nonprofit shops are a growing and successful venture for Friends groups. In a relatively small space, they extend the patron service, provide additional revenue, and promote the library.

The nonprofit library shop is very similar to a museum-type shop. It has an affiliation with a nonprofit organization (the Friends) and with a public nonprofit institution (the library). The Friends qualify as an exempt organization under Section 501(c)(3) of the Internal Revenue Code of 1954.

Before you have a store, you have to have a site, one usually agreed upon in consultation with the library administration and the trustees. This has to be in a well-trafficked area with adequate signage and handicapped accessibility. In general, the shop should be open during the busiest times of the day.

The setup can be a simple countertop with additional shelving units or a room with easy access. Keep in mind the type of merchandise displayed. Is it safer to have it locked away or on top of the counter? Fixtures can be borrowed from the library, acquired from local merchants, or purchased new or used. Signage is extremely important to indicate the store's location.

New libraries being built today often reserve prime space designed for easy accessibility for a retail store. It requires professional attention and it reflects the library and Friends to the community. The store design has to take into account adequate security, access, and lighting and present storage and display opportunities.

Action Point

Minneapolis, Minnesota

The Friends of the Minneapolis Public Library has operated a new and used book shop in the main library that in 1994 surpassed $100,000 in earned income. Over the years, the Friends Book Store has built a reputation not only for remarkable book bargains but also as the only volunteer-staffed book store in the metropolitan area. What began with volunteers continues to thrive in many important ways through volunteer commitment of time and energy.

Friends of the Library volunteers staff the store. The manager and assistant manager may be full-time or part-time, paid or volunteer. Retail experience is a definite advantage. The manager oversees the financial operations, the buying, and the display and promotions. In a large operation the assistant manager covers the daily floor operations and the orientation, training, and scheduling of the workers. Anyone considering starting a Friends book store or gift shop should remember that it is a business, it requires professional-quality attention, and it reflects the library to the community.

Resources

Friends who plan on setting up a library store may want to gather basic retailing business information by contacting the local Small Business Administration, Service Corps of Retired Executives (SCORE), Public Library Association's Retail Committee, or FOLUSA. The Museum Store Association (MSA) is the educational organization for nonprofit museum stores, which includes library stores. MSA has produced excellent publications for new managers and on opening stores. Trade shows by the George Little Company for buyers from museum and library stores are held in conjunction with large gift shows in major population areas. Some of these resources are listed in appendix A, or ask the advice of other shop managers, also listed in the appendix.

Budget Realities

Setting up a budget, keeping it up to date, and considering inventory investment compared with sales are of primary importance. The Friends should have help from accounting staff in setting up the books. Discuss various types of software with other, similar operations to see what would be most useful. A cash register is a necessity to keep track of your inventory. As with other financial dealings, record keeping should err on the side of too much detail. You'll need to keep track of what merchandise sells and keep the store solvent. You'll also have to meet the state sales tax requirements. An accountant can help you understand the federal and state tax implications, including unrelated business income.

Philosophy of Buying

Before you purchase any merchandise, decide on the image or ambience you want the store to reflect. The relatedness of the merchandise to the institution's collection is also very important. Providing the items needed by patrons, coordinating with library exhibits or events, and selling custom-designed products are ways to maintain the connection.

You
*Are Cordially
Invited
to*

*A Special
Christmas Opening
at*

*The
Library
Gift Shop*

**MAIN LIBRARY
325 SUPERIOR AVENUE
2ND FLOOR**

December 5 - 10

Members receive 25% off all Gift Items

HOLIDAY HOURS
*Monday - Saturday
11:00 a.m. - 3:30 p.m.
Sunday
1:00 p.m. - 4:00 p.m.*

Choose merchandise with a literary theme. Games, T-shirts, furniture, lamps, cards, jewelry, and clothing are just a few product lines that have literary merit. Many cards have designs from well-known book illustrators, feature famous quotes, or show a sketch of the library building. Games and toys should have educational value. You may be able to feature local writers and artists. See the items featured in the ALA *Graphics Catalog* for ideas.

Genealogy buffs are heavy library users, and special supplies for them are often provided. Obviously, research is done throughout the library, so note cards, pads of paper, pens, pencils, notebooks, and other paper supplies are needed. Also stock grants-writing publications, GED books, city-theme merchandise, books, book covers, book bags, city maps, magnifiers, umbrellas, and rain ponchos.

Special collections in the library can lead to other types of merchandise. Libraries with strong collections of early American, Revolutionary War, Civil War, or Western Studies materials can easily bring in merchandise that reflects these areas. Geology and biology materials and multicultural cards and crafts that are specific to the community can add to the shop's inventory without being a violation of the library's mission.

Sale of used books within a special section of the store is a way to recycle and provide additional revenue. Some stores set peddler-like carts in

the lobby outside the store with used books for sale. These can be moved to outdoor events as well.

Custom-designed products are a direct link to specific library collections or an architectural detail. These are unique to the institution and provide a higher profit margin. Some firms specialize in producing stationery and other products with individual motifs. It is a rare library that does not have some unique item that could be interestingly reproduced. Consider early photographs of the area, newspaper headlines, or old maps reproduced on note cards, calendars, and blank books.

Patrons and staff have the usual needs for cards and related items for birthdays, get-well wishes, and holidays. Wrapping paper and gift enclosure cards are also useful items to carry. Great care should be taken to carry only tasteful designs not usually found in other stores.

Merchandise selection is a trial-and-error process, but some preliminary work can help. Take an informal census of library patrons. Is the library in a business area or a tourist area? Do families primarily attend its events? Are many meetings held when the library store will be open? Do many school or university students use the library? The answers will help you define the store's patron base. Is there much competition in the area? If so, what sort of competition?

Throughout, the goal is to provide the library patron/shop customer with unique quality items that are competitively priced in a convenient location and to provide good customer service. The end result of this effort is profit.

18

Making the Computer Your Friend

Marcia Kuszmaul

Computers have become as ubiquitous as the IBM Selectric typewriter once was—and hundreds of times more useful. While we know we can live without a computer, why should we want to? The computer is a unique and valuable tool, an unprecedented workhorse that saves us time and effort and enables us to use information in countless creative ways.

This chapter is a basic guide to the world of computing and to some of the decisions your group will need to make as you integrate computers into the work of your organization. Many of you likely have taken the plunge already and may be considering upgrading hardware or computerizing additional processes. Others may just be getting started and are facing an initial buying decision. Buying a computer or upgrading a current system can be intimidating. It's an investment in money and time that you hope will have a big payoff. The good news is that while computers are complex, buying one and putting it to good use for your Friends group doesn't have to be complicated.

The computer world has its own terminology, but don't let that faze you. Figure 18 is a miniglossary of computer terms that you're likely to encounter. A librarian can direct you to additional computer reference sources.

Break down your buying decision into a series of simple steps:

1. How are you going to use the computer? What do you want to do with it?
2. What kinds of software do you need to do what you want to do?
3. What hardware do you need to run the software you want?
4. What kinds of service and support will you need?

A sacred adage in the library world is "information is for decision making." Nowhere is this more true than in making decisions about buying computer hardware and software. For each of these steps you'll be gathering information from friends and colleagues who use computers, salespeople, and computer magazines and books. Friends groups have the advantage of being affiliated with a library and

Figure 18. *Common Computing Terms*

Application	a software program that performs a specific task such as word processing, spreadsheet development, database management, etc.
ASCII	(pronounced "as key") a system for representing text as bytes of binary signals (*1*s and *0*s)
Baud	a unit of measure of data transmission approximately equal to bits per second
Bit	smallest unit of data in a computer expressed as either a *1* or a *0*
Byte	a measure of data equal to eight bits
Cache	a portion of memory or disk space set aside for quick access to the most recently used data by the processor
CD-ROM	(compact disc-read only memory) a format for storing digital information on a compact disc
Chip	an integrated circuit, usually manufactured on a very small piece of silicon
CPU	(central processing unit) the heart of the computer; the basic chip, made up of many components, that does the actual processing and calculations in a computer
Database	a software application for storing and retrieving data records in an organized manner
E-mail	(electronic mail) sending and receiving messages electronically with computers via modems
Floppy disk	also diskette or just disk; a light-weight, flexible magnetic medium for data storage encased in either a flexible or rigid plastic case; 3½" disks are more common now, although 5¼" are still used
Gigabyte (GB)	a unit of memory equal to 1,024 megabytes
Groupware	software that allows several people working on the same task to better interact and communicate
Hard disk	a large-capacity magnetic disk for storing data
Hard drive	a device installed inside the computer or in a separate device connected by cable for storing and reading data on a hard disk
Hardware	the physical parts of a computer

Icon	a graphic symbol that represents an object or process in the computer
Ink-jet printer	a printer that shoots ink on the paper in controlled amounts
Kilobyte (KB)	a unit of memory equal to 1,024 bytes
LAN	(local area network) a group of computers connected via cables so they can share peripheral hardware like printers or CD-ROM drives and share data
Laser printer	a printer that uses a laser to electrostatically charge a toner powder for high-resolution printing
Megabyte	a unit of memory equal to 1,048,576 bytes; common measure for hard-drive capacity
MIPS	(millions of instructions per second) a measure of a CPU's processing speed
Modem	a communications device that allows a computer to transmit data over phone lines to and from other computers
Monitor	the display device on a computer
Mouse	a small device used to control the cursor on the screen with "point-and-click" motions
Multimedia	combining sound, video, animations, or other media in one presentation
Operating system	the software in the computer that contains the instructions needed to run the computer's basic operations
Peripheral	a piece of hardware connected to a computer that gives it additional external capabilities, such as a printer, scanner, disk drive
RAM	(random-access memory) a temporary memory that stores data and instructions that a processor is working with at the moment; usually erases when the power is turned off
ROM	(read-only memory) a permanent memory that stores data; can only be read and is not changed or erased when the power is turned off
Software	a set of instructions written in computer language that controls a computer's functions
WAN	(wide-area network) a network of connected computers that covers a great geographical area

having access to librarians who are using computers every day and who can point you to helpful articles and books. Don't forget to "ask your librarian" in making your decisions.

What Do You Want to Do with Your Computer?

Too often people buying a computer start at the wrong end of the food chain. They buy a piece of hardware first, use the software that comes bundled with it or look for other software that runs on it, and only then figure out what they can do with what they've got. This can be a sure formula for frustration, and you risk not getting the most out of your investment in technology.

The best way to get started is to think through what your Friends group wants to do with the computer. Take a good look at your group's current activities and consider the things you would like to start doing or explore. Make two lists—"Things We Do Now" that you *could* do with a computer and "Things We'd Like to Start Doing" with a computer.

Your lists may look something like this:

Things We Do Now
- letters and other correspondence
- reports, proposals, and other documents
- annual budgets
- mailing lists
- membership directory

Things We'd Like to Start
- Friends newsletter
- fliers and ads for Friends programs and events
- turn-key Friends recruitment presentation
- membership/budget projections
- membership database
- electronic communications with library staff
- schedule of events
- volunteer hours database

Other questions you'll want to consider are

What are the activities that we do that are most repetitive?
What administrative tasks take the most time?
What kinds of lists or directories do we maintain?
How do we keep and update our member records?
What kinds of reports do we produce every year?
How do we communicate with members, the community, and the library staff?
How do we want to improve communications?

Another important question for Friends groups is "What does the library admin-istration do on their computers that the Friends group would want to do, too?" Does your Friends group ever produce a report or document that becomes a part of a larger document produced by the library? Talk with the library staff to find out how they use their computers. You will want your computer system to be com-patible with the library's so you easily can exchange documents and data.

Now that you know more about how you want to use a computer, you can determine what computer software to get. You want to think about software before you start looking at hardware because software controls the hardware and makes it do what you want to do.

What Kinds of Software Do You Need?

Software transforms a computer from a big box on a desk into a powerful information-processing machine. Software is a set of programming instructions that tells the computer what to do. The most important piece of software in your computer is the operating system, which controls everything your computer does and runs all of the other software you use. The operating system is the brains of the entire operation—it controls the main chip inside your computer, the microprocessor—and is the first type of software you need to consider.

The Operating System

The operating system is the software that controls the computer's hardware, man-ages the operation of programs, and coordinates the flow of data within the com-puter and between disks. To most computer users, the operating system will seem transparent. The software applications you actually use, such as word processing, database management, etc., "sit" on top of the operating system. However, it is the operating system that determines how easy your computer is to use; how many tasks it can work on at a time; and how data is stored, organized, and accessed.

While many operating systems have come and gone over the evolution of the personal computer, two distinct types are currently in use—the text-only DOS (Disk Operating System) and the GUI (Graphical User Interface) operating sys-tems like Windows, Macintosh, and OS/2.

DOS was the standard operating system for IBM and IBM-compatible com-puters prior to 1990. It is a text-based system in that all commands are typed as text. Apple first introduced the GUI for the Macintosh, and Microsoft followed with Windows, a GUI for DOS machines. GUI allows computer users to use a mouse to point and click on graphics, icons, and symbols to control processes. IBM also has introduced its own GUI operating system, OS/2.

Today, the key factors in choosing an operating system are ease of use and compatibility. The text-based DOS is not easy to use and will be found only on older machines. Among GUIs, Macintosh traditionally has held an edge over Windows for ease of use. However, Windows 95, Microsoft's newest upgrade that combines the Windows interface and DOS, has eliminated any ease-of-use advantage and has additional features that surpass Macintosh in some areas. OS/2 also gets high marks for ease of use but has technical features that tend to complicate processes for average users.

The second decision factor, compatibility, is especially important. While there are a few exceptions, most software is developed for a specific operating system and does not run on alternate systems. For one computer to be compatible with another—to share documents, to use the same software, etc.—both must use the same operating system. Before choosing an operating system, then, you should consider whether it is important for the Friends computer to be compatible with any other computers. For example, you may want to be compatible with the library's administrative computers or with the computers Friends members have at home or at work. Find out what operating systems these computers have before making a final selection.

Compatibility also is an important factor in the additional software choices available. Currently, most personal computers run the Windows operating system. Software developers, then, tend to create more applications for the Windows operating system than for other operating systems because the sales potential is greater.

While there are some computers on the market that will run both the Macintosh and Windows operating systems, they generally are engineered to run one best and the other only so-so. Some software is designed to run on both systems, and other software is available to translate data from one system to the other. In general, however, you will want to consider the compatibility issues outlined and standardize your systems as much as possible.

Once you have chosen an operating system, you are ready to shop for other software and, finally, the hardware that will put all the pieces together.

Applications Software

Rest assured, there is a software program for just about everything you would ever consider doing with your computer. However, there are a handful of basic types of software that will match most of your needs.

Word Processing

Word processing software is most like your typewriter, but oh so much more. Writing letters, reports, and countless other documents is much easier because of the way word processing software stores, retrieves, and allows you to change text.

With word processing software, you can compose and alter text before finalizing it by printing it or sending it to another computer. Text can be rearranged with easy cut-and-paste features. With simple key strokes or a few clicks of a mouse, you can completely alter the format of your document—change typefaces and type size, add bold or italic type for emphasis, change margins, and create columns and tables within your text without rewriting it.

Major features that make word processors so powerful include spell checking, grammar checking, automatic hyphenation, a built-in thesaurus, and search features that allow you to search entire documents to find specific words or word strings. In addition to basic document preparation, Friends especially will want to use word processing to create personalized letters for member communications, for membership promotion, and in advocacy efforts.

Two of the most common word processing programs are Microsoft Word and WordPerfect, which are available for both Windows and Macintosh.

Desktop Publishing

Desktop publishing combines word processing and graphic design to create a variety of professional-looking publications. These programs center around a layout application that combines and arranges text from word processing applications, graphics from paint and drawing applications, and scanned images all on one page.

The ability to manipulate and control so many different components makes layout software very useful for organizations like Friends groups that need to prepare high-quality, well-designed communications pieces on limited budgets. You should consider desktop publishing for fliers, brochures, newsletters, calendars, manuals, invitations, certificates, or just about any publication or printed document.

While desktop publishing requires more time to learn, it can save Friends groups considerable money over conventional typesetting fees and can greatly improve the overall look of your communications. Desktop programs often include predesigned templates for newsletters, brochures, and other standard pieces that allow you to choose from a wide variety of design styles. The program creates a customized look for you based on your choices.

Home Publisher (Adobe Systems) and Microsoft Publisher are easy to learn, cover all the essentials, and will help you produce great results immediately. Page-Maker (Adobe) and QuarkXpress are more expensive, more complex, but also more powerful. All are available for both Windows and Macintosh.

Making the Computer Your Friend

Graphics

With graphics drawing and painting programs you can create illustrations, manipulate graphics images on the screen, and insert them in your documents. Drawing programs, known as CAD (computer assisted design) are more precise than painting programs. CAD is object based, while painting programs generate bitmapped images made up of dots; therefore, painting program output looks very jagged when enlarged.

With graphics programs you can create your own artwork, but you also can import predesigned electronic clip art available on disk or CD-ROM. If you're not an artist, you'll appreciate the great variety of clip art available from commercial vendors and being shared through online bulletin boards. A number of vendors produce library-specific clip art.

Drawing and painting programs work much alike and are included in the popular integrated software packages such as ClarisWorks and Microsoft Works. Art Explorer (Aldus) and Dabbler (Fractal Design) are art packages that are especially good for drawing and special effects. For clip art, Art à la Carte is inexpensive and has fun graphics; Corel Gallery has 10,000 clip art images but is available only on CD-ROM.

Forms

A number of packages on the market allow you to design your own forms. These programs go beyond the preprinted forms that you can fill in by hand or with a typewriter. They can be stored on disk, retrieved on screen, filled in with data, and printed. Graphics from paint or drawing programs can be used to illustrate the form. The program guides you when entering data and shows you a preview of the completed form.

Spreadsheets

Computers are great number crunchers. With spreadsheet software you can perform all kinds of calculations and analyze numeric data. You can ask "what if" questions that allow you to develop budget projections based on different scenarios, and you can create graphs and charts as shown in figure 19.

In spreadsheets, data are entered in cells that are arranged in columns and rows on a work sheet. Formulas can be entered to add, subtract, multiply, divide, and perform other calculations. One work sheet can be linked to another. You also can enter text and use your spreadsheet program as a database for mailing addresses and creating simple directories.

Friends groups can make great use of spreadsheets to develop budgets, analyze costs, generate monthly financial reports and yearly statements, and more. Graphics features enable you to present information in interesting and compelling ways. For example, graphing membership growth from year to year or charting

Figure 19. *Sample Graph and Chart*

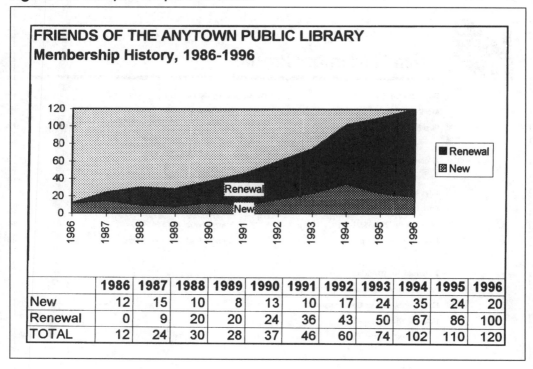

FRIENDS OF THE ANYTOWN PUBLIC LIBRARY
Membership History, 1986-1996

	1986	1987	1988	1989	1990	1991	1992	1993	1994	1995	1996
New	12	15	10	8	13	10	17	24	35	24	20
Renewal	0	9	20	20	24	36	43	50	67	86	100
TOTAL	12	24	30	28	37	46	60	74	102	110	120

actual dollars versus fund-raising goals are effective ways to communicate your activities to members, library staff, and your community.

For spreadsheet software, you can't go wrong with either Microsoft Excel or Lotus 1-2-3, two standard programs available for both Windows and Macintosh.

Databases
Your telephone Rolodex, your Friends membership directory, your list of city council members or county commissioners with information about dates of contact—these all are databases ripe for conversion to an electronic format with database software. Database programs allow you to enter "records" of information that can then be sorted, searched, or manipulated in countless other ways that make the information most useful for you. See figure 20 for a sample database record.

Databases are either flat file, which store information in fields on records that you can flip through and reorganize, or relational, which allow you to build links or relationships between information across fields for greater analysis and targeting. For example, a relational database would allow you to select from your database the

Figure 20. *Sample Database Record*

Friends Member Profile

Date Entered: 6-3-9X (the date you entered data in this form)

Member #: 146 Mr./Mrs./Ms.: Mr.

First Name: Gregory Last Name: Franklin

Address Line 1: 563 N. Springer St.

Address Line 2:

City: Anytown State: IL

Postal Code: 60498

Work Phone: 708-555-1212 Home Phone: 708-555-7890

Fax: same as home phone E-mail: gfrank@wherever.org

Personal Information

How Contacted: annual radio campaign

Employer: Whatever Corporation

Hobbies: Civil War history

Committees: Special Events

Comments

Good writer, interested in getting a newsletter started; board member, local YMCA

---

names of Friends members who live in a certain ZIP code, have children at home under 18, and are not currently committee chairs—perfect candidates for a new initiative with the schools in a particular district.

This added power comes at a price, of course, and is more difficult to use. Analyze your needs and intended uses carefully so you don't get stuck with a program that is more complicated than you need or, conversely, with a program that doesn't have the power to deliver the level of analysis you want.

Communications

Communications software allows your computer to communicate with other computers via telephone lines and a modem. Many communications software packages are available. Most come free when you purchase your modem, so you don't really have to make a choice.

Additional communications applications you will want to consider are electronic mail (E-mail), an online service, and Internet access. E-mail is a very basic communications application. It allows users to send messages to each other with attached documents and even voice messages and video clips.

Commercial online services also allow you to easily communicate with different computers. Services such as America Online, CompuServe, Microsoft Network, or Prodigy allow you to send e-mail without being on a network, access online libraries of information and special interest groups, and even go out to the Internet. These services typically are bundled on your computer. If you choose to subscribe, you will be charged a monthly use fee based on hours of use and perhaps transaction fees based on the nature of your online activity.

Online services and the Internet, the international network of government, university, corporate, and personal computers linked through communications protocols, are the hottest areas of development in computer communications. Your Friends group will want to consider how to make best use of the Internet and other online resources. A number of basic Internet books and Internet access packages are available. Your library likely is connected to the Internet in some way and may even have a "home page" area on the Internet for posting library information. Ask your library staff about how the library is using the Internet and how the Friends group can get involved.

Integrated Packages

Some applications are packaged together to provide different functions that operate together. These packages typically include word processing, spreadsheet, database, and communications capabilities. Linked so that they function together, the package allows a user to easily share information between, for example, word processing and a spreadsheet or a spreadsheet and a database.

These are excellent packages to consider for Friends groups. Many, such as Microsoft Works or ClarisWorks, are targeted for small businesses that need full functions but are not as sophisticated or powerful software as corporate office software. The advantages of these packages are that they use the same or similar commands across applications and cost less than what you would pay for the individual programs. Integrated software often is bundled on computers at purchase. The disadvantages are that each application in the integrated package is less powerful than the stand-alone programs.

If power is important to you, an alternative is to get a full suite of office software packaged together at a lower price—such as Microsoft Office, SmartSuite (Lotus), and WordPerfect Suite.

Utilities

Software utility programs can make day-to-day computing easier and help you take advantage of your computer's full capabilities. Utility programs don't actually do any work for you like the productivity programs described previously; they work on the computer itself to improve performance, make repairs, or diagnose problems.

Backup utilities help you quickly copy the content of your hard disk to diskettes or other storage media if the unspeakable occurs and your hard disk malfunctions. A repair utility can find and recover lost data from a deleted or damaged file. Other utility-like programs include enhancements such as notepads, calendars, appointment books, phone books, and calculators.

Multimedia Software

Multimedia software combines text, sound, graphics, animations, and video for a rich experience with information. Available only on CD-ROM, multimedia software is interactive. With a multimedia encyclopedia, for example, you can not only read about space flight, you can see animations that illustrate the dynamics of rocket power, watch a Saturn rocket lift astronauts into space, and hear recordings of prior broadcasts from the Moon.

Multimedia software is an exciting new medium for educational and library use. The multimedia format is ideal for encyclopedias, atlases, travel guides, adventure and educational games, and reference products of all kinds. For Friends groups, an integrated multimedia reference software that combines a dictionary that pronounces words, a world almanac, books of famous quotations, a ZIP code directory, and more can be an invaluable tool in sparking creativity and checking facts when preparing reports, proposals, and speeches. Microsoft's Bookshelf is the present top integrated reference program.

Software Buying Tips

Now that you have a better idea of the type of software you may want, here are a few tips to keep in mind when you're ready to buy.

> Never buy any software you haven't had a chance to test. If a store doesn't let you experience the software hands-on, go somewhere that does.
> Ask for a demonstration, in addition to having time to use the software by yourself.
> Ask friends or colleagues to show you some of their favorite software.
> Read the software box and make sure you understand the systems requirements. Some software will have required specifications and recom-

mended specifications. Always assume you need the recommended specs for the software to perform well.

What Hardware Do You Need?

Before you even start thinking about hardware, make sure you've done your home-work and have gone on at least one software shopping trip where you have decided which software packages match your needs, have tested the software, and have read the boxes to learn the system requirements. Only now are you really ready to make a good decision about hardware.

You can break down your purchase decision into two components—the parts of the computer that are inside the box and the parts that, for the most part, are outside the box. Inside the box are the microprocessor, computer memory (RAM), hard drives, floppy and CD-ROM drives, and busses and ports. Outside the box are the monitor, keyboard and mouse, printer, modem, and other peripherals. Many of the parts that used to be found outside, such as modems, have moved inside the box.

Inside the Box

A truism in the computer industry is that computing power and speed double every two years and prices are cut in half. So two years from now, the standard computer will be twice as fast and powerful as today's, and today's standard will cost half as much. Some experts would advise you to always buy as much power and speed as you can afford. Others would say that you should buy only the power you need, regardless of what's available. As in most things, the best path is somewhere in the middle. Always buy more than you think you need because once you start using your computer, you'll discover all kinds of new uses you hadn't planned for. At the same time, the most powerful machine on the market likely would be more than you would use for a couple of years, and you would pay top dollar.

Microprocessor
The microprocessor, also called the CPU for central processing unit, determines the power and speed of your computer. Processor chips are referred to by the number: 286, 386, 486, and Pentium are used in IBM compatibles. The higher the number, the more recent and more powerful the chip. Be aware of SX and DX suffixes—because of the way they process information, SX processors are slower than DX but consume less power.

The speed of a chip is measured in megahertz (MHz). The higher the MHz, the faster and more expensive the chip. A 100 MHz chip will run twice as fast as a 50 MHz chip. Speed is relative, however. Test drive a number of computers with different MHz ratings to get a sense of the trade-offs. Again, a good rule of thumb is to buy the latest chip and the highest speed you can afford.

RAM

Random Access Memory (RAM) is your computer's thinking cap. It provides temporary storage for all the data and instructions your computer is using at the moment. The more RAM your computer has, the faster it can process data and the more data it can handle overall. To determine how much RAM you need, consider how much memory your software requires, how much memory your computer can hold, and how much memory you can afford.

RAM commonly is measured in megabytes (MB). Software publishers are notorious for understating the amount of memory their software requires. If the box says the program requires 4 MB of RAM, count on needing 8 MB.

Always make sure your computer has room for installing additional memory. Most PCs can accept up to at least 32 MB of memory. And, as with power and speed, buy as much RAM as you can afford. *In fact, if you are faced with a decision between more RAM and more power, get more RAM.* The required minimum today is 4 MB; 8 MB usually is recommended. Buy memory at the same time you buy your computer, and your store will install it for you.

Another type of internal memory is cache, which stores the most recently used data and instructions. And—you've got it—the larger the cache, the better your computer will perform. Cache often is not listed in computer ads, and you may need to ask the salesperson for the amount of cache.

Disk Drives

Two main types of disk drives provide permanent storage for your data—the hard drive and the floppy drive. Hard drives are fast, capable of storing large amounts of data, and are inexpensive for the amount of storage you get. Floppy drives make it easy to load programs and to copy data on floppy disks for transporting.

Hard disks, too, are measured in speed and storage capacity. Speed is measured by access time in milliseconds (ms). With hard drives, the lower the number, the faster the drive. Any hard drive you consider should have an access time of no more than 20 ms. To determine how large a hard drive you should buy, add up the storage requirements for the various software applications you plan to use and then buy at least twice that amount. The very minimum you should consider is 200 MB, but 500 MB and up is standard on many computers you'll see advertised today. Hard drive capacity is relatively inexpensive, so don't cut corners here.

The 3½-inch diskette has replaced the 5¼-inch floppy as the standard for portable storage. Any computer you purchase today will have a 3½-inch floppy drive. Computers used to have a second 5¼-inch floppy drive. Consider a 5¼-inch drive only if you will be working with people who have much older computers that have only the larger drive.

Multimedia

Most home computers now offer full multimedia—a CD-ROM drive for playing multimedia software and a sound card. In recent years, there has been an explosion in multimedia software with a wide range of titles—multimedia encyclopedias, travel planners, enhanced music CDs with visuals as well as music, etc. Anyone making a new purchase should get a multimedia computer, and others should consider an upgrade kit.

Software reference programs such as Microsoft Bookshelf are an invaluable easy-to-use resource that you'll discover all kinds of uses for. Bookshelf combines a dictionary, book of quotes, almanac, encyclopedia, ZIP code directory, and more to literally provide you an entire reference shelf of information on one CD. Once you experience multimedia, you'll never go back!

Outside the Box

Monitor

Before you select a monitor, you should think about your video card, also called a graphics card, that is located inside the computer. The video card deciphers the instructions your computer sends to the monitor to display what you want to see. There are four standard video cards, with increasing degrees of sophistication— VGA, SVGA, 8514/a, and XGA. You'll want at least an 8-bit color SVGA, which will display 256 different colors, standard for today's colorful multimedia software.

Once you have selected your video card, it's easy to match it to a monitor. While it can be convenient to purchase your monitor from the same manufacturer as your computer, you don't have to. If you can get a better deal with a different brand, don't be afraid to mix and match—as you do with speakers and a stereo receiver.

In selecting a monitor, consider size and picture quality. Monitors are measured like television screens, diagonally from the corners. The standard size is 15 inches; you may want to consider 17 inches. Evaluate a monitor much the way you would a television screen—is the picture sharp in all parts of the screen? Are the colors too blue or too red for your liking?

Making the Computer Your Friend

Keyboard and Mouse

As with monitors, you can go with the same brand keyboard as your computer or pick an alternative. Most manufacturers make a standard 101-key keyboard. Test several to see if you like the responsiveness of one over another. You also may want to consider one of several ergonomic keyboards on the market specially designed to be easier on your wrists and provide a more natural finger positioning.

To work in a graphical interface environment such as Windows or Macintosh, you'll want that ubiquitous point-and-click device, a computer mouse. A Microsoft mouse or Microsoft-compatible mouse is the standard for PCs. Macs typically come with their own brand.

Printer

You want a laser printer. You would be very unhappy with the other types—dot matrix, ink jet, thermal—in a short while. Laser printers are fast and quiet, produce print-quality work, and accommodate a variety of type sizes, fonts, and graphics. Lasers are essentially for graphics design and desktop publishing. Prices have dropped to $500 to $2,000 and probably will continue to fall.

Printers are an item in which buying the "off brand" can hurt you. Stick with Mac for Mac and the "standard" Hewlett-Packard for PCs to ensure maximum compatibility with your computer.

Modems and Faxes

A modem is a device that lets your computer talk to other computers over the phone lines. Modems allow you to use electronic mail systems, online services, and the Internet and do other electronic data transfers between computers. You may not recognize an immediate use for one, and if you don't buy one at the time you purchase your computer, you always can install it later.

Modems can be internal or external. Internal modems, installed inside your machine, have the advantages of being out of sight and of not cluttering up your work space. The disadvantage is that internal modems are available to be used only by one computer. Sitting on top of your desk, external modems are easier to monitor and can be moved from one computer to another as needed. Internal modems are less expensive than external. In most cases, an internal modem will suit your needs just fine. You also will want to consider a combination fax/modem, which allows you to send and receive faxes directly from your PC.

As with your computer, get the fastest modem you can afford because the standard transmission rate, measured in bits per second (BPS), will only continue to increase. Ask for a Hayes-compatible modem, the standard.

Ready to Buy

Now it's time to shop. Before you head for the racks of computers, shop for service and support. Check with dealers to find out what their service policies are. Where would your computer be sent for repair? What additional warranties do they offer? Does the dealer pretest equipment? Are they willing to offer help over the phone? Do they offer classes?

You'll likely be checking out a local computer store, a national chain store, or a computer superstore. Don't hesitate to check out some of the mail order services, too. They generally offer lower prices as a trade-off to service, but some do provide good technical support via toll-free 800 lines.

Once you've identified a good source, do it! You know how you want to use your computer and what software will let you do that, and you have some ideas about what to look for in hardware. Now entrust yourself to the reputable, personable dealer you have checked out. You should have a wonderful experience and get the system that's just right for you and your Friends group.

Happy computing!

19

The Caring Core: Volunteers

Charlotte O'Dea

Woven into the day-to-day operations of organizations and agencies in America is the strong and colorful thread of volunteers. The United States is the only country in the world with this phenomenon of people giving freely of their time and talents to an organization for the enrichment of the organization and for the personal enrichment of the volunteer.

Every activity chronicled in this book as well as every Friends of the Library organization is dependent on volunteers. Most of us do not think twice about volunteering for something that we feel strongly about. It is a gift of self that should be treasured and appreciated by the receiving organization. This chapter will remind you of ways to show your appreciation as well as ways to manage this precious resource.

Showing Appreciation

Action Point

Canton, Ohio

In one library alone, Stark County District Library in Canton, Ohio, volunteers contributed more than 6,700 hours of service to the library and 2,100 hours to the Friends. The volunteers were honored by an annual luncheon.

Multiply the Canton example's astounding statistic by the number of Friends groups calculated to be in existence (about 3,500). Is there a way to thank them?

Luncheons, dinners, receptions, plaques, pins, certificates, and newsletter articles are some of the ways to try to say thank you to Friends volunteers. Luckily, most volunteers know they are needed, and while they appreciate recognition, they do not do their work to receive it but because they believe in the cause.

In some cases, volunteers are not Friends of the Library and are not interested in joining. They prefer to come in to the library, do their task, and leave. If they do not wish to join, it would be a mark of appreciation to give them "honorary status." If the librarian thinks it appropriate, let such volunteers receive the mail sent to "paid up" Friends. Sometimes, these volunteers can't afford the membership dues, but they appreciate the library for what it gives to them.

Recruiting

Members are offered the chance to volunteer through regular communication channels, as well as in the profiles many groups include in their membership forms. For example, a recruiting pamphlet for Rome-Floyd County Library, Georgia, shown in figure 21, asks potential volunteers to answer a number of questions. It also explains the areas in which volunteers could be of service.

Managing Volunteers

Volunteers give of their time freely. They bring special skills to the organization; they have a passion for the work they do. The least we can give them in return is a schedule of work and big thank you. The following guidelines will help your organization and its volunteers make the most of volunteers' time and talents.

Guidelines

Give each volunteer work and a job description. Some organizations actively recruit volunteers, compile a list of their work times and skills, and then never contact them to actually take on a job. If you select volunteers, make sure you are able to put them to work immediately. As you would do with anyone who is hired for a job, you need to interview prospective volunteers and furnish job descriptions.

Prepare a work schedule for volunteers. Once your volunteer is on board, make sure you work out a schedule for that volunteer—be it daily, weekly, or monthly. Make sure you contact the volunteer in advance if he or she is not needed on a certain day or if your schedule has changed. The horror of volunteers is to come to work and have no work to do or to find that the office is closed.

Integrate volunteers into the work force. Certainly, volunteers are not paid for their work; their remuneration is the pleasure of giving service. But we must remember to integrate them into the organization routine and workforce—not set

Figure 21. *Sample Recruiting Information*

Please answer the following questions. If you need more space for your response, use another sheet of paper.

1. How much time do you have to volunteer?
2. What skills do you have to offer?
   a. Can you type or use a computer? (Please describe)
   b. Do you prefer routine tasks?
   c. Do you prefer to work alone or with others?
   d. Do you write or speak well?
   e. Are you good at collecting useful data?
   f. Have you had any experience in working with children? (If so, please describe)
   g. Have you had any library work experience? (If so, please describe)
   h. Have you had any media experiences—press, TV, radio? (If so, please describe)
   i. Do you like to sell?
   j. What are your special interests or hobbies?
   k. What do you have to offer that's not mentioned here?

Volunteer Tasks Offered

Following are tasks Friends frequently volunteer to do. Please put a check mark in front of the categories that especially interest you.

Circulation: shelving, reading shelves, sorting due-date cards, miscellaneous tasks

Reference: filing, guiding patrons on the computer for InfoTrac, shelving magazines and newspapers, updating vertical files and picture files, help with special requests

Children's Department: checking out materials; checking in and shelving books; helping with story hour, summer reading, crafts

Audiovisual: checking out and checking in tapes, records, pictures, etc.; rewinding/cleaning returned tapes; previewing new materials

Special Collections: helping patrons locate materials, shelving materials, collecting historical and archival materials, instructing patrons in use of equipment

Talking Books: recording books, newspapers, Sunday school lessons, etc. and mailing to patrons; rewinding returned tapes; shelving returned materials; helping with newsletter typing, copying, folding, addressing, etc.

Extension Services: inputting collection on the computer, checking in and shelving books

Technical Services: processing new books, mending old books

Adult Literacy: becoming a certified tutor and a tutor trainer, helping with secretarial/clerical tasks

Video/The Library Literacy Channel: helping with the camera crew, hosting a local production, editing programs, writing grants

Gift Shop: selling merchandise, helping with scheduling, special displays, events, and inventory

Friends of the Library Office:

  clerical: keeping membership lists up-to-date, recording donations and notices sent, compiling the monthly report of volunteer hours

  book sale: working on publicity; sorting, pricing and packing books for storage; setting up for sale; selling; repacking after the sale; obtaining volunteers for the sale

  newsletter: writing articles, helping with mailings

  special occasions: hosting, planning refreshments, publicity, etc.

General: conducting tours, helping with publicity and library exhibits, pulling weeds, picking up trash, other tasks as needed

them apart. Volunteers take on these special duties for the skills they bring to the job and those they can learn and for the new friends they can make. When you are introducing your staff, always introduce your volunteers, making special note that they are regular volunteers in the organization.

Give volunteers feedback on their work. Volunteers need the positive feedback they get from supervisors. A big welcome when they come to work, a "good job" during the day, and a big thank you when they leave is so very important.

Recognize volunteers on an annual basis. Even though you may give them positive reinforcement at the work site, it is vitally important that some sort of public recognition be given your volunteers. As noted earlier in this chapter, you can recognize volunteers in various ways—volunteer tea, volunteer luncheon, special gifts ceremony, listing of the volunteer hours and the dollar equivalent for their work in an annual report, pins denoting hours of service, and special badges.

Evaluate each volunteer annually. Dedicated volunteers may be with you for years. They should be evaluated on an annual basis—to reconfirm their value to the organization, to correct any job dissatisfaction, and to gather suggestions for making the operation even better. Evaluation validates the volunteer's worth to the

WHY NOT ADD THIS TITLE TO YOUR COLLECTION...

Volunteer

FOR THE
FRIENDS
OF THE
KNOX COUNTY
PUBLIC LIBRARY

organization and gives the supervisor a better idea of how the volunteer perceives the organization and the particular job he or she is doing.

Do an exit interview when each volunteer leaves. An exit interview should be conducted with the volunteer to glean information about his or her particular job, ideas for improving the organization, and perception of what the organization is all about. This is invaluable information that can only make your organization better.

Volunteers and Library Staff

For a Friends group to survive with dedicated and appreciated volunteers, Friends and library staff must work together. The "care and feeding" of the volunteers falls on the shoulders of the officers of the Friends group or on the library director's staff and, in some cases, on trustees. The library director staff and trustees should work in harmony with the Friends and with the volunteers. With cooperation, projects will be completed swiftly and efficiently. The relationships built between library administration and Friends volunteers must be cemented early. If done properly, it will reap dividends for years to come.

Empower your volunteers. Volunteers come to a Friends group with a passion for their library and with specific skills they wish to contribute. Find out what those skills are, offer committee or library work, and empower your volunteers to get their jobs done.

Keep in contact with volunteers. Be sure you offer support to the volunteers working in the library. Touch base with each on a regular basis as he or she works through a project.

Get input from volunteers at board and committee meetings. Make sure those volunteers are included in the planning and execution process of a project that may take place at board meetings or committee meetings. The volunteers' "buy-in" is vitally important to the success of a project or the general harmony of the library.

Keep the library director, staff, and trustees abreast of volunteer work. Trustees, director, and staff must cooperate with the volunteers and be made aware of their projects. They must remember to say the "magic words" —thank you—to those volunteers working on a special Friends project or simply volunteering in the Library.

Give a collective thank you. The library administration must ultimately say the last thank you to the Friends

VOLUNTEERS ARE FRIENDS OF THE LIBRARY

A Guide For Volunteers

Rome-Floyd County Library
205 Riverside Parkway
Rome, Georgia 30161-2913
706-236-4610

through special recognition. Under no circumstance should the administration take the Friends group for granted. There must be continual communication and continual gratitude for the work of the Friends.

20

Friends of Special Libraries

Sandy Dolnick

Friends of special libraries inhabit a different part of the spectrum than most Friends groups do. Their world is defined by either their geography (for example, a military base or a religious institution) or by the audience attracted to their special collection. In some cases this can be a real asset for attracting membership because of the particular market or membership they attract. Development officers in special libraries often turn to Friends as a way to honor donors and to increase the base of outside involvement to help with the library endowment. Friends can sponsor special lectures, receptions, and social events with some cachet.

On the other hand, special libraries may be part of a larger institution that may not easily harbor a nonprofit membership organization in its midst. A bureaucracy may be inherent in a government or corporate environment that does not lend itself to cultivating the creation of a Friends group.

Some special libraries find it necessary to physically move their collections (which are kept intact) to a new home in a larger library to preserve their collections. This is a similar situation to that facing small museums who find the audience for their collections dwindling with the aging of the population.

Special libraries have, as all libraries do, some patrons that are more involved and care more about the library than others. These patrons may have special collections or resources that are also of interest to the library, making the cultivation of these people even more important. A Friends group, by any name, is one way to draw these patrons closer. Special programs can be underwritten by "friends" not part of an organized group. Since each library situation calls for special handling, the librarian has to take many variables into consideration to make an informed decision on how to best use these untapped supporters.

This chapter discusses Friends of military libraries. It also focuses on some types of special libraries, all successful.

Friends of Military Libraries

Margaret Johnson

Because of the ever-changing population, Friends of military libraries face unique challenges. However, they have proven to be successful, as the Focus example shows.

Military libraries are formed under the aegis of the Morale, Welfare, and Recreation (MWR) Fund. The Friends of Military Libraries Constitution and By-laws appear in appendix B.

FRIENDS OF MILITARY LIBRARIES

April - May Events

April   Author's Talk - Tuesday, 11 April 1530,
         at the Corry Station Library
   *Ralph E. Gaither, former Vietnam P.O.W.
   *Ruth M. Snyder, "Pecans Past and Present"
    and others © 1994
   *Phillip M. Thienel, "Seven Story Mountain,
    The Union Campaign at Vicksburg" © 1994
May   Annual Bargain Book Sale
         20 - 21 May at the Fifth Annual
         Armed Forces Day Celebration
         at Blue Angel Navy Recreation Park
         Sat. 10:00 - 6:00, Sun. 11:00 - 5:00

Great Minds Meet
at the Library

Contact your Military Libraries at 452-6394/4362 for information or to donate used books.

FOCUS

Corry Station Library, Naval Air Station Library Pensacola, Florida

The purpose of the Friends group is to assist the military libraries in focusing public attention on library programs, facilities, and activities as well as to stimulate the use of the libraries. The reasons for joining are familiar: Military libraries need support because of downsizing and decreasing budgets; funds raised by Friends supplement shortfalls in the library budget.

Special events are held at the library, including an author's panel with local authors: a former Vietnam P.O.W., a Civil War historian, and the local author of *Pecans Past and Present*. In addition, the library has offered an annual bargain book sale, held during the Armed Forces Day celebration; storytelling hours, held at the library; and a visit by the commanding officer in which he told the children about foreign countries and taught them to say hello in different languages. The commanding officer handed out certificates of achievement to youngsters completing the summer program.

News about the Friends is listed in the monthly publication of the MWR Department for the Corry Station community.

Friends of Association Libraries

A Friends group is supposed to call attention to its library. It is not always meant to raise funds. This is especially true in for-profit institutions. In the following Focus, the group accomplished its stated goals to the extent that it was no longer needed. This should not be perceived as a negative situation. The library was able to muster support when it needed it and call attention to itself in the midst of a large bureaucratic association. Sometimes all that is needed is a gentle reminder not to take the special resources offered by the library for granted.

FOCUS

The National Association of Realtors®

At the National Association of Realtors the energetic librarian was able to begin a successful group and newsletter. The success may lead to the demise of the group because some of its programs have been co-opted by other parts of the organization.

The parent organization for this library, the National Association of Realtors (NAR), holds an IRS status as a 501(c)(6) trade association. This status means that the NAR is a not-for-profit organization, but it is *not* charitable, which complicates the ability of its Friends group to qualify as a nonprofit organization capable of offering tax deductions to donors and members. Outright contributions cannot be deducted as business expenses.

The National Association of Realtors is a geographically dispersed organization. It is actually a federation of fifty-three state associations (including Puerto Rico, Guam, and the Virgin Islands) with more than 1,800 local boards of Realtors and with international cooperative agreements with more than 20 countries. All members currently have free use of the library, now called the Realtor Information Center, and the Center responds to more than 100,000 requests for information yearly from members, staff, and the outside public.

In 1987 the executive vice-president suggested that the library information services department form a Friends group. He had been involved with libraries for several years and viewed a Friends group as a vehicle for building

support with the NAR membership for the library information services department. The director of the department began the legal and organizational issues involved in developing the Friends group in 1988. In November 1988, the NAR library committee gave approval for the establishment of a project team made up of members of the committee to pursue this concept.

The project team recognized that a Friends group could provide greater visibility for the library, resulting in increased usage of and support for this resource. They also recognized the potential fund-raising benefits of a Friends group. The team grappled with the issue of benefits for Friends members, particularly given the restrictions imposed by the IRS. They decided to establish the Friends group and have the donation card and the newsletter both state: "An annual $5 donation is requested to help offset printing and mailing costs. Contributions may be wholly or partially deductible as a business expense. Check with your tax advisor."

To date, the newsletter is a triannual, four-page glossy publication with a lead article, director column, history column, real estate best sellers, popular books or subjects from this library, or any current topic that requires information dissemination.

Under the direction of the assistant director of the NAR Information Center, the Friends group has produced four major programs. The most popular of the programs was a standing-room-only auction with all proceeds going to the library. Other programs included Information South of the Border, with information on NAFTA and on real estate concerns in Mexico, Information on New Government-Required Appraisal Forms, and one on environmental concerns of the Realtor. Attendance at the programs is free, but a $5 donation is requested.

The funds from the newsletter and the programs cover the costs of the production of the newsletter and of augmenting the audio/video collection.

The major problem that the National Association of Realtors Friends group faces is its geographic dispersion. The contact between members is through the very popular newsletter and the occasional programs that the Friends group sponsors. Until 1994 the Friends group maintained official status with the association, first as a subcommittee, then as a task force. As of now, the Friends group does not have an official status in the NAR hierarchy because it holds no policy-making authority. The group is allowed to meet and can publish its meeting times in the official meetings calendar. The group can also sponsor programs, but there has now been an official information forum established that substitutes for the innovative programs that the Friends group had previously sponsored.

Without official sponsorship, there is some doubt as to the necessity or viability of the Friends group. There is little official support for the programs, and a tightened meeting schedule has all but erased the potential for adding another program. The newsletter remains a popular promotion tool and brings in several hundred dollars yearly to help offset the costs of the popular audio/video collection. However, the newsletter has become a staff-developed newsletter, and it is unclear if the Friends of the National Association of Realtors Information Center is worthwhile to continue as a formal Friends group. There will be a few more meetings for volunteers who are interested in keeping the Friends group as a visible entity of the association. Without significant new member support for a separate organized entity, the newsletter may continue but the actual group may dissolve.

Despite its successful programs NAR's Friends group faces challenges in finding firm footing in its association setting. Some more fortunate Friends in special libraries include the Friends of the National Library of Agriculture and the National Library of Medicine. The Friends of the J.P. Morgan Library have achieved wonderful results as well. Law libraries and state libraries are other areas where special collections and special users make Friends a viable proposition.

Friends of Special Libraries Throughout the World

Friends of special libraries exist all over the world. Some have been great successes within their respective niches. For example, the Icelandic Library for the Blind in Kópavogur, Iceland, organized the first Friends group in Iceland. They support purchases of materials for the library and sell Christmas cards as a benefit for the library. They used FOLUSA's resources to become established and con-

THE FAWCETT LIBRARY

NATIONAL RESEARCH LIBRARY FOR WOMEN'S STUDIES

Fawcett Library   Telephone:
London Guildhall University
Calcutta House   071-320 1189
Old Castle Street
London E1 7NT

sulted with the Friends of the Baltimore, Maryland, Library for the Blind and Physically Handicapped about that group's successful program. The Friends of the Wellcome Institute in London is part of the Wellcome Institute for the History of Medicine, which is connected to University College London. It has generated great support and has sponsored an impressive list of programs and publications. It sponsors travel programs and private collection tours. Members' benefits include access to a private dining room and reduced charges for library programs.

Each special library harbors the potential of amazing its patrons with unknown treasures in its collection. For that particular student or aficionado there is nothing to compare with the surge of adrenalin that comes with being surrounded by unplumbed materials of specific interest. The Fawcett Library has a unique collection that epitomizes a special library.

FOCUS

Fawcett Library
London, England

The Fawcett Library in London has a small but loyal group of Friends supporting the National Research Library for Women's Studies in London Guildhall University. Originally a society library housing a collection of pamphlets, leaflets, and governmental publications, it began as the London Society for Women's Suffrage in 1867. It became a major women's center attracting many prominent feminists including Vera Brittain and Virginia Woolf. Since 1977 the library has been maintained by the University with the help of the City Corporation and the Friends of the Fawcett Library. Also, many individual and corporate sponsors as well as donors of books, such as the women's press and Virago, have supported the library. Its fascinating collection includes books, pamphlets, periodicals, ephemera, archives of suffrage organizations and their successors, newspaper clippings, photographs, illustrations, posters, and more than fifty banners. The materials are so unique that they lend themselves well to reproductions, and there are postcards of the banners carried in the large suffrage demonstrations between 1908 and 1912.

Silhouette of Emily Wilding
Davison by Baron Scottield c1912.

21

Some Friends in Detail

This chapter consists of detailed histories of a variety of Friends organizations. Included are the Friends of the Columbia University Libraries (including a short history of Academic Friends), Friends of the New York Public Library, Friends of the Free Library of Philadelphia, and Friends of the San Antonio Public Library. These groups represent established organizations from distinct types of Friends: academic, special, large public library with a Foundation involved, and a city library. Each demonstrates that Patience and Fortitude are necessary for a Friends group to succeed.

FOLUSA is often queried about how and where the first Friends originated. One answer is given below in the Columbia University Library section. However, it should be noted that the Friends of the Library of Hawaii was founded in 1879 by Honolulu's business leaders, merchants, and Hawaiian royalty as the Honolulu Library and Reading Room Association. The efforts of the association brought a grant from Andrew Carnegie in 1909 to build Hawaii's first public library. The association has maintained its vitality and has become a state Friends of the Library group, part of the FOLUSA network.

Friends of the Columbia University Libraries

Kenneth A. Lohf; updated by Anthony W. Ferguson

The association of academic libraries and Friends has been a long and venerable one, dating from the time of Sir Thomas Bodley. This distinguished diplomat under Queen Elizabeth I spent the last fifteen years of his life forming a library, not for himself, but for Oxford University. He inspired others from his group of "Honourable Friends" (a title the Bodleian Library uses today for its benefactors) to donate their books to the library as well as "stirring up other men's benevolence,"

as he stated his policy. Thus was formed the concept of library benefaction. When he died in 1613, his charitable notion was to remain dormant for nearly 300 years.

The first official group of Friends was that of the Bibliothèque Nationale in Paris "La Société des Amis de la Bibliothèque Nationale," founded in 1913. This group signaled the beginning of a new era for academic libraries. Their support became broadbased, and contributions were made by quantities of individuals rather than by a single benefactor. In 1925 the Friends of the Bodleian Library was officially established. At approximately the same time, the Friends of the Harvard Library was founded, largely through the efforts of Archibald Coolidge, at that time a professor of history and director of the Harvard Library.

Columbia Friends

In 1926 in New York, Professor David Eugene Smith, who had retired from his Columbia University teaching position, founded the Friends group at Columbia. It was among the first such associations to be organized at an academic institution in America. The initial ingredients that went into the making of a successful Friends organization were great teachers who were lovers of books and generous alumni who did not forget the inspiration of their professors. Smith, a much-loved teacher, was also a prodigious collector of rare mathematical books, manuscripts, and instruments. He became a major benefactor of this library. He was also successful in inspiring other potential donors to support the program of the Friends, notably George Arthur Plimpton, who became chairman in 1928 and later bequeathed his magnificent library of rare books and medieval and Renaissance manuscripts.

Shortly after failing health forced Smith to give up his Friends activity, the Friends association died, testimony to the fact that the success of such an organization often depends on one individual's energy and enthusiasm. Smith's activities did, however, establish a pattern of support for academic libraries in the decades to follow—to influence the donation of books and to secure funds for the enrichment of the collections.

The Columbia Friends was born again in 1951, and the mission of the group, as stated in its constitution and bylaws, remains:

> To promote and further among the alumni and the public an interest in the Libraries of the Columbia Corporation, to provide ways to give them a fuller understanding of the role of the research library in education, to serve as a medium for encouraging gifts and bequests in support of the Columbia University Libraries, and generally to assist Columbia Univer-

sity in showing through exhibits, programs, publications, and by other means the resources of the University and its Libraries.

The aim of each Friends association varies according to the situation at the individual library, but the previous statement underscores the basic premises under which most such groups operate. Most importantly, implied in its purposes are promoting the understanding of the library among a wider group of individuals than librarians and scholars themselves and fostering a favorable climate for support of the library over a broad range of possibilities. The governance and the program of each Friends group, however, varies according to the local situation and need. For instance, a Friends group at a small college may find frequent meetings at the library of the greatest usefulness, whereas an ambitious publishing program might be the best means of communication among members at a large university in an urban area.

Administration

There is a degree of contradiction in the operation of academic Friends groups. On the one hand, a broader interest among outsiders can usually be attracted if the library and the Friends group are independent of each other, thus giving more freedom for support and for suggesting new means of benefaction. At the same time, the library and Friends group should cooperate closely so that outside support remains in agreement with the goals of the library and its parent academic institution. These dual objectives can be satisfied through the structure and management of the association. A member of the professional library staff might assist in an active way in the operation of the group, and the head librarian could provide liaison with the library and its objectives without intruding directly into the functioning of the Friends group.

The governance of the academic Friends group is normally entrusted to a council or board, its members usually appointed by the trustees of the college or university upon nomination by the president of the university. Nominations to the council are made for such terms of office as will result in continuity of operation. The continuing success of each Friends group rests finally on its ability to attract dedicated and active council members who will promote the programs of the group and extend support and membership.

Membership

The members of academic Friends organizations come from a variety of sources, depending on particular places, individuals, and purposes. Persons on or near the campus, such as faculty, university officials, and librarians, may form the primary group. Persons among the alumni who have shown a specific interest in book collecting and libraries will form an important segment of any academic group, but caution may have to be exercised in this area so that there is no conflict with alumni groups. In large metropolitan areas, the group may seek support from among the professions and the community at large; these membership efforts will doubtless be modified by the activities of other competing Friends groups in the area. Depending upon the goal of a specific group, membership might be unlimited and support sought from the widest possible source. For a library with a more specific program, Friends membership might be limited to those individuals who could best assist the institution in reaching such goals. Broad support across great numbers is not necessarily the best means to an end. A focused support among dedicated individuals might accomplish achievable goals more effectively and efficiently.

Funds

Operating funds derive primarily from dues, and each Friends organization will devise a schedule of classes of membership, such as regular, sustaining, patron, benefactor, etc., with each class having a corresponding level of contribution. In addition, a special membership for the institution's active and retired staff members might encourage their participation. An honorary membership for individuals who have made distinguished contributions of their time or resources might be devised. Corporate matching grants, a relatively recent development, are another important source of income. Dues contributions also provide funds for the support of such projects as the acquisitions of important first editions and manuscripts, endowments of library positions or book funds, purchase of equipment, or the furnishing of a room, to mention only a few of the projects that have been achieved by successful groups.

Activities

Interest in a particular library and its resources can best be stimulated through a series of meetings and receptions, ranging from an annual dinner meeting with a featured speaker to a reception opening an exhibition centering around an important library acquisition or commemorating a literary or historical anniversary. Libraries and Friends may sponsor annual awards, such as the Frederic Bancroft Prizes in American History and Diplomacy at Columbia and the Donald F. Hyde Awards for Distinction in Book Collecting at Princeton.

The publications of the Friends group are an important means of communicating to the members at large the projects and activities of the organization. The frequency of publication is important to maintain contact with a far-flung membership. For example, the *Columbia Library Columns*, published since 1951, is issued two times a year. The publication dates generally conform to the meetings of the Friends and serve to record those meetings.

The magazine primarily contains articles of general interest related to the library's collections. Each issue includes an account of individual gifts received during the preceding period. Entitled "Our Growing Collections," the account serves as a printed record of benefactions and indicates to the members of the organization how the resources of the library are developing, thus stimulating additional gifts.

Other publications might include a newsletter, a bibliographical journal, keepsakes based on important books or manuscripts in the collection, and exhibition catalogs. Publications such as catalogs and monographs may generate income to extend the publishing program and may stimulate donors to provide grants for publications. At Columbia, *Columbia Library Columns* is supplemented by *Books & Bytes,* a newsletter designed to keep the Friends apprised of new developments in the Libraries.

The numbers of Friends groups at academic libraries have increased substantially during the past thirty years. Hardly any institution of any standing does not now have a thriving organization stimulating interest in its library's development of research resources among faculty, alumni, and other individuals. While Friends groups may at times assist in fund-raising efforts, the book and manuscript collections in the humanities, the arts, law, medicine, and other specialized areas are their chief interests. Time and changing needs of libraries may place greater emphasis on the fund-raising potential of academic Friends, but it would appear that the most successful among them achieve these goals as well if they are successful in their literary pursuits.

The Friends of the New York Public Library

Fran Q. Tschinkel, Manager of Public Affairs

The New York Public Library is a private, nonprofit corporation created in 1895 by the consolidation of the privately financed reference libraries of John Jacob Astor and James Lenox with the Samuel Jones Tilden Trust. It now consists of four research and eighty-two branch libraries.

From its inception, the library has depended on a unique private–public partnership to fulfill its basic mission to offer "free and open access to the accumulated wisdom of the world, without distinction as to income, religion, nationality or other human condition."

Your Invitation to Join
The Friends of The New York Public Library

Celebrate
The New York Public Library's
extraordinary century of public service to New York,
the nation and the world
by becoming a Friend of the Library.

Your generous contribution
will entitle you to many special privileges
during the Library's year-long Centennial Celebration.

More important, your gift will help
the Library continue to fulfill its critical mission—
to provide free access
to the world's accumulated wisdom—
now and during the next 100 years!

R.S.V.P.
by May 1, 1995

Special Centennial Events
for Friends are listed
on the back of this invitation.

Some Friends in Detail

The library has always received financial support from generous individuals and has counted on dedicated volunteer service in numerous capacities. The term "Friends of the New York Public Library" was first used in the fall of 1970 in conjunction with a small direct-mail appeal to encourage donations to the library. During the years that followed, special events were held to thank these donors, including exhibition openings, lecture luncheons, and unique trips.

In 1979 steps were taken to formalize the Friends group and to clarify the role of volunteers at the library. Membership categories were established with a structure of benefits for each donor level. A direct-mail test program begun in 1976 under the direction of the library's development office was expanded, and membership in the Friends group became the focus of this fund-raising effort.

Volunteer activities such as conducting public tours, lobbying, office services, and other critical functions have grown tremendously, first under the direction of a Friends steering committee and, since 1984, under the Volunteers of the New York Public Library group through the leadership of its executive council.

The Friends Program Today

Today the Friends program functions primarily as a fund-raising activity. It is charged with the task of attracting new donors through large cold-prospect mailings, renewing and upgrading the support of current contributors who give up to $1,249 annually, and servicing these donors through a specially designed program of membership activities.

There are six categories of Friends membership:

Library Associate: These donors give $25 to $39 and receive the quarterly *New York Public Library News.*

Friend: These donors give $40 to $64; they receive the quarterly *New York Public Library News;* a personalized membership card; invitations to member-only previews, lectures, and seminars; opportunities to travel with the Friends; discounts of 10 percent in the library shops; special shopping weeks with an additional discount; and an invitation to the gala holiday open house.

Participating: These donors give $65 to $99; they receive all of the benefits of the Friends membership plus two additional invitations to the holiday open house and advance notice of the public education programs.

Supporting: These donors give $100 to $249; they receive all of the benefits of the above categories plus invitations to VIP openings of major exhibitions, invitational tours with curators of the library's collections, invita-

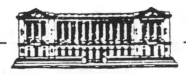

tions to a special lecture–luncheon series at a nominal fee, and twelve bookplates for their own libraries.

Patron: These donors give $250 to $499; they receive all of the previously described benefits plus a special library publication and the annual report of the library.

Sustainer: These donors give $500 to $1,249; they receive all of the previously described benefits plus a major exhibition catalog.

Donors of $1,249 or more become conservators of the library and receive invitations to special conservator programs, including the annual conservators' dinner. This program is administered by a paid coordinator who is part of the annual-fund staff.

Donors of less than $25 are not members of the Friends group, but they do receive renewal solicitations and are encouraged to upgrade to the basic membership level.

In 1995 there were 43,000 donors who gave from $1 to $1,249, and 25,000 qualified as members of the Friends. (See the Focus in chapter 8 for a description of how Friends of the New York Public Library are acquired and renewed and chapters 8 and 14 for events for members.)

The Friends program is managed by a paid staff of four—a manager, an assistant coordinator, an associate, and an assistant. In the fall of 1996 the New York Public Library will announce the Second Century Campaign.

The Friends of the Free Library of Philadelphia

Michael Nichols, past president

History

The Friends of the Free Library, which was established in 1973, had a membership of 3,600 Friends, including 40 Friends groups in 53 branches of the Free Library system. Its mission was the advocacy and support of the Free Library of Philadelphia and its branches. It is a separate and independent organization from the Free Library—a key factor for its advocacy efforts to be successful. Funding of the budget was primarily from contributions of members, supplemented by contributions from foundation and corporate donors. The Friends managed a gift shop and a used book store, of which the gift shop was, at best, at a break-even level, whereas the book store generated good revenue.

Some Friends in Detail

The success of a nonprofit organization in carrying out its mission effectively is the strength, dedication, and commitment of its staff and board of directors. The day-to-day operation of the Friends is overseen by a full-time executive director and an administrative staff of two. The gift shop and book store each have full-time managers supported by both part-time employees and volunteers.

The board of directors has twenty-five members and consists of a diverse group of outstanding individuals from the corporate, educational, legal, and grass roots communities. As with many nonprofit boards, a core group of directors actively serves on committees and questions and comments on actions at meetings.

A citywide coordination of Branch Friends groups must be facilitated in a manner that contributes to effective advocacy efforts. In 1979 the idea of a coalition of all the Branch Friends groups, called the Alliance of Friends, was conceived. It comprised the presidents and co-chairs of the Branch Friends groups. The alliance provides a focus for grass roots volunteers to exchange ideas, plan strategies to support the Free Library, and coordinate the advocacy efforts with the goals and activities of the Free Library.

A quarterly newsletter, a joint effort of the Friends and the library staff, keeps the membership and Alliance of Friends informed about Free Library activities, issues, happenings, and upcoming Friends programs. The Friends sponsor several programs during the year coordinating with the Free Library, including the annual Black Writer Conference Reception, Young Library Readers Program, and Read Together Coalition's "Love Is Reading Together" Week.

The Present

Currently, the membership of the Friends has grown to 9,000 strong with the Alliance of Friends comprising 51 Branch Friends groups representing 4,000 members citywide. The prime mission still remains advocacy. The source of funding has undergone a major change that has enabled the Friends to grow in numbers; to remain a strong, separate, and independent organization; and to be viewed citywide as *the* advocacy group for the Free Library System.

Relationship with the Free Library of Philadelphia

If it is to be successful in advocacy to further the aims, usage, and public understanding of the Free Library of Philadelphia, the Friends of the Free Library of Philadelphia must be perceived as independent and separate from the Free Library's administration.

The relationship between the Free Library of Philadelphia and the Friends of the Free Library has changed markedly. It began with a strategic need of the Free Library.

From its beginning in 1973 the Friends organization, as an independent, self-funding entity, raised contributions by memberships, foundation and corporate donors, and sales of the gift shop and book store. In 1992 the Free Library began to lay the groundwork for a major citywide fund-raising campaign to benefit branches, enhance technology, and expand programs. Accordingly, an apprehension arose that in raising funds through a major citywide campaign many of the same contributors, particularly at the grass roots level, would be contacted by the Branch Friends in their own fund-raising efforts. From the standpoint of the Free Library, the objective was to have one prime fund-raising entity throughout the city. This would eliminate confusion among potential contributors who might be approached by different Library entities and, more importantly, to clearly delineate that the purpose of all fund-raising was to strengthen the Free Library of Philadelphia.

The other element of the Free Library's proposal was that the mission of the Friends was advocacy with membership fund-raising being the responsibility of the Free Library's Foundation. Without question, this aspect raised major concerns with board members of the Friends—how do we obtain funds to perform our mission? What happens to our independence? If we have our independence, how effective can the Friends be as advocates for the Free Library? How will the Friends survive?

This was a watershed period in the history of the Friends. It could define the future relationship with the Free Library as one of cooperation and team effort to achieve a common objective for the greater success of all the entities in the library family. Or it could be one based on uncertainty and territoriality, thus achieving significantly less as entities because of overlapping goals.

With a goal to ensure that the Friends remain separate and independent, the president of the Free Library of Philadelphia drafted an agreement. In agreement were the chair of the board of trustees of the Free Library of Philadelphia and the president of the Free Library Foundation. The primary mission of the Friends remained the same—advocacy for the Free Library of Philadelphia.

Fund-raising is limited to a select group of foundation and corporate donors and sales from the gift shop and the book store. The major source of our funds now comes from a single entity. The Foundation is recognized as the prime fund-raising arm of the Free Library and the membership list of the Friends is an element of this fund-raising. Accordingly, the agreement calls for the Foundation to remit to the Friends a quarterly payment based on an amount established at the beginning of each year. This arrangement ensures a minimum level of funds to the Friends that may be supplemented by funds raised from its list of donors.

This arrangement has brought about an important change in coordinating efforts and building teamwork to accomplish common strategic goals and objectives. The need to work cooperatively is clearly seen by the staffs and the board of the Free Library, the Foundation, and the Friends. One noteworthy event is an annual dinner meeting attended by all board members of the three entities to develop ideas for increasing contributions, programs, and involvement at the grass roots level. It is a font of ideas, teamwork and cooperation.

The major accomplishment spawned from this agreement is the significant increase in memberships in the Friends of the Free Library—the number has more than doubled to 9,000 contributing members. This was accomplished through direct mailings by the development office of the Foundation as the major fund-raising entity working in cooperation with the Friends of the Free Library, a feat that could not have been achieved had the Friends continued on the path to raise its own funds. An essential element of the citywide fund-raising campaign is to establish a grass roots contribution effort. Since the Friends' strength is at the grass roots community level, the Friends staff is developing a program, in cooperation with the Foundation's development office, to encourage the neighborhood and communities to participate in the campaign.

The Friends of the Free Library of Philadelphia has made major changes based on results from appropriate financial and audit procedures. As in many organizations today, the Friends had to take steps to ensure our financial viability. The board of directors and executive director streamlined the staff, making use of volunteers, and decided to close the gift shop.

The relationship among the Free Library administrators and staff, board of trustees, and board of directors of the Foundation has evolved into one noted for its cooperative effort, coordination, and teamwork to achieve a common objective—to make the Free Library of Philadelphia a stronger and more vibrant cultural and educational institution serving the neighborhoods and communities of Philadelphia into the twenty-first century.

The Friends of the San Antonio Public Library

Mary McAfee, past president

The Friends of the San Antonio Public Library was founded in 1964 by people from the greater San Antonio–Bexar County area who believed that a good

public library is essential. The Friends membership is about 700 as of this writing, of which about half are life memberships. From its modest dues and its donations and gift/memorial fund, the group fills needs and offers services that are beyond the budget of the library.

The Friends maintain an extensive archive on theater history in San Antonio. Each year the organization provides financial aid to three librarians so they can attend the Texas Library Association Conference, and it honors a local author or artist with the Arts and Letters Award celebration. The group also accepts donations for books to honor people or as a memorial. A bookplate attached to the book names the honored person.

In 1989 the Friends helped to pass a bond issue of $46.5 million for the library and its eighteen branches. The bond funds are to build two new branch libraries and renovate six existing ones. The big push for a new central library came true with the May 20, 1995, opening of the "Enchilada Red" building.

The Friends have supported the library with volunteers, funds, and anything else that they are asked to do. In 1990 the Friends were able to persuade the San Antonio city council to allow Friends to sell the books that are weeded from the libraries. That year, the Friends had their first annual book sale followed by one each year since. The proceeds, usually more than $20,000, go to the director of the library for the wish list. Each branch manager asks for specific items that are needed at that location.

A wonderful spinoff of the book sale is that the Friends founded their Book Cellar in the basement of the Hertzberg Circus Museum on the banks of the San Antonio River downtown. The Book Cellar is staffed by volunteers and since 1990 has given over $60,000 dollars to the library for books, etc.

The Hertzberg Circus Museum is owned by the San Antonio Public Library. The building is an old San Antonio Public Library building and contains a one-of-a-kind collection of circus memorabilia collected by Harry Hertzberg and others. The Friends have been able to pay for restoring many of the priceless posters. Among valuable items are the carriage of Tom Thumb and Mr. Hertzberg's rare-book collection.

In 1991 the first of our Branch Library Friends groups was formed. To date there are twelve including the Texana/Genealogy Friends that has just been formed. These groups pay the regular member dues amount and then $3 each for the special branch membership. The money generated from the dues and special book sales held at their branch libraries is used for that particular library. The assistant director of the San Antonio Public Library attends every Friends board meeting and advises the Friends board of needs. The Friends have a very good working relationship with the library director and staff. We invite you to come visit us!

Some Friends in Detail

Appendix A

Gift Shops

Resources

Data Banque Profiles: Libraries. Denver: Museum Store Association, 1990. Comparative data on store operations, management, merchandise mix, etc.

"Library Stores in Public Libraries," in *1995 Librarian's Yellow Pages,* 170–2. Larchmont, N.Y.: Garance, 1995. A brief article and list of 47 library stores.

The Manager's Guide. Denver: Museum Store Association, 1992. Basic guidelines for the new store manager.

The New Store Workbook. Denver: Museum Store Association, 1994. Guide to remodeling, expanding, and opening the museum store.

Strauch, K. "Selling Points—Shops in the Library." *Wilson Library Bulletin* 68 (Feb. 1994): 45–7.

Sweetland, J. "At Library Stores, Business Is Booming," in *1993 Librarian's Yellow Pages,* 6A–10A. Larchmont, N.Y.: Garance, 1995.

Theobald, M. M. *Museum Store Management.* Nashville, Tenn.: American Association for State and Local History, 1991.

Associations

Museum Store Association
501 S. Cherry St., Ste. 460
Denver, CO 80222
(303) 329-6968

Public Library Association
Committee on Retail Outlets in Public Libraries
Chair, J. M. D'Oliveira
c/o Library Foundation of Los Angeles
630 W. Fifth St.
Los Angeles, CA 90071

Library Stores in Public Libraries

Compiled from the *Librarian's Yellow Pages*

Alaska
Janel Feierabend, Mgr.
Friends of the Library Shop
Z. J. Loussac Public Library
3600 Denali St.
Anchorage, AK 99503
(907) 261-2952

Arizona
Christine Hippensteel, Mgr.
Friends Gift Shop
Chandler Public Library
25 S. Arizona Pl., Ste. 111
Chandler, AZ 85226
(602) 786-2315

California
El Cajon Friends Bookstore
El Cajon Public Library
200 E. Lexington
El Cajon, CA 92020-4519
(619) 579-4454

Norma Van Riper, Mgr.
Friends, Books & Things
Oxnard Public Library
251 South A St.
Oxnard, CA 93030
(805) 385-7508

Kitty Taylor, Community Events
Forgotten Books and Other Treasures
Santa Ana Public Library
26 Civic Center Plaza
Santa Ana, CA 92701
(714) 647-5269

Norma Callero, Manager
Library Foundation Store
Thousand Oaks Library
1401 E. Janss Road
Thousand Oaks, CA 91362
(805) 497-6282

K. W. Carlson, Chair
Friends of the Library
San Juan Capistrano Regional Library
31495 El Camino Real
San Juan Capistrano, CA 92675
(415) 364-8092

Jennifer D'Oliveira, Mgr.
The Library Store
Central Library of Los Angeles
630 W. 5th St.
Los Angeles, CA 90071
(213) 228-7550

Olga Wrobel, Chair
Friends Gift Shop
Huntington Beach Library
7111 Talbert Ave.
Huntington Beach, CA 92648
(714) 842-4481, ext. 2213

Aileen Hoy, Buyer/Mgr.
The Library Shop
Palos Verdes Library District
701 Silver Spur Rd.
Palos Verdes Peninsula, CA 90274
(310) 377-9584, ext. 241

Ronald Thomas, Mgr.
The Book Stop
Chula Vista Public Library
365 F St.
Chula Vista, CA 91910
(619) 691-5000

Jack Buchanan, Dir.
Friendshop
Santa Maria Public Library
420 S. Broadway
Santa Maria, CA 93454
(805) 925-0996

Ann Morris, Mgr.
Palm Springs Library Store
300 S. Sunrise Way
Palm Springs, CA 92262
(619) 323-8298

Colorado
The Library Store
Denver Public Library
10 W. 14th Pkwy.
Denver, CO 80203

Kay Wells, Coord.
Friends' Books
Elic Library
Pikes Peak Library District
5550 N. Union Blvd.
Colorado Springs, CO 80918
(719) 531-6333, ext. 1460

Kay Wells, Coord.
Friends' Books
Penrose Public Library
Pikes Peak Library District
20 N. Cascade
Colorado Springs, CO 80901
(719) 531-6333, ext. 1460

Delaware
Colleen Shivone, Coord.
Used Book Shop
Wilmington Public Library
10th & Market St. S
Wilmington, DE 19801
(302) 571-7407

District of Columbia
Elena Tscherny, Exhibits & Programs
    Coord.
Books Plus
Martin Luther King Library
901 G St. NW
Washington, DC 20001
(202) 727-6834

Anna Lee, Retail Mktng. Officer
Madison Sales Shop
Library of Congress
Washington, DC 20540
(202) 707-7715

Florida
Kathryn Porter, Chair
Largo Friends Bookstore
Largo Library
351 E. Bay Dr.
Largo, FL 34640-9793
(813) 587-6715

Jessica Roberts, Mgr.
Friend's Corner
S. Regional Broward Community
  College Library
7300 Pines Blvd.
Pembroke Pines, FL 33024
(305) 963-8825

Hannah Wilner, Mgr.
Friend's Gift Shop
Broward County Main Library
100 S. Andrews Ave.
Fort Lauderdale, FL 33301
(305) 761-1845

The Friend's Used Bookstore
Deerfield Beach Percy White Library
837 E. Hillsboro Blvd.
Deerfield Beach, FL 33441
(305) 360-1380

Terry Kutolowski, Branch Mgr.
The Friends' Used Bookstore
W. Regional Broward County Library
8601 W. Broward Blvd.
Plantation, FL 33324
(305) 831-3300

Laura J. Murru, Coord.
Friends of the Library Book Store
Orange County Library System
101 E. Central Blvd.
Orlando, FL 32801
(407) 425-4694, ext. 496

John Beale, Mgr.
Friends of the Library Bookstore
Seminole County Public Library
215 N. Oxford Rd.
Casselberry, FL 32707
(407) 339-4000

Illinois
Stephanie Davis, Mgr.
Harold Washington Library Center
400 S. State St.
Chicago, IL 60605
(312) 747-4112

Indiana
Book Sale Room
Lake County Public Library
1919 W. Lincoln Hwy.
Merrillville, IN 46410
(219) 769-3541

Louisiana
Teresa Roberts, Mgr.
Friends of the Library Giftshop
Lafayette Public Library
P.O. Box 3247
Lafayette, LA 70502
(318) 261-5785

Maryland
Averil Kadis, Buyer
Pratt Place, The Library Shop
Enoch Pratt Free Library
400 Cathedral St.
Baltimore, MD 21201-4484
(410) 396-5494

Massachusetts
Maureen Boyda, Mgr.
The Book N'More Store
Worcester Public Library
3 Salem Sq.
Worcester, MA 01608
(508) 799-1655

Michigan
Trudy Pinto, Mgr.
Friends Gift Shop
Livonia Public Library
32777 Five Mile Rd.
Livonia, MI 48154
(313) 421-8306

Minnesota
Martin Olson, Mgr.
Friends of the Minneapolis Library
　Book Store
Minneapolis Public Library
300 Nicollet Mall
Minneapolis, MN 55401
(612) 372-6667

Missouri
Nancy Volpe, Mgr.
Dewey Co.: The Library Shop
Kansas Public Library
311 E. 12th St.
Kansas City, MO 64106
(816) 221-2685

New York
Hope Van Winkle, Mgr.
The Library Shop
New York Public Library
Fifth Ave. & 42nd St.
New York, NY 10018-2788
(212) 930-0800

Ohio
Thea Bailey, Mgr.
The Library Store
Columbus Metropolitan Library
96 S. Grant Ave.
Columbus, OH 43215-4781
(614) 645-2617

Mary Scelsi, Co-Dir.
The Library Gift Shop
Cleveland Public Library
325 Superior Ave.
Cleveland, OH 44114
(216) 623-2821

Elaine Michael, Mgr.
The Library Friends' Shop
Public Library of Cincinnati/Hamilton
　County
800 Vine St., Library Sq.
Cincinnati, OH 45202-2071
(513) 369-6920

Pennsylvania
Sarah Oates, Mgr.
Andrew's Alcove
Carnegie Library of Pittsburgh
4400 Forbes Ave.
Pittsburgh, PA 15213
(412) 622-8871

Friend's Gift Shop
Free Library of Philadelphia
1901 Vine St., Logan Sq.
Philadelphia, PA 19103-1189
(215) 567-4562

Rhode Island
Josephine Carson, Mgr.
Friend's Book Store
Newport Public Library
300 Spring St.
Newport, RI 02840
(401) 847-8720

South Carolina
Tim Jarrell, Mgr.
The Friendshop/The Teashop
Richland County Public Library
1431 Assembly St.
Columbia, SC 29201-2828
(803) 799-9084

Texas
Jeff Weber, Mgr.
The Library Store
Dallas Public Library
1515 Young St.
Dallas, TX 75201
(214) 670-1400

Virginia
Nancy Lowe, Buyer
Friendshop
Virginia Beach Central Library
4100 Virginia Beach Blvd.
Virginia Beach, VA 23452
(804) 431-3025

Washington
Helen DuPuy, Mgr.
Friends Shop
Seattle Public Library
1000 Fourth Ave.
Seattle, WA 98104
(206) 386-4100

Wisconsin
Christine Murphy, Admin. Asst.
The Book Cellar
Milwaukee Public Library
814 W. Wisconsin Ave.
Milwaukee, WI 53233-2385
(414) 286-3000

Sample Constitutions

Friends of Libraries U.S.A. (FOLUSA) activities are coordinated through the office of Sandy Dolnick, executive director and founding president of FOLUSA. The board of directors, FOLUSA's governing body, is made up of Friends of all types of libraries and from all regions of the country as well as corporate supporters from book- and library-related businesses and liaisons from other library organizations.

The structure of this umbrella organization provides a backup and support network for Friends of the Library groups, library associations, and individuals. The very quality that makes a Friends group so valuable to its library—its interest in the particular institution—makes it difficult for most Friends groups to see a role outside their own community. FOLUSA helps to open up the lines of communication to the larger library community, allowing Friends groups to participate in library events on a national scale and bringing them new ideas and resources to use to enhance their local programs.

Friends of Libraries U.S.A.

CONSTITUTION

Article I.

Name
   1. The name of this association shall be Friends of Libraries U.S.A. (FOLUSA)

Purpose
   2. The purposes of this association are as follows:
      (a) To encourage and assist the formation and development of Friends of Library groups in the United States.
      (b) To promote the development of excellent library service for all residents of the United States.

(c) To provide a means for Friends of Library groups to have access to information and ideas that will prove useful to them in the operation of their organizations.

(d) To make the public aware of the existence of Friends of Library groups, and of the services they perform.

Location

3. Friends of Libraries U.S.A. shall have and maintain in the State of Illinois a registered office at the headquarters of the American Library Association, currently located in the city of Chicago, county of Cook.

Article II.

Membership

Membership in the association is open to any persons, corporations or organizations who share in the purposes of the association, upon payment of dues.

Article III.

Governance

1. A Board of Directors will be the means of governing the association. It shall be elected by the membership.

2. Officers of the association shall be the President, Vice-President, Secretary and such other appointed officers as the Executive Committee shall determine. Committees of the association shall be a Nominating Committee, an Executive Committee and such other committees as may be appointed by the President.

Vacancies

3. The Board of Directors may choose any member of the Board to fill any officer vacancy until the next regular election.

Terms of Office

4. Officers of the association shall serve for terms of one year, except that the Treasurer shall be appointed.

5. Members of the Board shall serve for terms of two years except that one-half of the Initial Board shall serve for a term of one year.

6. No elected officer or Board member shall serve for more than three successive terms in the same capacity.

Compensation

7. No Board member shall receive remuneration for service on the Board.

When authorized by the Board, reimbursement may be made for travel and other out-of-pocket expenses in discharging official duties.

8. No part of the net earnings of the association shall inure to the benefit of any member, official or individual, and no part of its activities shall involve attempts to influence legislation, to carry on propaganda, or to intervene in a political campaign on behalf of any candidate for public office and any election filed pursuant thereto except as allowed within the meaning of Section 501(c)(3) of the Internal Revenue Code.

Article IV.

Annual Meeting

1. The annual meeting of Friends of Libraries U.S.A. shall be held in conjunction with the annual conference of the American Library Association.

Board Meeting

2. A meeting of the Board of Directors shall be held annually in conjunction with the American Library Association Midwinter Meeting.

Special Meetings Notice

3. Special Board meetings may be called by the President or by any members of the Board constituting one-half of its members.

4. Notice of each annual meeting of the Board of Directors shall be mailed at least fourteen days before the meeting.

Official Periodical

5. The Friends of Libraries U.S.A. periodical shall be the official means of communication with the members of the organization.

Proxy

6. Members of the Board shall be entitled to vote by proxy at Board meetings.

Article V.

Amendments

This Constitution and its Bylaws may be amended by a majority of the Board members following at least 60 days notice in writing of such proposed changes.

Article VI.

Dissolution

Upon dissolution of Friends of Libraries U.S.A. or winding up of its affairs, the assets shall be applied and distributed as follows: after payment of obligations all remaining assets shall be transferred or conveyed to the American Library Association *if* it is then an exempt organization under the provision of Section 501(c)(3) of the Internal Revenue Code, or, if not, to one or more organizations which have operations or perform services similar to the Friends of Libraries U.S.A. anywhere in the United States and are exempt under the provisions of Section 501(c)(3) of the Internal Revenue Code of 1954 or the corresponding provisions of any federal tax law which shall be in effect.

BYLAWS

Article I—Membership

Classes
1. There shall be such categories of membership as the Board may from time to time determine.

Dues
2. Membership dues shall be set by the Board of Directors.

Fiscal Year
3. The fiscal year shall be from September 1 through August 31. A membership year shall begin in the month a member joins and end eleven months after that date.

Resignation
4. Any member may resign by filing a written resignation with the Secretary at any time.

Transfer Roll Rights
5. Membership is not transferable or assignable.
6. The current membership list will be kept by the FOLUSA office.
7. (a) Each member is entitled to one vote on each matter submitted to a vote. In the case of an organization, or a corporation, the vote shall be cast by the chief executive of that organization, or by whomever that group chooses to delegate responsibility.
   (b) Subscription(s) to the Friends of Libraries U.S.A. periodical(s) shall be part of the rights of each member.
   (c) Members may use the official emblem of this organization on their stationery or official publication, when shown with the words, "member of." Use of the official emblem does not indicate endorsement of the

activities of any group by Friends of Libraries U.S.A. Stationery or official publications bearing the official emblem must be filed with the office of the Executive Director annually.

Article II—Meetings

Quorum

1. Members of the association represented in person or by proxy, shall constitute a quorum at any meeting of the members except that in the presence of less than ten, a lesser number may adjourn the meeting from time to time.
2. Members of the Board of Directors must constitute one-third of the whole group to provide a quorum for the transaction of business at any Board meeting, in person or by proxy, provided if less than one-third of the directors are represented, a majority of the directors present may adjourn the meeting from time to time.

Article III—Officers

Composition

1. There shall be not less than twenty elected members of the Board of Directors.
   (a) Officers shall be the President, Vice-President, Secretary and Treasurer.
   (b) The Executive Director, ALA Liaison and all past Presidents shall have full voting rights at Board meetings.
   (c) Liaison representation from related organizations may be appointed by the FOLUSA Board to serve with the same rights and terms as regular board members. Designation of such a representative may be suggested by the related organization. Alternatively, a regular FOLUSA board member may be designated by the board to act in liaison capacity to the related organization.
2. The Nominating Committee shall request suggestions for nominations from all members in appropriate publications.
3. Any voting member may submit a candidate for nomination, in writing filed with the Nominating Committee, at least sixty days prior to the balloting date at which the Director or Directors are to be elected.
4. No person shall be elected a Director without his or her prior consent.
5. Balloting for elections shall be by mail.
6. The term of office for the newly elected officers and other members of the Board shall begin following the annual meeting of the association.

Article IV—Contracts, Checks, Deposits and Funds

Contracts

    1. The Board of Directors may authorize any officer or officers, agent or agents, to enter into any contract or execute and deliver any instrument in the name of and on behalf of the association; such authority may be general or confined to specific instruments.

Checks

    2. All checks, drafts, or other orders for the payment of money, notes, or other evidence of indebtedness, issued in the name of the association shall be authorized by the Executive Director of the organization.

Deposits

    3. All funds of the association shall be deposited and invested from time to time to the credit of the association, in banks, trust companies or other financial service institutions.

Gifts

    4. The Board of Directors may accept or reject on behalf of the association any contribution, gift, service, bequest or device for the general purposes or for any specific purpose of the association.

Article V—Honors

Officers

    1. The Board of Directors may from time to time appoint honorary officers to act in an advisory capacity only.

    2. The Board of Directors may from time to time establish certificates or other awards which may be awarded as the Board of Directors shall elect.

Article VI—Meeting Procedures

Procedure

Except as otherwise stated in the Constitution and Bylaws, all proceedings of this association shall be governed by Robert's Rules of Order, Revised.

Article VII—Records

Records

The Friends of Libraries U.S.A. office shall keep correct and complete books and records of account. The Secretary shall keep minutes of the proceedings of the meetings of the Board of Directors and committees having any authority of the

Board of Directors. FOLUSA shall keep at its registered office a record giving names and addresses of the members entitled to vote. All books and records of the association may be inspected at the office of FOLUSA by any member, or his agent or attorney; for any purposes at any reasonable time.

Article VIII—Audit

Audit
The books of this association shall be maintained and audited at the close of the fiscal year according to the procedures of the American Institute of Certified Public Accountants.

Article IX—Committees

Committees
1. The President may appoint committees to conduct activities of the organization, or to assist the Board of Directors.

Dissolution
2. A committee shall be considered dissolved upon completion of its task and acceptance of its report by the Board.

Article X—Annual Reports

Annual Reports
Annual reports shall be submitted to the Board in writing at the time of the annual Reports meeting and shall be retained by the Executive Director.

June 1995

Friends of the Richland County Public Library, Inc.

BY-LAWS

Article I—Name

The name of this organization is the Friends of the Richland County Public Library, Inc.

Article II—Purpose

The purpose of this organization is to establish closer relations between the Richland County Public Library and the people it serves; to promote informed interest in its function, resources, services, and needs; to confer with the Board of Trustees and the staff of the Library on matters relating to the welfare of the institution; to stimulate and receive gifts, endowments and bequests for the benefit of the Library; and to support the development of a program for the extension and improvement of the Library's services and resources.

Article III—Governing Board

1. The management of the affairs of the Corporation shall be in the control of a governing board which shall not exceed thirty in number and the members of which, in the first instance, shall be elected by the corporation.
2. Each Board member shall be elected for a term of two years and may be reelected to similar terms, provided, however, that a Board member may serve no more than six consecutive years without retirement for at least one year.
3. At each annual meeting, members of the governing board shall be elected by the membership to serve for two years or until their successors are elected and qualified. Any Board member who has more than three consecutive unexcused absences from regular Board meetings or who has more than six unexcused absences from formal Board functions in any twelve-month period may be retired from office by a majority vote of the Board.
4. The governing board reserves the right to elect members to the governing board to fill the unexpired term of members who resign between annual meetings, even if the remaining members are less than a quorum. Directors so elected shall hold office until the next annual meeting or until their successors shall be duly elected and qualified, unless sooner displaced.
5. During the last quarter of each year, the Board shall designate a Nominating Committee of at least one Board member with at least two other

members of the Friends to propose a list of new Board members to fill any vacancies for the next year. This list may be adopted by majority vote of the current Board for submission to the annual meeting of the Friends. The Nominating Committee shall make all reasonable efforts to nominate a slate of directors that will ensure that all geographical areas of Richland County are represented on the Board.

6. Additional nominees may be submitted from the membership by petition of at least ten members, submitted ten days prior to the annual meeting.

Article IV—Officers

1. The governing board shall elect the following officers to serve for terms of one year: President, First Vice-President, Second Vice-President, Secretary, and Treasurer. During the last quarter of the year, the Board shall designate a committee of at least three Board members who shall present a list of nominees for consideration by the Board. The Board may select from the nominees presented or may nominate additional members of the Corporation. Officers shall be elected by a majority vote of the Board members present.

2. The President shall be the chief executive officer of the Corporation and shall preside at all meetings of the Corporation. The president shall have the power of appointing committee chairmen.

3. The First Vice-President shall assume the duties of the President in his absence or inability to perform.

4. The Second Vice-President shall be responsible for the planning and coordination of the Annual Meeting of the Corporation, shall assume the duties of the First Vice-President if the First Vice-President is absent or unable to perform.

5. The Secretary shall make and keep a permanent record of all business transacted by any meeting of the Corporation and any meeting of the governing board and shall maintain a permanent file of all official correspondence of the corporation and a list of members of the Corporation.

6. The Treasurer shall make and keep a permanent record of all monies of the Corporation and all transactions involving money of the Corporation. The Treasurer shall report the financial affairs of the Corporation as required by the governing board, but not less often than annually.

7. The Executive Committee, composed of the President, immediate past President, the two Vice-Presidents, the Secretary and the Treasurer, shall have the powers of the governing board between meetings and actions of

the Executive Committee shall be submitted to the board for ratification at its next meeting.

8. In addition to the above duties and any other duties provided in these by-laws, the officers shall have such authority and perform such duties in the management of the Friends as may be provided by the Board.

9. All officers shall be elected by the Governing Board and shall hold office for such term as may be prescribed by the Board. Any officer elected or appointed may be removed with or without cause at any time by the Board.

Article V—Membership

1. The membership of the Corporation shall consist of all persons who have paid the annual dues fixed by the governing board.

2. For the purpose of fixing annual or other dues, the governing board may divide the membership into classes, but such division shall not affect the voting rights of members as hereinafter set forth.

Article VI—Membership Meetings

1. The annual meeting of the members shall be held in the first quarter of each year at a time and place designated by the Governing Board in a written notice.

2. At each meeting of the Corporation, each member shall be entitled to one vote, either in person or by proxy.

3. Special meetings may be called at any time by the President and shall be called upon the written request of four or more members of the Governing Board or ten percent (10%) or more of the members of the Friends.

4. Notice of the annual meeting and of any special meeting shall be given to all members in writing, stating the time and place of the meeting, at least five days before such a meeting. The members present shall constitute a quorum at such meetings. Proof of notice shall be filed with the Secretary.

Article VII—Governing Board Meetings

1. Regular meetings of the Governing Board may be held at such time and at such place as determined by the Board. The Secretary shall send written notice to all members of the Board at least three days before a regular meeting.

2. Special meetings of the Governing Board may be called by the President upon three days written notice to each member of the Board. Special meet-

ings shall be called by the President in like manner and on like notice at the written request of three (3) directors.

3. At all meetings of the Governing Board, six (6) members shall constitute a quorum for the transaction of all business, and the vote of a majority of the Board members present at a meeting where a quorum is present shall be the act of the Governing Board.

Article VIII—Notices

1. Notices to Governing Board Members and members shall be in writing and may be delivered personally or by mail or telegram. Notice by mail shall be deemed to be given at the time when deposited in the post office or a letter box and addressed to the members at their addresses appearing on the records of the corporation.

2. Whenever a notice is required to be given by any statute, the certificate of incorporation or these by-laws, a waiver thereof in writing, signed by the person or persons entitled to such notice, whether before or after the time stated therein, shall be deemed equivalent to such notice. In addition, any member attending a meeting of the membership in person or by proxy without protesting prior to the conclusion of the meeting the lack of notice thereof to him, and any Board member attending a meeting of the Governing Board without protesting prior to the meeting or at its commencement such lack of notice shall be conclusively deemed to have waived notice of such meeting.

Article IX—Finances

1. The fiscal year of the Corporation shall be the calendar year. The Treasurer, in consultation with the Executive Committee, shall prepare an annual budget during the last quarter of the year to reflect the best estimate of the expenses and income of the Corporation for the next year. This proposed budget shall be presented to the Board at the first meeting of the succeeding year for approval or revision. The approved budget shall be submitted for adoption by the Corporation at the annual meeting of the Corporation along with a final report of the prior year's financial statements.

2. The funds of the Corporation shall be deposited in such demand deposits or other insured investments as the Board may direct. No disbursement shall be made from these funds without the signatures of two authorized persons, one of whom must be the President or Treasurer of the Board.

3. All notes, bonds, or mortgages shall be executed on behalf of the Corporation by the President and Secretary, and then only upon appropriate resolution of the governing board.
4. The Treasurer shall furnish bond in such amount as may be deemed adequate by the governing body.

Article X—Event of Dissolution

In the event of dissolution of the Corporation, all real and personal property then owned by the Corporation shall be conveyed, transferred and paid over to such charitable corporations or purposes in such shares, amounts and proportions as the governing board shall select and determine as being most in furtherance of the Corporation's purposes and in no event shall any of the assets of the Corporation accrue to the individual benefit of any member of the governing board, officer, member or any other private individual except that the governing board may, in their discretion, pay reasonable salaries for work actually performed and may reimburse members of the governing board and officers for reasonable out-of-pocket expenses.

Article XI—Amendments

1. The Governing Board shall have power to amend, repeal or adopt by-laws at any regular or special meeting of the Board. However, any by-law adopted by the Board may be amended or repealed by vote of the members at the annual membership meeting or any special meeting.
2. If any by-law is adopted, amended or repealed by the Board, there shall be set forth in the notice of the next annual meeting of the members the by-law so adopted, amended or repealed, together with a concise statement of the changes made. Any notice of meeting of the Governing Board or members at which by-laws are to be adopted, amended or repealed shall include notice of such proposed action.

Friends of The Carnegie Library of Pittsburgh

BY-LAWS
September 1989

Article I—Name

Section 1. The name of the organization shall be FRIENDS of The Carnegie Library of Pittsburgh.

Article II—Purpose

Section 1. The purpose of the organization shall be to maintain an association of persons interested in The Carnegie Library of Pittsburgh; to focus public attention on resources and services; to receive and encourage gifts, endowments and bequests to the Library; to support and cooperate with the Library in developing library services and facilities for the community; and to support the freedom to read as expressed in the American Library Association Bill of Rights.

Section 2. No part of the net earnings of the corporation shall inure to the benefit of any member, trustee, official or individual. The corporation shall not engage in propaganda or intervention in any political campaign on behalf of any candidate for public office. No substantial part of the activities of the corporation shall involve attempts to influence legislation.

Article III—Membership

Section 1. Members Membership in the organization shall be open to any individual, association, organization or corporation interested in the purpose of the organization. Membership is active upon payment of annual dues.

Section 2. Dues and classifications Membership dues and classifications shall be as set, from time to time, by the Board of Directors.

Section 3. Voting privileges Each individual member and a representative of each association, organization and corporate member, in good standing, shall be entitled to one vote on each matter submitted to a vote at any meeting of the members.

Section 4. Removal   Any member who has not paid dues for a period exceeding 14 months shall forfeit all rights and privileges of membership and shall be removed from the membership rolls.

Article IV—Meetings

Section 1. Annual meeting   An annual meeting of the members shall be called each year by the Board of Directors for the purpose of reporting on the previous year's activities and plans for the current year and electing of Board members.

Section 2. Special meetings   Special meetings of the members may be called upon the request of 20 or more members and shall be held within 3 weeks of the date of receipt by the President of such a request. The President may at his/her discretion, and shall, upon order of the Board of Directors, call special meetings of the members.

Section 3. Notice   Written notice of meetings and the business to be transacted thereat shall be sent to each member at least 14 days in advance of the meeting, except that notice of the annual meeting and any meeting called to consider (1) the assumption of a liability of the organization in excess of the organization's current assets less outstanding obligations, or (2) dissolution of the organization, shall be mailed to each member at least 20 days in advance of such meeting.

Section 4. Quorum   The members present at any regularly scheduled meeting shall constitute a quorum for the transaction of any business which may properly come before the meeting. The acts of a majority of the members present shall be the acts of all members, except that (1) the assumption of a liability by the organization in excess of the organization's current assets less outstanding obligations, or (2) dissolution of the organization shall require the approval of at least ¾ of the members present.

Article V—Board of Directors

Section 1. Authority   The Board of Directors shall have full power to conduct, manage and direct the business and affairs of the organization.

Section 2. Terms of office   The Board of Directors shall consist of at least 11 directors elected by a majority vote of members present at the annual meeting. Each director shall be elected for a 3 year term with the exception of the initial board which shall consist of 11 directors, having terms of which as nearly as may be, ⅓ shall expire each year, appointed by the Director of The Carnegie Library of Pittsburgh. Directors may not serve more than 2 consecutive terms.

Section 3. Nominating committee   The President shall appoint a nominating committee composed of at least 4 voting members of the organization, one of whom shall be a board member. The committee shall present nominations to the Board at the Board meeting prior to the annual meeting. The names of those nominated to fill expired terms shall be sent to the general membership with the notice of the annual meeting. Elections shall be held at the annual meeting and new Board members shall assume their duties at the close of the annual meeting.

Section 4. Vacancies   The Board of Directors shall have the power to fill vacancies on the Board by a majority vote of the remaining members of the Board. A Board member so elected shall serve for the remainder of the unexpired term. A vacancy may be declared if a Board member fails to attend 3 consecutive Board meetings without notice. Prior to declaring a vacancy, the Board must notify the Board member of its intentions.

Section 5. Meetings   An annual meeting of the Board of Directors shall be held immediately following the annual meeting of the members. Special meetings of the Board may be called at the discretion of the President. Notice of the time and place of the Board meetings shall be given to each Board member not less than 7 days before the time of such meeting. Notice of any special meeting shall also include the purpose of the meeting.

Section 6. Quorum   A majority of the members of the Board of Directors shall constitute a quorum for the transaction of any business which may properly come before the meeting. The acts of a majority at such a Board meeting shall be the acts of the Board.

Article VI—Officers

The officers of the organization shall be a president, a vice president, a secretary, a treasurer and such other officers as the Board of Directors may appoint, all of whom shall be members of the Board. All officers shall be elected annually by the Board from its members at the annual meeting of the Board. In addition to the power and duties set forth in these By-laws, each officer shall have such additional powers and duties as the Board may determine.

Article VII—Duties of Officers

Section 1. President: to preside over and conduct meetings of the members and of the Board of Directors; to appoint committees and to be an ex-officio member of all committees except the nominating committee.

Section 2. Vice president: to perform the duties of the president in the absence of the president and to assist the president as requested.

Section 3. Secretary: to take attendance and minutes at all meetings of the members and the Board of Directors; to maintain membership files and records; to send meeting notices and to conduct the correspondence of the organization.

Section 4. Treasurer: to keep and maintain the financial records of the organization and to review such records with the Director and appropriate financial officers of The Carnegie Library of Pittsburgh with respect to the solicitation and receipt of dues, contributions and gifts, as well as expenditures.

Article VIII—Executive Committee

Section 1. The executive committee shall consist of the officers of the organization and the chairperson of each standing committee. The Director of The Carnegie Library of Pittsburgh shall serve, without voting privileges, as an ex-officio member of the executive committee.

Section 2. The President of the Board of Directors shall serve as chairperson of the executive committee.

Section 3. The executive committee shall exercise, in the intervals between meetings of the Board of Directors, all of the powers of the Board that may lawfully be delegated in the management of the affairs of the organization or such lesser powers as may be specified from time to time by vote of the Board.

Section 4. The executive committee shall perform, or cause to be performed, an annual audit of the organization's books of accounts.

Section 5. All actions of the executive committee shall be reported to the Board of Directors.

Section 6. The executive committee shall meet on a regular basis as determined by the President.

Section 7. A majority of the members of the executive committee shall constitute a quorum.

Article IX—Committees

The Board of Directors may, by resolution adopted by a majority of the Board members, establish standing or ad hoc committees to include one or more members of the Board. Each committee shall serve at the pleasure of the Board.

Article X—Branch/Department Council

Section 1. There shall be a Council whose purpose is to insure communication, provide mutual support and encourage coordination of activities among all The Carnegie Library of Pittsburgh FRIENDS' groups. The Council will meet at least three times a year.

Section 2. Membership in the Council shall be made up of one representative from each of The Carnegie Library of Pittsburgh's branch and department FRIENDS' groups and one member from the Board of Directors to be appointed annually by the President.

Section 3. The Board appointed Council member shall serve as chairperson of the Council and shall be responsible for reporting Council activities to the Board of Directors.

Article XI—General Funds and Liability

Section 1. General funds shall be deposited to the master account of the FRIENDS of The Carnegie Library of Pittsburgh and shall be disbursed by the treasurer upon the authorization of the Board of Directors.

Section 2. Monies raised by Branch/Department FRIENDS' groups for the support of their local Branch/Department shall be kept in separate bank accounts and those monies shall be managed by the local FRIENDS' groups. Quarterly reports of financial activity in these separate bank accounts must be submitted to the treasurer of the organization in a designated format.

Section 3. An auditor appointed by the Board of Directors shall audit the books of account at the end of the fiscal year which will run from January 1 to December 31.

Section 4. To the fullest extent that the laws of the Commonwealth of Pennsylvania permit elimination or limitation of the liability of Board of Directors members, no Board member or officer shall be personally liable for monetary damages as such for any action taken or any failure to take any action as a Board member.

Section 5. Each Board member and officer of the organization and each other person denominated by the Board as so entitled shall be entitled as of right to such indemnification by the organization and to such rights and privileges related thereto or may from time to time be provided in the By-laws.

Section 6. Neither the Board of Directors nor the officers shall have any authority to borrow money or incur an indebtedness or liability, other than current expenses, in the name of or on behalf of the organization.

Section 7. No contract shall be entered into and no obligation shall be incurred beyond the amount on hand or in the bank after deducting therefrom, or providing for, the total of all unpaid accounts and unpaid obligations and liabilities.

Article XII—Amendments

These By-laws may be amended, upon recommendation of the Board of Directors, at any meeting of the members, after notification in writing to each member at least 14 days before the meeting at which the voting is to take place.

Article XIII—Dissolution

Section 1. In the event of the dissolution of the corporation, and prior to the completion thereof, all liabilities and obligations of the corporation shall be paid, satisfied and discharged, and all of the remaining assets, property and income owned or held by the corporation shall be expended or applied to the purposes of the corporation, or one or more of such purposes, by transferring and conveying such assets, property and income to one or more corporations or organizations organized and operated exclusively for religious, charitable, scientific, literary or educational purposes, to which exemption from income taxes has been granted under Section 501(c)(3) of the Internal Revenue Code of 1986 (or the corresponding provision of any future United States Internal Revenue Law), and no part of such remaining assets, property or income shall be distributed to members or to any other persons whatsoever.

Revised 9/90

Friends of Military Libraries

CONSTITUTION AND BY-LAWS

Article I—Name

This organization shall be known as Friends of Military Libraries, and hereinafter referred to as FRIENDS.

Article II—Purpose

The purpose of the FRIENDS group is:

1. Assist military libraries in focusing public attention on library programs, facilities, services, and activities.
2. Stimulate use of library's resources and services.
3. Raise funds to enhance and improve the overall operation of the library, to include encouraging and receiving gifts and/or donations for use and benefit of the library.

Article III—Membership

Section 1. Membership is open to all eligible MWR patrons and members of the civilian community, nominated and approved by the Executive Board, interested in military libraries and sponsored by an eligible patron.

Section 2. The holder of an individual or family membership shall be entitled to one vote at all regular and special meetings of FRIENDS. Young Friends (under 16) and affiliates are not entitled to vote.

Section 3. There is no minimum age to be a member, however, individuals under the age of 16 years of age will be designated as (non-voting) Young Friends.

Section 4. There will be four categories of membership and corresponding dues:

      A. Individual — (One person) .... $ 5.00
      B. Family — (More than one person) $10.00
      C. Young Friend — (Under the age of 16) .... $ 2.00
      D. Affiliated — (Any private business or organization
                         wanting to support military libraries) $25.00

Article IV—Dues

Section 1. The dues of FRIENDS shall be determined by the Executive Board in August and published in September, payable annually on the first of October. Persons new to the area may pay their initial dues on a prorata basis. Membership dues will be effective from 1 October through 30 September of each year.

Section 2. Members in arrears after one month will be ineligible to vote in FRIENDS elections or on expenditure of funds. Members whose dues are in arrears may rejoin by paying back dues.

Article V—Meetings

Section 1. Regular meetings will be held at least twice each calendar year at a time and place designated by the president.

Section 2. The Executive Board shall meet at least once each month at a time and place designated by the president.

Section 3. One-fourth of the number of active members present, in good standing, will constitute a quorum at any regular meeting.

Article VI—Executive Board

Section 1. The Executive Board shall consist of elected officers, program coordinator, and at-large members of the group that have been appointed by the elected officers.

Section 2. The Executive Board shall approve all fund-raising and other activities, by a simple majority of the board members present. A majority of the board members shall constitute a quorum.

Section 3. In case of a tie, the president shall cast the deciding vote.

Article VII—Officers/Duties/Nominations/Elections/Term of Office

Section 1. Office/Duties: (Members filling the President, Vice-President, Secretary, and Treasurer shall be 18 years of age or older.)

A. *President* shall: schedule and preside at all meetings of FRIENDS; appoint members to positions requiring qualifications or special skills/ knowledge, to include project coordinators; appoint committee chairpersons as required; decide on all matters not requiring a vote by the board of directors and/or general membership; be elected by a majority vote of the membership present at elections and shall preside until the next election.

B. *Vice-President* shall: assume the presidency if a vacancy occurs; preside in the absence of the President; be elected by a majority vote of the membership present at the elections and shall preside until the next election.

C. *Secretary* shall: attend all meetings of FRIENDS and maintain an accurate written record of all business; conduct all correspondence for FRIENDS, e.g. publicity, history, minutes, letters; be responsible for maintaining a current roster of active members and project coordinators; be elected by a majority vote of the membership present at the elections and shall preside until the next election.

D. *Treasurer* shall: establish and maintain records of the checking account; submit financial reports to the Commanding Officer annually outlining the financial status and activities of FRIENDS; prepare and submit to the board of directors, at scheduled meetings, a written financial statement covering financial transactions subsequent to the last meeting/report; collect all incoming revenue, make all payments and other disbursements, and maintain accurate records of the FRIENDS treasury; notify FRIENDS Secretary of members delinquent with their dues; be elected by a majority vote of the membership present at the elections and shall preside until the next election.

E. *Program Coordinator* shall: be a member appointed by the current president to serve as the central point of contact for all programs and activities initiated by FRIENDS during the elected term of the president, to include being the coordinator for committee activities and serving as the committee representative; be a voting member for the board of directors.

Section 2. There will be a nomination committee consisting of three members appointed by the President two months prior to the annual election. This committee will present the proposed slate not later than one month prior to the election.

Section 3. Officers of FRIENDS shall be elected in September of the current year by a written ballot, to assume office on October 1. A majority of the vote cast shall constitute an election.

Section 4. Should simultaneous vacancies occur in the office of President and Vice-President, a special election will be held to fill these vacancies.

Article VIII—Amendments

These By-Laws may be amended at any regular meeting, providing a quorum is present and if notice of the proposed amendment or amendments has been given at the previous meeting.

Article IX—General Provisions

FRIENDS constitution and any by-laws shall be incorporated by a majority vote of members present at a general membership meeting. Any proposed revisions shall be promulgated thirty days in advance of the meeting at which the revision will be voted upon. Any revision will be approved by a majority vote of members present at a general membership meeting. All changes must be submitted to the Commanding Officers, NAS Pensacola and NTTC Corry Station. All funds raised and related activities of FRIENDS shall be for the sole purpose of supporting military library programs.

Article X—Dissolution

Upon dissolution of the FRIENDS, all assets shall be equally divided and revert to and become property of military libraries designated by the Executive Board for use at the library only.

Friends of Libraries U.S.A. Fact Sheets

#1
How to Organize a Friends Group

1. Determine the purpose of the group and the need for a group. This should be done with the librarian and a small core of concerned citizens.

2. Select a steering committee to reflect your community and the needs of the group. It is important to have access to a lawyer, PR and advertising talent, and high-profile leaders.

3. Work on federal and state tax-exempt status with a lawyer's help so that when you collect dues, they will be deductible. At the same time work on a constitution and bylaws.

4. Define your dues structure and membership categories.

5. Decide on a membership brochure, artwork, and how you will reproduce and distribute the brochure.

6. Begin your publicity campaign in the community. Be sure to involve elected officials, trustees, and other interested parties.

7. Decide on a tentative schedule for the first year to involve new members on committees as soon as they join.

8. If fund-raising is important, have your campaign in place and goals set. People like to know where their money is going (see Fact Sheet #2).

9. Set an opening meeting date. Plan your program carefully. Have a *brief* agenda for the first annual meeting.

10. Develop a long-range plan for Friends. Reevaluate it periodically.

For more information and ideas, join Friends of Libraries U.S.A., 1700 Walnut St., Ste. 715, Philadelphia, PA 19103.

#2
Fund-Raising

1. Obtain tax-exempt status. There will be lawyers in your area who will do this for you on an in-kind basis.

2. There is always competition with other worthy projects. Present your case with facts, benefits, and reasons for giving.

3. Project confidence in the fund-raising organization by having community leaders head the campaign. This encourages donors to give with the knowledge that their gifts will be used wisely and effectively.

4. Personal contacts—eyeball to eyeball—have never been challenged as the best way to approach prospective donors.

5. Leadership gifts are important. Go after the biggest donors first. Send the right person at the right time to the right prospect for the right amount.

6. Advise prospects about what will be done with their gifts. Maximize what your organization does with donations. Minimize expenses.

7. Canvass your population. Address any audience that will sit still . . . women's clubs, veterans' organizations, civic clubs, church and synagogue groups, library groups, and PTAs. Stay with your audience, but lead them in your presentation.

8. Accept cash, checks, or pledges. Ninety percent of the people who make pledges honor them. In-kind gifts are appropriate, as are memorials and endowments.

9. Remember: Leadership is the key!

10. Finally—*Don't forget to say thank you* to both workers and donors!

Join Friends of Libraries U.S.A. and learn what other groups are doing! Write to: Friends of Libraries U.S.A., 1700 Walnut St., Ste. 715, Philadelphia, PA 19103.

#3
A Checklist for Planning Successful Programs

1. People lead busy lives; don't hold a program just because there is space in the calendar. Have a clear idea of the program purpose.

2. The program committee should be large enough to handle the necessary tasks so that no one person feels too overburdened. Call on other committees for support depending on the type of program.

3. Publicity is a key ingredient. Have experienced people be responsible for publicity, and determine media contacts and deadlines.

4. Set up a realistic timetable so that all concerned have a clear expectation of the time involved.

5. Evaluate each event afterward. If your audience evaluations are good, don't be discouraged if a program doesn't draw the numbers you expect. Often, unforeseen events can change the attendance at a program.

6. Look for other community organizations to share the responsibility of the program. Two invitation lists are better than one, and you can expose more people to Friends of Libraries.

7. Some potential pitfalls: poor timing, inadequate notification, careless organization, unclear delegation of responsibilities, not enough participants involved, inadequate or poorly timed publicity.

8. Possible sources of ideas and materials: *FOLUSA's News Update, Friends of Libraries Sourcebook* published by ALA, books, local interest, political necessity, current trends.

For more information and ideas, join Friends of Libraries U.S.A. Write to Friends of Libraries U.S.A., 1700 Walnut St., Ste. 715, Philadelphia, PA 19103.

#4
How to Organize an Academic Friends Group

1. Obtain support of the library administration, the development office, and the administration of the parent institution.

2. Establish a liaison position in the library with a specific time designated for Friends activities.

3. Select a steering committee of concerned people from the alumni, faculty, student body, and local community. Include a liaison with the development office. It is important to have access to the institution's lawyer, PR and advertising talent, and high-profile leaders.

4. Define your dues structure, membership categories, and prerequisites.

5. Clarify tax status of *Friends groups or of the parent institution* so that when you collect dues they will be deductible *by the member.*

6. Define the mission to be fulfilled by the Friends, and develop a constitution and bylaws reflecting this mission.

7. Decide on a membership brochure, artwork, and how you will reproduce and distribute the brochure.

8. Begin your publicity campaign. Be sure to involve university public relations and development offices, the alumni office, and the local media.

9. Decide on a tentative schedule for the first year to involve new members on committees as soon as they join.

10. Set a date for an opening meeting. Plan the program carefully. Have a *brief* agenda for first annual meeting.

11. Develop a long-range plan for Friends. Reevaluate it periodically. When fundraising becomes feasible, develop a campaign and set goals (see Fact Sheet #2).

For more information and ideas, join Friends of Libraries U.S.A. Write to: Friends of Libraries U.S.A., 1700 Walnut St., Ste. 715, Philadelphia, PA 19103.

#5
How to Organize a Junior Friends of the Library Group

1. Decide on goals for the group. These could include motivation to use the library, physical help in the library, decorating, help with story hours, etc., or a combination of these. Parents or a member of the Friends usually serve as adult leaders. Staff members must not be expected to assume this responsibility. However, they should be involved with program ideas, projects ideas, publicity, and scheduling.

2. Target the age range of members, based on the availability of adult sponsors. They can include grades K–1, 2–4, 5–8, 9–12. Start with a workable group; you can always expand your goals.

3. Set dues, even if they are very low. It increases the importance of the group. The adult Friends may set aside funds for Junior Friends, especially in the formative stages, and provide refreshments, membership cards, etc.

4. Hold an organizational meeting. Depending on the age of the group, present bylaws and discuss potential programs and projects.

5. Select/elect officers, if desirable.

6. Appoint committees, being sure to involve everyone in at least one committee. Suggested committees: Program, Projects, Membership, Publicity.

7. Potential projects for Junior Friends include Junior Great Books, decorating for holidays, clipping for files, sponsoring various contests, giving book reviews for peers, and helping with story hours and community festivities.

8. Always keep the business portion of meetings brief.

9. Keep work and fun projects in balance.

10. Do not let adults assume responsibility for planning. Members should make decisions with the *assistance* of adults, being careful not to plan projects that are too ambitious.

For more information, join Friends of Libraries U.S.A. and be part of our network of Friends of the Library groups. Write: Friends of Libraries U.S.A., 1700 Walnut St., Ste. 715, Philadelphia, PA 19103.

#6
How to Organize a Friends of a School Library Group

1. Determine the purpose of the group. The goal might be the improvement of the library media program; objectives would include a volunteer group, involvement of parents, children, alumni, and faculty.

2. Identify and develop a core of lay leaders; the librarian and administration are resources whose involvement and approval are crucial to success.

3. Acquaint the Friends with the basic philosophy and requirements for an effective media program. Define the organizational structure and the dues structure.

4. Develop a membership campaign.

5. Plan an orientation program for volunteers and demonstrations for other members. Explain school policies and procedures and pertinent state and national standards.

6. Begin your publicity campaign. Use letters to parents, news articles, and speeches emphasizing how school libraries can make a difference in the education of children.

7. Keep careful records, and periodically evaluate the program.

8. Build in recognition for Friends and volunteers.

9. Decide if Junior Friends could be an adjunct program (see FOLUSA Fact Sheet #5).

For more information and ideas, join Friends of Libraries U.S.A. Write: Friends of Libraries U.S.A., 1700 Walnut St., Ste. 715, Philadelphia, PA 19103.

#7
Holding a Readathon

A Readathon is an event held for a limited time, featuring a variety of people consecutively reading out loud. The materials read, the age of the readers, the time elapsed, and the site may vary.

1. Decide on a theme or hook: literacy, favorite books, children's books, etc. This is necessary for publicity.

2. Pick out a site: library steps, city hall, village fair?
   Consider logistics: What are rain plans (tent)?
   Consider heat, cold, wind, and street noise.
   You'll need rest rooms, refreshments, and chairs for readers; reading material for those who come unprepared. Are permits needed? Do police have to be notified?

3. Decide on a time span for the Readathon: 2 hours, 4 hours, 12 hours, 24 hours? Decide on the length of time for each reader—3–5 minutes is suggested. Stick to it!

4. Line up readers and an excellent emcee. Use public figures from government, sports, business, academia, entertainment and literary fields, ethnic communities, and local clubs and fill in with Friends. Ask the mayor to be the first reader.

5. Get the best audio system possible. Test it. Book a photographer. Make plans for getting an audience.

6. Prepare and send out news releases and public service announcements. Get support from local media—have you included them in your list of readers?

7. Follow up publicity releases with phone calls.

8. Have banners or signs at the site for maximum publicity.

9. Have adequate volunteers available for the event.

10. Follow-up: Write thank-you letters, send pictures to local papers and newsletters, and evaluate the event for the next time.

For more information, join Friends of Libraries U.S.A., 1700 Walnut St., Ste. 715, Philadelphia, PA 19103.

#8
How to Revitalize Your Friends Group

1. Define problem areas for the group (or board of directors). Confidential phone calls to directors or membership dropouts will help.

2. Give a party for members and past members only. It should be fun and have refreshments and music. Any excuse will do for the party: holiday, author, recognition, social evening. A private home will make it special.

3. Be sure to include the dropouts and get small amounts of help from many people to ensure attendance. Have various people be responsible for bringing food and necessary articles.

4. Send out preevent and postevent publicity with names and photos. Make the Friends look like a fun and meaningful group.

5. With the information you should now have, reevaluate your goals and objectives. Did you have too broad a mission? Were you stressing fund-raising to the neglect of other activities?

6. Reorganize the board of directors, adding positions and breaking down responsibilities so that individuals do not have too great a burden. Enlarge committees.

7. Review the benefits of membership, making sure they are in line with what your community expects.

8. Review communications to members; are they being kept informed? Are you taking advantage of the materials FOLUSA provides through *News Update* and programs?

9. Consider enrolling new members as a year-round effort, not limited to a certain period. Be sure brochures are available at every event and at the library desk.

10. Be sure to appreciate and recognize efforts of every magnitude. Recognition is of primary importance to volunteers.

For more information, join Friends of Libraries U.S.A., 1700 Walnut St., Ste. 715, Philadelphia, PA 19103.

#9
Getting Involved with Literacy Programs

Two of every five Americans are illiterate. An even greater number are aliterate—able to read but not interested in doing so. Libraries and Library Friends can make a difference. Following are some steps to help others along the path that means so much to us.

Direct Service

1. Participate in local literacy groups as a trustee or member of an advisory committee.
2. Generate financial resources by helping the library or literacy groups apply for federal, state, and local funds and by developing corporate and foundation grants.
3. Donate funds for (a) tutor and student recognition, (b) public awareness campaigns, (c) social events to foster enthusiasm, (d) materials for adult new readers, (e) general operations for new or existing programs.
4. Donate equipment or space.
5. Volunteer to (a) be a literacy tutor, (b) help in the office, (c) provide child care, (d) provide transportation for students or tutors.

Indirect Service

1. Create a committee within the Friends board to maintain contact with literacy programs. Network with other organizations to ensure a proactive campaign for literacy by the library.
2. Create or join a citywide council in conjunction with the mayor's office.
3. Educate business, labor, and industry leaders about literacy issues and encourage their contact with literacy providers. Send letters to business leaders. Publish a newsletter. Sponsor an informational conference or luncheon.
4. Compile a resource directory on community literacy programs.
5. Provide programs and speakers for other organizations on the problems of illiteracy and the work of literacy agencies.
6. Initiate activites such as a marketing campaign for literacy services.

Join Friends of Libraries U.S.A. and learn what other groups are doing: Write to Friends of Libraries U.S.A., 1700 Walnut St., Ste. 715, Philadelphia, PA 19103.

#10
Planning a Book and Author Event

1. Line up a cosponsor for the event. A local newspaper, department store, or bookstore are good options.

2. Decide on author(s), working with a date of the planned event. Invite local or regional authors when possible. You may also want to take advantage of promotional tours. Be realistic. Don't expect Toni Morrison to speak! Contact authors far in advance through their publishers' publicists. The *Literary Market Place* is a good source of information.

3. Invite the cohost to introduce the author. Ask hosts to share costs with in-kind services, such as printing the program, invitations, or free ads in their publications. Make plans for getting advance and follow-up coverage in the media.

4. Ask local merchants to donate cheese, wine, goodies for a preevents reception. Be sure to give credit for the donations on the program, in news releases, and during introductions.

5. Make a fuss. Authors like to be catered to. Offer to entertain them at cocktails, dinner, a quick tour, etc., if they are interested. Many authors enjoy talking to a writing class if time permits.

6. Make sure you invite the county chair, mayor, chancellor, heads of departments, local council representatives—the men and women who make decisions concerning the library. Often this makes an appropriate event to honor someone who has made a special contribution to the library.

7. Remember, most authors are there to sell books. Plan in advance to have copies available for sale and autographing. This is very important. Order more than you expect to sell. You can always return them, but authors are upset if books run out. This is also a way to earn 40 percent of the proceeds, if you order yourself instead of through a bookstore.

8. Make sure someone is familiar with the author's work and can talk knowledgeably with him or her about it.

9. Consult the *Friends of Libraries Sourcebook* for detailed program planning outlines to check your final arrangements.

Join Friends of Libraries U.S.A. and learn what other groups are doing! Write to Friends of Libraries U.S.A., 1700 Walnut St., Ste. 715, Philadelphia, PA 19103.

#11a
Friends and Trustees

Friends and trustees are citizens who choose to help their local libraries. Their goals are similar, but their paths to achieve them differ. The following guidelines are designed to help clarify their joint missions and facilitate working together for the good of the library.

Friends are citizens who value the service of public libraries and volunteer to help them. Friends usually operate with a self-elected board of directors, representing the community.

1. Friends may be future trustees and trustees future Friends; however, there should be no overlapping boards.
2. Friends are kept informed of the library's plans, progress, and problems.
3. Friends recognize that they do not perform a policy-making role for the library, but they should feel that their opinions are valued by the trustees.
4. Friends support trustee board decisions.
5. Friends serve as "connecting links" between the library and community, interpreting one to the other.
6. Friends supplement what cannot be provided by the library budget with funds, materials, equipment, and services. Friends decide how to spend their money after conferring with the librarian and the library board.
7. Fund-raising by the Friends is done with the knowledge of the trustees and in coordination with the library director.
8. Individually and collectively, Friends use their influence to assist the library in obtaining desired financial support, representing the library point of view to legislators and the media.
9. A Friends written policy should include representation or liaison with the trustees.
10. Friends learn more by joining Friends of Libraries U.S.A. and their state organization.

For more information, write to: Friends of Libraries U.S.A., 1700 Walnut St., Ste. 715, Philadelphia, PA 19103.

#11b
Trustees and Friends

Trustees are a small number of people elected or appointed to represent the community and, as a body, are legally and officially responsible for the operation of the library.

It is the responsibility of the trustees board to employ the best person possible as library director, to adopt a long- and short-range plan for library service to meet the needs of the community, and to implement policies needed to carry out the plan.

1. Trustees officially adopt a budget, working with the library director. Budget hearings should be attended with the library director and with a representative of the Friends.

2. A "wish list" of items not covered by the budget should be made available to the Friends to aid them in their fund-raising effort.

3. Trustees serve as "connecting links" between the library and community, interpreting one to the other. Individually they uphold adopted policies of the board.

4. Trustees value and encourage input and opinions of Friends, recognizing that this is representative of the community.

5. Individually and collectively, trustees should act as advocates of libraries and present the library point of view to their locally and nationally elected legislators and leaders.

6. The library policy should include representation or liaison with the Friends.

7. Trustees should attend Friends' events whenever possible.

8. At least yearly, the library board should plan a joint meeting to discuss mutual concerns with Friends. This can be done in conjunction with a breakfast or dinner meeting.

9. Trustees should belong to the American Library Trustee Association (ALTA). Membership includes a subscription to the journal, *American Libraries*.

For more information, write to: ALTA, 50 E. Huron St., Chicago, IL 60611.

#12
Designating a Literary Landmark

1. Select a landmark that is tied to a literary figure or work or its author.

2. Identify a group or individual who will be responsible for the site and guarantee its continued designation.

3. Compile background material that corroborates the role of the site and a bibliography of the author's work and related writings.

4. Apply for Literary Landmark designation by writing to Rosemary Jones, FOLUSA/Literary Landmarks Register, 901 E. Las Olas Boulevard, Ft. Lauderdale, FL 33301.

5. Discuss cooperative efforts for cosponsorship with other local or state groups (e.g., historical society, Federation of Women's Clubs, Chamber of Commerce, Restaurant and Hotel Association, colleges and newspapers).

6. Identify a speaker on the subject for the ceremony. It is also probable that there is an individual to honor who has made a special effort on behalf of the site.

7. Plan a public event. Line up a cosponsor for the event. A local newspaper, department store, or bookstore are good options (see Fact Sheet #10: Planning a Book and Author Event).

8. Invite local decision makers who finance cultural institutions and invite people on mailing lists of the cosponsors.

9. Check the *Friends of Libraries Sourcebook* for detailed program planning outlines to check your final arrangements.

Join Friends of Libraries U.S.A. and learn what other groups are doing! Write to Friends of Libraries U.S.A., 1700 Walnut St., Ste. 715, Philadelphia, PA 19103.

#13
Checklist for Advocacy

1. Consult with the library staff to define problem areas for your local library regarding current and pending legislation and local legislative support.

2. Develop a clear, specific strategy with limited, easily understood objectives regarding those areas or persons you wish to influence. One or two action items a year is realistic.

3. Find ways to communicate your story. Form a communications task force; don't hesitate to ask for *pro bono* help. Illuminate the issue. Produce a one-page fact sheet as a handout.

4. Consider everyone in your community as a potential ally. "All politics is local."

5. Ask politicians to be of assistance. Work with their staff. Work with potential candidates for office.

6. Use any method you can: hand-delivered notes, phone calls, letters to local media, and telegrams. Use the resources of the Friends to find local connections to decision makers.

7. Keep in touch and involved with the opposition. Keep issue oriented; don't personalize the conflict. The next issue may be one you agree on.

8. Plan immediately for the next issue, taking advantage of what was learned.

9. Establish permanent contacts with political staff. The personal touch is very important.

Join Friends of Libraries U.S.A. and learn what other groups are doing! Write to Friends of Libraries U.S.A., 1700 Walnut St., Ste. 715, Philadelphia, PA 19103.

#14
Board Development Strategy

1. Keep your board of directors relevant. The original board may not reflect the current needs of your organization.

2. Established terms of office and rotation of leadership are vital to a dynamic organization.

3. Turnover of a portion of the board of directors should occur periodically and should be a part of the bylaws of the organization. Good members can be retained by membership on committees or by asking them to serve again after a lapse of a year or two.

4. Consciously review the roles and responsibilities of the board each year as changes occur on the board and within the library institution.

5. The context of the mission of the group defines who should be on the board. Choices might include: prominent citizens from various constituencies; members of emerging communities; politicians; specialists in law, marketing, computers, and accounting; and givers and doers in the community.

6. Nonvoting liaisons to the board can include prospective board members, liaisons to other groups, those concerned with the governance of the library, local philanthropies, and school and other cultural institution administration for outreach development.

7. Establish a human resources committee for the cultivation of new board recruits and their orientation.

8. A continuing long-term appraisal of the needs and performance of the board is necessary.

9. Younger officers and key people in corporate settings and smaller companies are an excellent and often neglected source of board members. They can help with leadership, financial support, advocacy, and volunteers. They want to be seen as good citizens and should be given a visible role.

Join Friends of Libraries U.S.A. and learn what other groups are doing! Write to: Friends of Libraries U.S.A., 1700 Walnut St., Ste. 715, Philadelphia, PA 19103.

#15
Moving to Center Stage in the Community

Friends of Libraries groups have to become visible players in the life of the community to have equal footing with other, perhaps more socially involved, nonprofits.

1. Inventory the notable organizations and associations in the community. Identify those that do and do not have a library voice among their leadership. Make it your goal to place a voice on those boards where it is lacking.

2. The library director or a member of the Friends or board of trustees should participate in the Rotary Club; the Chamber of Commerce should be aware of the necessity of a good library system to the business economy.

3. City or villagewide celebrations should list the library as one of their sponsors. Whether it's a display at the library or a booth or float at the event, the library should participate through its Friends.

4. The Friends should set up a correspondence committee to write guest editorials for local publications about the library or to write a periodic column in local newspapers. Letters to the editor are another opportunity to gain attention.

5. Nurture media contacts and provide advance notices when there is a special Friends program. Don't abuse this, as TV time and editorial space is limited.

6. Local elected government officials should be on the Friends regular mailing list even if they're not members. They should receive invitations to library events followed up with phone calls when there's a good photo opportunity. They should also be invited for occasional private briefings on library issues.

7. Ask for liaisons to other institutions or clubs or invite a representative from them to brief your board about events or issues of mutual interest. Plus, serve on community boards as a representative of the library.

8. Coproduce when possible if there is some event or display in the community that could be further illuminated by a library program. Don't be afraid of capitalizing on the interest generated.

9. Take advantage of any opportunity or venue to bring up the library. The Friends should provide a speaker's bureau with information from the library.

Join Friends of Libraries U.S.A. and learn about other groups! Write to Friends of Libraries U.S.A., 1700 Walnut St., Ste. 715, Philadelphia, PA 19103.

#16
How to Organize a Friends Foundation

The primary reason to form a foundation is to create a funding source separate and distinct from the regulations and restrictions that apply to any governmental institution. The foundation can establish its own rules and buy equipment or provide services for the library without regard to competitive bidding, committee approvals, etc. The library Friends group and the library foundation are clearly separate groups. The foundation is usually formed when larger amounts of money are needed than can be raised by the Friends group, and these funds can then be invested until they are disbursed.

1. Contact a lawyer to develop documents pertaining to foundations, such as articles of incorporation and bylaws (necessary for limited liability), and to obtain federal and state tax-exempt status.

2. Select a steering committee or board of directors that will reflect your community and the needs of your library. Define your needs and mission statement with this group.

3. It is usually helpful to have lawyers, bankers, and public relations and marketing people as well as high-profile community and corporate leaders serve on the full board.

4. It is often necessary to hire a director for the foundation with fund-development experience. Disbursement of the funds is normally decided between the foundation board and the library director.

5. Monies raised are often best looked after and invested by bank trust companies or other money managers. A survey of your community will help you determine where to place your funds.

6. Opportunities abound for fund-raising. The Friends of Libraries U.S.A. *News Update* and its office can provide many ideas. The foundation is an excellent vehicle to promote a deferred-giving program.

7. Be sure to involve elected officials, library trustees, and other interested parties in the development of the foundation.

8. Develop a long-range plan for the foundation, and periodically reevaluate it with your foundation board of directors and the librarian.

9. Maintain a liaison to the Friends of the Library and to the trustees to keep open lines of communication.

Join Friends of Libraries U.S.A., 1700 Walnut St., Ste. 715, Philadelphia, PA 19103.

Broward County Library Foundation's Children's Reading Festival

The following is a proposal for corporate sponsorship opportunities connected with one of Broward County Library Foundation's newest fund-raising efforts. Notice how it is positioned to appeal to a wide audience but has specific targets within the proposal that satisfy various sponsor needs.

"LOVE ME, READ TO ME"
1996 CHILDREN'S READING FESTIVAL

Thousands of children and their families will attend a countywide Children's Reading Festival over the weekend of April 22, 1995, at the Broward County Main Library. This year we will celebrate with the theme book *The Little Engine That Could*. The Festival will be preceded by a special in-service day on Friday for teachers, librarians, child care providers, and educators from around the state.

The Festival includes creative activities, storytelling, favorite storybook characters, musical and dramatic performances, events with authors, and opportunities for children to read and perform themselves.

Activities take place inside and outside the Main Library in downtown Fort Lauderdale, the streets surrounding the library, and sites of the Downtown Cultural Arts District.

The Children's Reading Festival is dedicated to promoting a literate and educated society—a nation of readers.

The Audience

Three million people visit the thirty branches of the Broward library system each year. More than 500,000 children and adults participate in family programs and activities throughout the year.

An estimated 1.2 million readers will be exposed to media promotion of the Festival.

An estimated 35,000–40,000 will attend the 1996 Children's Reading Festival (1995 figures were 35,000 attendees).

One thousand teachers, librarians, and child-care providers are invited to attend an in-service professional conference. Approximately 300 attend.

Goals

1. To present special activities and events for children that will delight their imaginations, stimulate their minds and bodies, and encourage reading and learning
2. To involve families through dynamic cultural and educational programs and hands-on activities
3. To share information with parents and educators about the importance of reading aloud to children
4. To present in-service training for professionals about current developments and innovations in children's literature
5. To promote reading as essential to learning for now and into adulthood
6. To expand the children's collection throughout the library system
7. To increase awareness of the library as a valuable community resource in the education of children
8. To increase awareness of other community organizations dedicated to children and families

Benefits to Sponsor

The opportunity to associate with a proven, well-established community-wide event, the ONLY event of its kind in South Florida.

Anticipated audience at the 1995 Festival is at least 35,000. The *Sun Sentinel* is the major media sponsor. WPBT2 Public Television is another media sponsor. Media sponsors provide approximately $100,000 in promotional time/space. Other corporate sponsors include Blockbuster Entertainment Corporation, NationsBank, American Airlines, Motorola, Target Stores, the City of Fort Lauderdale, and the Friends of the Fort Lauderdale Library.

Support for the Festival provides the sponsor with comprehensive, positive exposure throughout South Florida.

The Festival provides the sponsor with the opportunity to promote its image and products, generate in-store traffic with special cross-promotions, and increase awareness among your key demographic of families and children. It also provides you with a $100,000 promotional campaign linked with reading, literacy, and the South Florida community.

Title Sponsorships include:

Great Book Giveaway

The Great Book Giveaway allows the sponsor expanded media exposure and increased awareness for specific product(s) and sampling tied to this special promotion within the Festival. The Great Book Giveaway provides FREE BOOKS for children who redeem "coupons" or an identifying product label at the Festival. Anyone coming into the store or purchasing the product and providing the label/coupon at the Festival will be given a FREE BOOK from the contributing sponsor. The sponsor's name will also be acknowledged with a bookplate inside each book. Elements include:

- Special media campaign with sponsor's logo included in all event advertising.
- Retail outlets give coupons to customers who exchange them at Festival for a free children's book. Special title area for promotion manned by library staff during Festival. Special signage provided.
- Promotion of Great Book Giveaway in all libraries and participating schools and education centers.
- Costumed mascots for guest appearances at selected stores prior to Festival.
- Special media campaign in *Sun-Sentinel* valued at $30,000.

Sponsorship: $17,000

Performance Stages

The Festival has three stages designated for major sponsors. All activities and performances on these stages will be acknowledged to title major sponsor.

Sponsorship: $15,000

Food for Thought

A special promotion to tie in products could be worked out with coupons/labels. This would all be promoted under the Foundation's efforts to provide educational resources for children and families.

Books and educational materials would be purchased for children's libraries tied to product purchases. The library card campaign could also be tied into promotion. Sign-up for card at selected stores with special purchase, with percentage of proceeds designated for Festival or Foundation efforts.

Sponsorship: $10,000

Children's Authors

The Festival brings in noted children's authors for readings, book signings, and writing classes for children.

Sponsorship: $10,000

Museum Row

The Festival will provide booths for local and regional museums and galleries to display art and art-related activities. These include the Morikami Museum (Japanese and Asian-American art), Fort Lauderdale Museum of Art, Young at Art, and Broward Children's Museum.

Sponsorship: $7,500

Arts and Crafts

Hands-on activities related to the arts and education, including face painting, puppet making, drawing, computer games, and the art of storytelling.

Sponsorship: $5,000

Library Card Campaign

Children and families are encouraged to sign up for library cards at the Festival. All those who sign up will be given incentives, e.g., photos, games, puzzles, books, etc. Special prepromotion with library card sign-ups in selected areas around the community is available.

Sponsorship: $5,000

Exhibits

The Festival will feature several national touring exhibits especially designed for children and families on such topics as health care, fitness, environment, recycling, parenting, animal care, education, performing arts, and cultural arts. Sponsorship is per exhibit.

Sponsorship: $5,000

Health/Fitness Area

The 1996 Children's Reading Festival will once again provide a special health and fitness area for children and their families. This year's theme book is *The Little Engine That Could.*

Themes of self-esteem, pride, achievement, and participation will be stressed with all of the activities that will be provided in the Health and Fitness area. Activities will include:

- Health and fitness Olympics
- Health and nutrition presentations
- "Leaders Are Readers" Read-In
- Rap "Slams"

Prizes will be awarded, and children will be recognized for their participation with special incentives.

Sponsorship Opportunities

Great Book Giveaway	$17,000
Performance Stages	15,000
Food for Thought	10,000
Children's Authors	10,000
Museum Row	7,500
Arts and Crafts	5,000
Library Campaign	5,000
Activity Areas	5,000

Health Care/Fitness
Environment/Recycling
Animal Care
Education
Parenting
Performing Arts
Cultural Arts

Benefits
County-wide promotion will acknowledge sponsors

- The *Sun-Sentinel's* participation ensures extensive publicity and promotion. The *Sentinel* provides a series of ads promoting the Festival up to six weeks prior to the Festival (valued at approximately $60,000).
- Other media sponsors ensure wide exposure through television and radio.
- Sponsor will be included in all publicity and promotion released by the library and the Foundation. Promotion materials include

    100,000 "Love Me, Read to Me" programs distributed to all library branches and through schools in Broward County

    50,000 flyers distributed through county libraries, schools, and family and children's organizations

    50,000 bookmarks distributed through county libraries and family and children's organizations

    25,000 programs

    25,000 copies of monthly library calendar, *Bookings*

    6,000 copies of Foundation newsletter, *Focus*

    300 posters distributed throughout county

    Banners displayed at selected library branches, main library, and selected sites throughout county

Bus signs on all county buses

Signage at all Festival sites

- Recognition of sponsorship and introduction of sponsor at opening ceremonies of Festival
- Recognition at special dinner honoring sponsors

Additional Benefits

- Visible leadership role in a major county-wide project associated with children and families
- Opportunity to reach thousands of young children and families by providing positive, family-oriented activities
- Opportunity to provide programs that would not otherwise be available for children and families
- Opportunity to associate with the Broward County Library
  The Library is one of the few institutions that has a county-wide network reaching *all* segments of the population. Broward County residents like the library, and they use it! A recent study commissioned by the County states,
    The library system is well utilized by the county's citizens. . . . The library system might well serve as a model for the delivery of cultural and educational services on a county-wide basis.
- Opportunity to associate with other major corporate sponsors who support county efforts

Conclusion

With your generous support the Foundation will be able to expand the scope and impact of the 1996 Children's Reading Festival. Thousands more children and families can attend and enjoy a weekend filled with activities and events designed to celebrate the joys of learning.

We continue to grow and provide programs and services to our community through private support. The library system is now the twelfth largest public library system in the country with a population base of 1.2 million residents and more than 500,000 children and families who participate year-round in library programs.

It is only through the private support of organizations and individuals in our community that we can provide quality programming like the Children's Reading Festival. This private-public partnership has produced a major effort that has reached thousands of children and families to send a powerful message:

Read . . . Learn . . . Grow

We look forward to working with you to help spread this vital message.

Thank you for your generosity and consideration.

Model State Friends' Cooperative Framework

	Library Director
General Administrative	Administer daily operation of the library including personnel, collection development, fiscal, physical plant, and programmatic functions. Act as technical adviser to the board and ensure staff representation at all Friends' board meetings.
Policy	Apprise board of need for new policies as well as policy revisions; implement the policies of the library as adopted by the board; keep Friends apprised of all library policies.
Planning	Coordinate and implement long-range planning process with board, Friends, staff, and community. Long-range plan coordination will include preparation of appropriate status reports.
Marketing	Coordinate and implement an ongoing marketing program.

Source: Connecticut State Library, Association of Connecticut Library Boards, and Friends of Connecticut Libraries.

Trustee	Friends
Recruit and employ a qualified library director; maintain an ongoing performance appraisal process for the director.	Support quality library service in the community through fund-raising, volunteerism, and serving as advocates for the library's program.
Identify and adopt written policies to govern the operation and program of the library including personnel, general operating, and collection development policies.	Support the policies of the library as adopted by the library board; adopt a constitution and bylaws for the Friends.
Ensure that the library has a long-range planning process with implementation and evaluation components. The process should include input from Friends, community, and staff. Support the librarian, staff, and Friends in carrying out the library's program.	Provide input into library's long-range planning process and remain knowledgeable as to the status of the plan.
Ensure that the library has an active marketing program.	Promote the library program to the public.

<table>
<tr><td></td><td>Library Director</td></tr>
</table>

	Library Director
Fiscal	Prepare an annual budget for the library in consultation with the board and Friends; present current report of expenditures against the budget at each board meeting; make the Friends aware of the special financial needs of the library.
Legislative	Educate board and Friends regarding current local, state, and federal library laws and pending library legislation.
Meetings	Provide written reports at and participate in all board and Friends meetings; ensure that there is a staff liaison to the Friends.
Networking	Affiliate with the state and national professional organizations and attend professional meetings and workshops; make use of the services and consultants of the Connecticut State Library, Association of Connecticut Library Boards, Inc., and Friends of Connecticut Libraries, Inc.

Trustee	Friends
Secure adequate funds to carry out the library's program; assist in the preparation and presentation of the annual budget.	Conduct fund-raising that complements the library's mission and provides funding for special library projects.
Be familiar with local, state, and federal library laws as well as pending library legislation.	Serve as advocates for local, state, and national library issues; represent the library program to legislators.
Attend and participate in all board meetings and see that accurate records are kept on file at the library; comply with Freedom of Information regulations; appoint a liaison to the Friends' board to attend their meetings.	Maintain a liaison to the board of trustees to attend all their meetings. Executive board members should attend and participate in all Friends' executive board meetings.
Attend regional, state, and national trustee meetings and workshops, and affiliate with the appropriate professional organizations. Make use of the services of the Connecticut State Library and Association of Connecticut Library Boards, Inc.	Affiliate with state and national Friends' organizations and attend their meetings and workshops. Make use of the services and consultants of the Connecticut State Library as well as Friends of Connecticut Libraries, Inc.

Index

Janet Russell

Sandy Dolnick is the nation's leading expert on volunteer support for libraries. As founder and executive director of Friends of Libraries U.S.A. Dolnick has spent her career advocating and aiding the efforts of community volunteer supporters of libraries.

Founded with a membership of 110 local groups, FOLUSA has grown twenty-fold over the last fifteen years to encompass more than 2,500 Friends groups reaching more than 1 million members in all 50 states. Since becoming its executive director in 1985, Dolnick has built FOLUSA into a comprehensive program of education, information, and advocacy.

In addition to managing the daily operations of FOLUSA, Dolnick maintains an active schedule of speaking engagements and consulting assignments with Friends groups throughout the U.S.A. She is the editor of a number of publications about libraries and volunteers and continues as an active supporter of a number of community organizations.